GURPS

CYBERWORLD™

High-Tech Low-Life in the One-and-Twenty

By Paul Hume

Additional Material by Chris W. McCubbin

Edited by Jeff Koke
Cover by Keith Parkinson
Illustrated by Dan Smith

GURPS System Design by Steve Jackson
Loyd Blankenship, Managing Editor
Laura Eisenhour, Art Director
Page Layout and Typography by Jeff Koke
Cartography by Laura Eisenhour
Production by Laura Eisenhour; Color Production by Derek Pearcy
Print Buying by Monica Stephens

Playtesters: Lane Boyd, Andrew Hartsock, Fred McCabe, Kevin McCabe, Robert Patton, Derek Pearcy,
Marlon Stout, Rob Thomas, Robert Wheeler, Charlie Wiedman, Todd A. Woods, Dustin Wright and Steven Zieger.

ISBN 1-55634-235-7

PRINTED WITH
SOY INK™

1 2 3 4 5 6 7 8 9 10

CONTENTS

INTRODUCTION

This paryen with the steel eye was holdin' forth on how the proles get drigged by ProGov, when the nerks joined the party. No surprise. When three streetfolk talk revolutseeya, it's an easy bet two are dreamin' and the third's a sneetch for the heat.

The goons' matte-black combat suits seemed to soak up the light. Not local heat. They was carryin' burners as well as the standard-issue pocket rockets. Only the nerks get that kinda bangbang to play with. A laser took out the gent with the steely glance and I was under the benches by the time the gyrocs started flyin', and wishin' the plast was a little thicker.

I pulled my stinger and was glad to see the nerks were in monocrys, not plate. The needles made that whipcrack sound, and Gospodin Nerk by the window Gaussed out. By now, bullets and needles was flyin' everywhere, and between them and the throw weight from the nerks, the place was gettin' unhealthy. I clicked my teeth and the legs fired up, launchin' me on a flat trajectory through the glass. Two more flatblacks was posted outside the window. They was slower than me.

GURPS Cyberworld is a cyberpunk sourcebook set 50 years in the future, almost halfway through the "one-and-twenty" (21st century). Where **GURPS Cyberpunk** jacked the **GURPS** system into the virtual reality of cyberpunk fiction, **GURPS Cyberworld** presents a detailed setting for adventures and campaigns.

There are some differences between this book and the campaign setting described in **GURPS Cyberpunk. GURPS Cyberpunk** described a "mature" TL8 technology. Lasers and gyrocs were the standard sidearms. Cyberwear was chromed and slicked-down and well-behaved, and often you couldn't tell it from the original meat. In **GURPS Cyberworld,** the world at large – where you and I live – is at *early* TL8. There's still a lot of TL7 tech around, and TL8 toys are for the wealthy and powerful. People still shoot each other with primitive things like bullets. Most TL8 bangbang is mil-spec only. Cyberwear is not an off-the-shelf proposition you can buy on every street corner. And when you do get it, it is more likely to have raw welds and breadboard microcircuits than polished chrome and synthiskin camouflage. A hacker with a cyberdeck is one in a million, and as far as most Net computers are concerned, he's a god.

Apart from these details, there are a few other little changes from the world we know in 1993. The Provisional Government and its enforcement arm, the NERCC, maintain a police state in the U.S. The leading technological power on Earth is the economic alliance formed by Japan and the Commonwealth of Independent States (formerly the USSR). Australia is a depopulated wasteland, victim of a lab-born plague virus. The korps, the keiretsu, squeeze the world a little tighter each year – they might as well. It ain't popped yet, right?

Fun place. Nice to adventure in, not so nice if you gotta live in it. You don't like it? Kakoy' oo'zhas, paryen! That's too driggin' bad! So fix it, livewire. If you think you can . . .

About GURPS

Steve Jackson Games is committed to full support of the **GURPS** system. Our address is SJ Games, Box 18957, Austin, TX 78760. Please include a self-addressed, stamped envelope (SASE) any time you write us! Resources now available include:

Pyramid. This bimonthly magazine includes new rules and articles for **GURPS**, as well as information on our other lines: **Car Wars, Toon, Ogre Miniatures** and more. It also covers top releases from other game companies – **Traveller, Call of Cthulhu, Shadowrun**, etc.

New supplements and adventures. We're always working on new material, and we'll be happy to let you know what's available. A current catalog is available for an SASE.

Errata. Everyone makes mistakes, including us – but we do our best to fix our errors. Up-to-date errata sheets for all **GURPS** releases, including this book, are always available from SJ Games; be sure to include an SASE with your request.

Q&A. We do our best to answer any game question accompanied by an SASE.

Gamer input. We value your comments. We will consider them, not only for new products, but also when we update this book in later printings!

BBS. For those who have home computers, SJ Games operates a multi-line BBS with discussion areas for several games, including **GURPS**. Much of the playtest feedback for new products comes from the BBS. It's up 24 hours per day at 512-447-4449, at 300, 1200 or 2400 baud. Give us a call! We also have discussion areas on Compuserve, GEnie, and America Online.

Page References

References to the **GURPS Basic Set,** Third Edition begin with a B – e.g., p. B102 means p. 102 of the **Basic Set,** Third Edition. HT means **GURPS High-Tech,** a UT refers to **GURPS Ultra-Tech,** and a C refers to **GURPS Cyberpunk.**

About the Author

Paul Hume is a freelance author who lives and works in Wheaton, Maryland.

GURPS Cyberworld is his first project for Steve Jackson games, but he has written and co-written innumerable books for FASA and others, including **Shadowrun, Second Edition, Grimoire** and **Shadowbeat.**

1 A WORLD ON THE EDGE

In a dark corner of the New York megasprawl, an appliance store faces the street, its vidscreens and thriddie boxes showing snow through the plastiglass storefront. Nobody is on the street this early, except for a stray dog, so the flickering screens play to an audience of one.

As if on cue, all the screens change to display a korp logo over a computer-generated Earth spinning in slow motion. The Earth fades to a vector-graphic globe with continental outlines, then a slow dissolve to Bink and Bett sitting behind a light blue-gray desk, with the worldscreen behind them.

Bink flashes the camera a knowing smile. "'Hayo gozaimas, paryeni. I'm Bink Bentley."

"And I'm Bett Bartley."

"And here's SatNews, Jan-one-forty-three. Population worldwide partied down last night, making much welcome to 2043."

Behind the cheerful twosome, the worldscreen displays laserflash shows and holo-pyrotechnics over Hermitage in Petrograd, Kremlin in Moskva, Commonwealth Congress Building in Minsk, all capitals of the various Republics. During the montage, the screen expands to take up the whole picture.

Bett's voice creeps in over the video. "In the Commonwealth, folks made bolshoyeh praz'navoon'yeh, closing the year of celebrations marking the Big Five-Oh . . ."

The video spits out a scratchy oldvid of USSR flag being lowered for the last time on January 1st, 1992.

". . . half a century since the old Soyuz went dodo, back at the threshold of the one-and-twenty. The celebration also marked the 20th anniversary of the Joint Economic Agreement that started the Russo-Japanese Economic Union. Russky-Pres Malashev . . ."

The worldscreen brings up a much more recent shot – Russian President Andrei Malashev and Japanese Premiere Tadeo Takahashi, drinking toasts; behind them, a huge window looks out on the Earth, hanging against a backdrop of stars.

". . . and Prime Minister Takahashi, celebrating the occasion at TenTan's main orbital facility, wished the crowds in Yeltsin Square and elsewhere 'Snoh'veem Goh'dum!' via hololink."

The shot pulls back from the worldscreen, showing Bink and Bett, with their permanent smiles.

"And 'Happy New Year' back at 'em, Bett. In the U.S., ProPrexy Hammond and ProCon leaders holo-hosted the traditional Times Square blowout, and indicated that the National Recovery Plan for the past year had come in far above predictions."

Once again, the worldscreen spins around and grows to cover the entire view. Now it shows Provisional President Hammond addressing a bustling crowd in Times Square. Hammond's voice, a powerful grandfatherly lilt, comes echoing over loudspeakers.

". . . and in the light of these advances, made by the dedication and sacrifice of the American people, I feel confident in predicting that the state of emergency will end much sooner than expected, allowing the Provisional Government to step down and, God willing, institute free elections in the very near future . . ."

The scene dissolves back to Bink, head and shoulders only. The korp logo fills up the worldscreen behind him.

"A holocopy of President Hammond's full New Year's address is available on any SatNews d/l node for a nominal charge. And while you're there, paryeni, don't forget to browse all our hot SatNews libefiles – all the news, all the time, on SatNews.

"Elsewhere, less fun-making for the New Year. A joint NERCC/FBI operation ended last night in a krovvy-red shootout at the state line between Arizona and Sonora, where a coyote operation had been ferrying unauthorized Scale Three citizens from the Low Six to the Upper Forty-Eight."

Without losing Bink's upbeat discourse, the camera pulls back to take in combat footage on the screen behind him – a chopper strike on a convoy of half a dozen ramshackle trucks. The footage is intercut with starlite- and IR-enhanced helmet-cam footage of ground fighting and mop-up. The scene is eeirily macabre with only Bink's warm voice for a soundtrack.

Talkin' One-and-Twenty

Babooshka: (Russ.) Grandmother. Granny. Old-fashioned.

Bolshoyeh: (Russ.) Big. Great. Large.

Coyote: Someone who smuggles illegal transients from Mexico to the U.S.

Dyadooshka: (Russ.) Grandfather. Gramps. Old-fashioned.

Go dodo: To become extinct or obsolete.

'Hayo gozaimas: (Jap.) Hello.

Khorosho: (Russ.) Good. OK. Fine.

Korp: Multinational corporation. A keiretsu.

Krovvy: (Russ.) Bloody.

Livewire: Informal term of address.

One-and-twenty: The 21st century. Up-to-date. Modern.

Paryen: (Russ.) Pal. Friend. Chum. (pl. paryeni)

Praz'navoon'yeh: (Russ.) Celebration. Party.

Snoh'veem Goh'dum: (Russ.) Happy New Year.

TD: Tolliver's Disease.

Toller: Tolliver's Disease.

Touchdown: Tolliver's Disease.

A World on the Edge

Firstworld/Lastworld

People used to talk about "First World" nations (industrially developed), "Third World" nations (a.k.a. "emerging" nations, ones with no industrial infrastructure to speak of), and so on.

On the Edge, it boils down to firstworld and lastworld. Anyone in the middle tends to slug their way into the former or get sucked down into the latter.

The firstworld includes the United States, United Europe, the Commonwealth of Independent States, the Central Asian Federation, the Israeli Empire, Japan, most of the republics, free provinces in Canada, and Chilentina. Maybe the Third Revolution's China is at firstworld levels, too, if anyone knew just what was going on in there.

The lastworld is almost everywhere else. Some lastworld nations are tough, with a decent level of tech available, but it's all imported. They shovel out resources and they get tech-toys back. Most of them are in the same bind the Third World was in last century, with a few big boys at the top raking off most of the loot, and the streetfolk, the villagers, the farmers living off the crumbs.

"The commissioners for the Southwestern and Mexican regions issued a joint statement that all due care has been taken to respect the reserved rights of the Mex C-3s involved. Over half the coyote's cubs came out without a scratch. Khorosho job, fellas."

The camera cuts to Bett. "On the Cuban front, General Ormiston's weekly press briefing denied the rumors that U.S. overflights of the Camaguay region had encountered SmartSAM batteries. The general noted that Operation Cuba Libre timetables have been adjus–"

The screen goes black for a second, then flashes in bright red letters "[CLASSIFIED CLASSIFIED CLASSIFIED]." After 30 seconds, the image of Bett re-emerges on the screen ". . . penalties for unauthorized media activity in a designated combat area."

Back to a double shot of Bink and Bett. Bink speaks.

"And in the Antarctic, a missile barrage hit the Korsakov-Shimadzu Korp's Resource Probe base camp, spilling blood under the midnight sun. The 'Spear of Gaia' ecoterrs claimed responsibility for the raid, which dusted twelve korpers and dropped twice as many into the doctanks. The ecoterr hit burned a cool million rubyen worth of hot korp tech as well. In a press conference, K-S spokesmen reported that the base camp would soon be back in operation, with all functions khorosho within 24 hours. Sound efficient? You bet. That's just one example of the kind of performance you can expect from Korsakov-Shimadzu. We'll be back after this message, which shows you a few others."

Trendy, upbeat music slides in from the background, and the screens fade to the SatNews logo. Then the scenes cut to a Korsakov-Shimadzu advertisement.

In the deserted alley, with the first sounds of a sleepy populace waking the city in the background, the stray dog wanders off toward dawn to find some food.

Looking Backways Twentywards

Fifty years from now the world is on the Edge. The edge of what? Of heaven or hell? Of an explosion of technology and information, or just an explosion?

From 2043, looking back to 1993, here's a quick rundown of the events that pretty much destroyed the forms and norms that Dyadooshka and Babooshka used to know, and left us on the Edge.

1990-2000: Slipping into Chaos

The Commonwealth of Independent States

The Soviet Union was formally dissolved on January 1, 1992 and its member republics formed the Commonwealth of Independent States. In its early years, the CIS faced economic collapse, shortages in agriculture and industry, violent ethnic wars, and the coup attempts of 1991, 1993, 1995 and 1996. More than once, the Commonwealth almost fell apart in a welter of suspicion and old hatreds.

Russia remained the strongest voice in Commonwealth affairs, despite some early attempts to avoid Slavic, and specifically Russian dominance in the CIS. The Slavic republics gave up trying to please the other member states. The death of Yeltsin, from an anonymous sniper's bullet during the National Front's uprising of '96, was the pivotal point. His successor, Dmitri Breslov, made it clear that while Russia was prepared to cooperate with the Commonwealth, it would no longer subordinate its own national concerns merely to calm the fears of the other republics. Russian economic and military intervention on behalf of ethnic Russians in other republics became a continuous and escalating cause of tension in the CIS throughout the rest of the decade.

The TD Pandemic

Tolliver's Disease, a highly contagious retroviral plague, broke out in 1997. Modern transportation let TD move like lightning across the world scene. As epidemiology identified the pattern, international travel and even travel from one city to another shrank to a trickle. Most countries slapped ferocious quarantine restrictions on travelers. In some regions, panicked residents indulged in do-it-yourself "public health measures" that left thousands dead or wounded.

Cities became polarized between two major categories. The "have-lots," those who did not flee to the less dangerous suburbs and exurbs, could afford privately-enforced security, medical ID checkpoints, protected public transport and other measures. Corporate and government employees could either commute between the hellish cities and the relative heaven of exurbia, or live in high-security "endominiums" – self-contained complexes of apartments, shops, offices and other facilities that kept the plague-stricken world safely locked o-u-t. The "have-nots" could afford neither flight from the city nor security within it. They carried on as best they could. As jobs moved out of the cities in ever-increasing numbers, or became restricted to those who could satisfy the high standards set by the korp enclaves, social services broke down under the increased demands of the urban poor.

The Toller was joined by diseases of poverty in many firstworld cities: cholera, typhus, kwashiorkor, beriberi.

Justin Tolliver identified the virus responsible for the disease in 1999. An effective treatment was developed in 2008, but it was, and is, expensive, and only the most having of the have-lots could afford it. A vaccine was developed in 2019 but did not go into global distribution until 2021.

Self-preservation dictated that the wealthy nations and corporations provide vaccination at little or no cost to poorer populations. Rumors abound that adulterated vaccine or outright placebos went to some areas.

Tolliver's Disease

Tolliver's Disease (TD, touchdown, the Toller) is a retroviral infection which affects primates, including *Homo sapiens*. It can be spread by aerosol droplet infection (sneezing, coughing), by intimate contact or, in the later stages, by contact with the discharge from a victim's lesions.

Anyone with the Immunity to Disease advantage is immune to TD, as is anyone who has been vaccinated against it. Most PCs will receive this vaccination along with the usual round of childhood immunizations (polio, DPT, measles, HIV). People from a lastworld country, or those with a negative Status might not be immunized. Anyone who has survived TD is also immune.

Susceptible individuals can contract it when they are exposed to a carrier, or are in an area where TD has broken out (see p. B133).

An infected person displays no symptoms for 2d days; during this period there is no test that can accurately diagnose the disease.

After this time is up, the victim is infectious and anyone exposed to him may catch the disease. The carrier still displays no symptoms, but standard medical tests will easily reveal the presence of Tolliver's virus. Tests require lab facilities of TL7 or better, and a successful roll vs. Diagnosis+4. This phase lasts the carrier's HT+1d days.

Continued on next page . . .

A World on the Edge

Tolliver's Disease infected one person in three between 1997 and 2021. In areas with high population density, the infection rate approached 70%. Three-fourths of the plague's victims died, over a billion people in all, and many of the survivors suffered nerve damage, hideous scars and other side effects. Occasional outbreaks of TD still occur, even in firstworld areas.

Tolliver's Disease (Continued)

After this time, the victim develops symptoms and must start making HT rolls. He may die. During this period, victims are highly contagious. Roll daily vs. HT using the following numbers.

A victim under no medical care whatsoever rolls vs. HT-8.

Someone under TL7 medical care with full hospital facilities rolls against HT-5.

If under TL8 medical care with full hospital facilities, the roll is vs. HT-3. Specific treatment for Tolliver's Disease makes the roll vs. HT+3. TL8 facilities offer such care for $5,000 per day – it involves tailored monoclonal antibodies designed specifically for each patient.

Any other medical care, or simply complete rest, good diet, and palliative treatment for pain, secondary infections, etc., allows the roll at HT-7.

Each day that the roll *fails*, the patient loses 2d points of HT (3d on a critical failure). This is general damage and is treated as shown on p. B126. Once the patient's HT drops below 0, he becomes comatose, or helpless in delirium, and stays that way until he is cured and his HT returns above 0. The patient's ST and DX are reduced by half his HT loss, and if either one reaches 0, the patient is rendered helpless by the disease.

Once the disease reduces HT by half, the patient breaks out in a distinctive rash. When HT drops to 3 or less, the rash develops into open lesions with an unpleasant discharge. If the disease reaches this stage, the victim will be permanently scarred. Reduce Appearance by three steps. A character with Average (or lower) Appearance becomes Hideous. Because the scars are unmistakable, the survivor *also* suffers the Social Disease disadvantage (see p. C25), even though he is no longer contagious. Someone rendered Hideous by the disease would thus suffer -5 on reaction rolls, instead of -4. Cosmetic surgery can restore Appearance, of course, and eliminate the telltale signs of TD.

Once a HT roll succeeds, the patient recovers damage normally (see p. B128). Each successful recovery restores 1 point of lost HT, ST, and DX.

The End of NATO

As the threat of the Soviet Union faded into history, and as Europe became more and more independent of the United States, the stresses on NATO became intolerable. The European governments were less tolerant of U.S. dictates. The U.S. was increasingly reluctant to expend scarce dollars "defending" allies who were patently not in danger from anybody. Divergent foreign policies were also a source of friction.

The situation in the Balkans, especially in what had been Yugoslavia, forced the growing dissent into the open. With the situation growing worse, several countries formed a peace-keeping force in late 1993, designed to force a cease fire between the warring factions. The United States, with social pressure on the government to focus on the worsening domestic crisis, would not commit ground troops to this effort.

After several days of acrimonious negotiations, the other governments turned authority in the matter over to the Conference for Security and Cooperation in Europe (CSCE). In early November, joint forces from the European Community moved into the Balkans, without a U.S. presence.

This rift marked the beginning of the end for NATO. Over the next decade, as the U.S. reduced troop concentrations in Europe, and European governments minimized their commitment to NATO, the organization withered away, and was formally dissolved in 2003.

2000-2010: Political Turmoil

The Central Asian Federation

In 2003, a series of confrontations between the governments of the Asiatic republics of the CIS and the Slavic majority reached a peak. A rising tide of nationalism in the southern republics, fuelled by petrodollars and military support from certain Islamic governments, led to the secession of the republics of Kazakhstan, Uzbekistan, Turkmenia, Tadzhikistan and Kyrgyzstan. Violent rioting took thousands of lives, as ethnic Russians and local inhabitants took to the streets, and army units fired on rioters and on each other. Not coincidentally, the political turmoil disrupted production at a number of the Commonwealth's richest oil fields.

The formal secession was proclaimed on July 9, 2004, in a joint declaration by the Central Asian governments at a summit held in Frunze, capital of Kyrgyzstan. On September 12, after a good deal of rhetoric, some military maneuvering and civil disorders, the Commonwealth recognized the secession. Behind the scenes, Kazakhstan threatened to escalate to a nuclear response in the event of military intervention by the Commonwealth, or any of its member republics.

South Africa Aflame

In 1998, a general election returned a government dominated by the African National Congress, headed by the elderly but still intensely charismatic Nelson Mandela. However, while the ANC espoused moderation, more extreme parties received enough support to gain a strong voice in the new government.

Disruptive anti-white initiatives on the part of more radical officials, in defiance of official policies, plagued the Mandela administration. New outbreaks of factional violence among adherents of the ANC, the New African and the Zulu

Confederation parties, and the Pan-African Coalition, further weakened the government.

In 2004, a coup mounted by hard-line Afrikaaners seized control in Pretoria, Johannesburg and Cape Town. Conflicting loyalties splintered army and police units. Many – often the best armed and trained – supported the coup, augmented by paramilitary forces from the ultra-conservative Boer population. Others supported the elected government. Still others joined burgeoning secessionist movements in Natal, the Orange Free State, and the Transvaal.

The South African civil war continued for 12 years; when the violence stopped, the southern part of Africa had split into a half dozen new nations.

The fighting had an immediate global impact, however, as resources produced in South Africa stopped flowing into the world economy. Gold prices tripled in the first two weeks of fighting. Panic buying in chromium, manganese, platinum and other strategic resources produced by South Africa followed, driving world stock markets into free fall.

The Grand Slam

In 2006, stock markets and investment systems all over the world crashed. The downward spiral of boom and bust from preceding decades, coupled with the devastating effects of the TD pandemic, the South African Civil War and petrodollar manipulations by certain Middle Eastern governments all culminated in one massive global collapse. Even the strongest currencies suffered double-digit inflation. Weaker economies disintegrated completely. Unemployment in the firstworld approached 35%. In the developing nations, it was nearly 50%.

Tech Timeline 1990-2000

1998: Advances in plasma display technology allow commercialization of multimedia personal computers. "Virtual reality" goggles and multi-purpose control surfaces are demonstrated, but limitations on processing speed make them impractical for serious use.

Sustained "hot fusion" reaction is demonstrated at Hiromatsu Power's research facility on Hokkaido.

Megabyte chips (Intel Decade, Taizu 1998-10/6) are introduced, becoming the basis for the next generation of computers.

1999: Royal Motors, Canada, and General Motors, U.S., unveil the Lectra series of electrical commuter cars, with a top speed of 50 mph. They run for 6 hours on a single charge of their nickel-hydride batteries, which can be recharged on household current.

As part of the same move toward alternative power sources, new formulations of methanol fuels are developed by several firms, despite covert attempts at sabotage by several OPEC nations.

The Human Genome Project is formally established as part of the search for a cure for Tolliver's Disease. Resources from 14 nations are committed to the formal genome mapping effort.

Hurricane Abner

The first hurricane of the 1998 season exceeded all previous records for ferocity. It ripped a swath of destruction across the Caribbean, devastated Cuba, and then turned sharply northwest to rake the U.S. coast. Seaboard cities from Charlotte, South Carolina, to Baltimore, Maryland, were hit by winds approaching 150 mph, and a storm surge that was measured at 35 feet in some areas. Killer thunderstorms spun off from the main mass, spreading lesser damage over the remainder of the coast. The death toll was estimated at 7,200, and property damage was in the billions of dollars.

A highly controversial joint report by government scientists was published in 1999, presenting results that suggested Abner's unprecedented fury fit prediction models based on global warming. Arguments about the report were still going on in 2000, when Hurricane Marko did a repeat performance along Abner's route. Since then, weather statistics show a 10% increase in hurricane frequency, and a 25% percent increase in the energy levels of the worst storms.

Abner and its successors on the hurricane hit parade stoked the urban panic caused by Tolliver's Disease in coastal cities, and accelerated the middle-class exodus to the 'burbs, especially 'burbs on higher ground in seaside regions.

Similar cyclonic weather patterns have appeared in the Pacific and Indian Oceans.

A World on the Edge

The reconstruction of the global economy took the better part of a decade. When it was done, national currencies had taken a back seat to the monetary systems of the major economic communities and the biggest multinational corporations.

Unrest in China

In the generation prior to the Grand Slam, the People's Republic of China had been emerging from economic isolation. Doctrinaire hard-liners almost threw away China's great opportunity to join the mainstream of global trade by imposing strict controls on Hong Kong's marketplace when control of the former crown colony reverted to Beijing in 1997. However, a bloodless coup within the Party leadership in 1999 restored a more liberal faction to control, and Chinese participation in world trade increased substantially between 1999 and 2006. China extended its deficit, and began to raise its quotas of foreign imports. Chinese industry retooled to apply technology introduced from the more developed nations.

Caught off-balance in the transition from the austerities of hard-line rule to the reforms of the liberal leadership, China was hit hard by the Grand Slam. Famine was an immediate threat in many regions, and an outbreak of Tolliver's Disease in the industrialized northeastern Harbin region threw gasoline on the smoldering embers of civil disorder.

The country was virtually cut off from the rest of the world as its leaders struggled, murderously, among themselves. The conflict culminated in the Third Revolution, in 2014, which finally restored a semblance of order.

The Non-Election of 2008

The dollar went into a nose dive during the Grand Slam, bottoming out in 2008 with an annual inflation rate of 800%.

Federal programs were cut, then cut again, throwing intolerable strain on local budgets. Government services broke down at virtually every level. During the record heat waves of August 2007, martial law was in effect in almost a third of the U.S. as authorities tried to prevent a final collapse into anarchy. The abdication of federal authority was formalized by the Local Powers Act of 2009, in which Congress granted wide latitude to governors, mayors and even private institutions, authorizing extraordinary powers to preserve order during emergencies. Needless to say, these local forces did not always use this power wisely.

In this climate, extremists from all points of the political compass drowned out moderate voices. Half a dozen political parties now existed where for generations power had effectively been divided between only two. Coalition politics was a new game in the U.S., and both the politicians and the electorate were slow to figure out the rules. The presidential election of 2008 failed to return a majority for any of the five major candidates.

Under the 12th amendment of the Constitution, when the electoral college fails to return a majority for a single candidate, Congress is authorized to elect the next president from among the three candidates who received the most votes. December 2008 saw more intense politicking in Washington, D.C. than anything in the previous 200 years.

A coalition ticket was hammered out. The presidency went to the inoffensive Centrist Democrat candidate, Walter Burris. The vice-presidency went to Archconservative candidate Martin Patterson, as the price for his supporters' votes. Under-the-table deals split the cabinet positions and other appointments among various power blocs. The end result was to leave the executive branch virtually paralyzed by the conflicting politics of this ad hoc coalition.

Tech Timeline 2000-2010

The immediate impact of the Grand Slam put a damper on most technological advances during this decade, but several major developments stand out.

2001: Experimental designs for prostheses using enhanced neurotransmitter therapy and micro-neural laser surgery are applied in clinical trials. This is generally regarded as the first step towards full-function cyberwear development.

2002: Increased processing speed allows the first virtual-reality interface for general computing use, on MetaPulse Systems' high-end workstation. The lack of software specifically designed to take advantage of VR hampers the spread of the new technology for several years. The advent of VOS-21, in 2008, puts the new technology over the top. VOS-21 combines an operating system with development tools, both designed to accommodate the potential of virtual-reality controls. By 2012, VR interfaces are as common as mice were by the mid-1990s.

2003: Driven by the oil shortages of the Petroslam, firstworld governments and korps allocate significant funding to development of viable synfuels to reduce dependence on oil.

Power-cell technology is demonstrated by Kunstler Mettalurgischen Erforschung, GmbH. Production costs of key components keep the technology from commercial use until zero-g refining techniques make the necessary materials available at acceptable costs in the 2020s.

2007: A man-portable laser weapon system delivering damage comparable to a modern firearm is demonstrated. Power requirements preclude its development for field use for over two decades, until power cells become more widely available.

2010-2020: Unity Through Force

The Patterson Presidency

On April 17, 2010, President Burris was assassinated during a speech in Cincinnatti. The assassin used a rocket launcher and had fitted the missile with an anti-personnel warhead. The flechettes also took out three local Congressmen, the mayor, four Secret Service agents and several dozen bystanders. The assassin was killed in an exchange of fire with police and federal agents.

Vice President Patterson was sworn in as head of the government within hours. His first official act was to declare a day of mourning for his predecessor. His second was to impose martial law on Cincinnati, and order Federal troops into the city to, in his own words, "comb through the city house by house, and if need be, brick by brick, until the nest of traitors is exposed and exterminated." Government press releases revealed that a "revolutionary cult" calling itself the Army of Satanic Order had been responsible for the assassination of President Burris. Shortly thereafter, a block of tenements in downtown Cincinnati was reduced to flaming rubble by units of the Army and the Ohio National Guard, and government spokesmen reported that the cultists had been tracked down and dealt with. President Patterson issued an executive order the following week, calling for the apprehension and investigation of individuals with a history of involvement in "occult" organizations and activities, including Wicca, Satanism, the Rosicrucians, Spiritualism, the OTO, the Michaeline Order, the Golden Dawn, Transcendental Meditation, the SCA, investigators of ESP, and fantasy roleplaying games.

As conditions in the U.S. worsened, the Patterson administration demonstrated a brutal ability to maintain order and keep crucial resources moving through the economy.

The Canadian Collapse

Internal conflicts in Canada increased following the rejection of yet another draft Constitution in 1996. Quebec swung into a phase of extreme regionalism, and Premiere Jean-Baptiste Corbec was elected in 1995 on a platform of increased autonomy for the province.

When the Grand Slam hit the Canadian economy, the battered federal government in Ottawa was unable to preserve national unity. Each province, perhaps genuinely, perhaps perversely, seemed intent on a particular, mutually exclusive solution to the crisis.

The oil industry in the western half of the country was already ill-disposed toward the central provinces, where auto makers had diligently worked to develop cars powered by synfuels and electricity, and had lobbied for strict regulation of internal-combustion vehicles. The busy port cities of the coasts had suffered disproportionately, in their view, from Tolliver's Disease, and their citizens charged that Ottawa had been more concerned with checking the spread of contagion inland than in helping the areas most harshly afflicted.

The end result was the virtual dissolution of the Canadian confederacy in 2007, followed by its formal dissolution in 2010. The individual provinces of Canada became autonomous nations, though they conducted most of their internal commerce within the new Canadian Trade Community exactly as they had under the federal government. The resource-rich areas of the former Northwest Territory became a joint protectorate of the provincial governments. The Yukon Territory, however, petitioned the state of Alaska for union, and became part of that state, and thus of the U.S., in 2016.

A World on the Edge

ECUs

The hardest currencies in 2043 are Economic Community Credit Units. A multilingual pun has spread into usage in most languages, and these units are called "ecus" (ay-kyooz), which was the name for an old French currency in the Renaissance. The ecus are:

The rubyen: ECU of the CIS and its largest trading partner, Japan;

The eurotaler: ECU of United Europe;

The neodollar: ECU of the United States and its North American trading partners.

After the ecus, the most stable currencies are hard, firstworld money and "keiretsu marks" (K-marks, Korpmarks) issued by the top 10 multinationals.

Details on currency and exchange can be found under *Economics* on p. 59.

Patterson received an 80% margin of the vote in 2012, an overwhelming mandate from the 16% of the electorate that actually cast ballots. A coalition of the extreme conservative parties (Archconservative, True American, and Neo-Capitalist) swept Congress as well. With the executive and legislative branches of government working on a common agenda for the first time in over half a century, the U.S. economy began to recover from the ravages of the Grand Slam and the TD pandemic. Popular support for the President's ambitious recovery programs increased at the grassroots level, especially after the U.S. invasion of Cuba in 2013 (see below). The conquest of Cuba was hailed by the congressional coalition that supported the President as, in the words of Senator Barbara DiNunzio (True American Party, PA.), "proving that Americans can still defend their own."

During Patterson's first term as an elected President, Congress ratified a bill to repeal the 22nd Amendment, which limits the number of terms a President may serve. This was ratified by the states in 2018, during Patterson's second term. Patterson was elected to his third term in 2020. There was no presidential election in 2024.

The Cuban Invasion

Fidel Castro died of natural causes in 1997; upon his death, Cuba was wracked by internal struggles for power. In 2002, a moderate socialist government, under President Raul Guzmán, was finally established.

Relations between the Guzmán administration and Washington were cool at best. After Castro's death, Cuban emigrés in Florida actively sought to establish a Cuban government of their own, and the U.S. openly supported this faction. In addition, the U.S. continued to maintain its naval base at Guantanamo as an extraterritorial enclave, which has been a sore spot with Cubans for almost a century.

The Guzmán government continued to operate Cuba's VVER nuclear reactor, constructed on the island in the early 1990s by Russian engineers, despite continued complaints from the U.S. that a severe accident at the unsafe facility could expose the southeastern U.S. to radioactive contamination. Since the reactor produced over a third of Cuba's electricity, shutting it down was not an option that the Guzmán government was willing to entertain.

On March 14, 2013, the fishing boat *Sweet Charlene,* out of Key West, was hailed by a Cuban patrol vessel in the vicinity of the Nicholas Channel. When the *Sweet Charlene* failed to heave to, and attempted to flee, the Cubans fired upon the boat, killing two crewmen, and boarded.

There is much that is murky about the incident. U.S. sources claimed, and maintain to this day, that the *Sweet Charlene* was in international waters. The Cubans, equally stubbornly, claimed that the boat was within 12 miles of its coast.

Cuba took the fishing boat and its six surviving crewmen into custody, holding them at a facility at Matanzas. President Patterson ordered a joint-forces rescue operation set in motion to extract the crew. On March 27 there was a pitched battle at Matanzas, between Cuban military and U.S. forces, mostly Navy SEALs and Delta Force. This left 14 Americans dead, including the six crewmembers of the *Sweet Charlene*. In retaliation, Cuban forces shelled the U.S. base at Guantanamo. There were no casualties, and the Cuban government immediately claimed that the shelling was the unauthorized action of a local military commander. The commander was placed under arrest by the Guzmán government, but events were now completely out of control.

President Patterson signed the executive order authorizing the bombing of Havana on March 28, at the same time that Congress passed the "Matanzas Resolution," calling for war with Cuba. Under a full invasion by U.S. forces, Cuban resistance crumpled. President Guzmán signed the articles of surrender on June 3, 2013.

Despite loud protests from the Organization of American States (OAS), Cuba was made a territory of the U.S., first under a military government (2013-2017), then a territorial government appointed by Congress (2017-2024). Cuba, along with the "Low Six" in Mexico, was granted "reserved" statehood by the Provisional Congress in 2025.

The Third Revolution

In 2014, eight years of civil war in China ended when the Third Revolution took power.

No one is entirely sure which factions joined to form the Third Revolution. Certainly elements of the former 4th People's Liberation Army, under the command of High General Liao Shiu-Doh, formed the backbone of the Revolutionary Force of Peace, as the Third Revolution's military arm was called. But General Liao never appeared as a member of the new government. Shuo Tsao, who was a minor official in Mongolia under the old regime, appeared on broadcasts, in China and internationally, as the spokesman for the Third Revolution, but whether Shuo participated in forming the policies he announced to the world is unclear.

As the Third Revolution extended its sway over China, it erected a "Bamboo Curtain," more impenetrable than anything Mao ever managed. It launched remarkably sophisticated virus programs into any telephonic switching system that attempted to link into China. It firmly denied foreign interests any entrance to the country. It expelled resident foreigners and nationalized all their holdings.

The Third Revolution did maintain a stream of exports, including very creditable copies of slightly outdated computer-chip designs and other first-decade technologies. These found a ready market in lastworld nations.

From 2014 to 2022, the Third Revolution consolidated its position as the sole ruler of China. A system of buffer states, semi-autonomous areas ruled by warlords, was created along China's frontiers.

The NERCC

In 2017, Patterson and the Congress created an extraordinary body, the National Emergency Resource Coordinating Commission, to oversee all matters of commerce and production deemed essential *in the Commission's own view* to the prosperity and security of the United States. Adam Hammond, the dynamic CEO of the multinational North American Technologies Corporation, became a "dollar-a-year man" to head the NERCC.

The NERCC demonstrated its approach to local obstacles that, "in its view," presented a danger to the public welfare. When power workers at the main fusion plant in Schenectady went on strike, NERCC forces isolated the plant, while the computer specialists overrode plant controls, locking the strikers out of the main

Tech Timeline 2010-2020

2012: The European Space Agency unveils Arrow, a variation on the Sanger/Horus spaceplane design. Arrow consists of two component vehicles, each capable of multiple launches and landings, with minimal downtime between missions. In the same year, Russia unveils the Archangel, an inexpensive single-launch vehicle built on the "BDB" (Big Dumb Booster) model. Archangel is capable of lofting a very large payload into orbit at reasonable cost.

2014: North American Technology unveils its first gigabyte chip (the NAT 10-2-9). Combining its immense speed and capacity with the MPSC (Massively Parallel Single Component) instruction set developed by NAT and the Shimadzu Corporation, gigachip technology drives the next quantum leap in computer performance and sophistication.

2015: High-temperature superconducting materials, operating at temperatures as high as -100°F, are demonstrated by the Japan Center for Superconductive Studies, a government-sponsored consortium of researchers from many companies.

China introduces a strain of rice that thrives under the increased temperatures and UV exposure that threaten the "rice-bowl" nations of Southeast Asia due to the greenhouse effect. This is the first of a number of gene-engineered plant products offered on international markets by the Third Revolution.

2016: Construction of Kosmozavot Tenno Tanjo (Space Factory Heavenly Birth) begins under the joint auspices of Russia and Japan. Even before its completion in 2031, KTT develops a number of products using processes difficult to reproduce on Earth's surface. Some, like the metallurgical refining techniques needed for power cells, are adapted for Earthside use. Others, like the zero-g environment needed to produce nanotools, remain a monopoly of the orbital factories.

A World on the Edge

Secure Observation Facilities

These facilities combine the best (or worst) features of concentration camps and ghettos. Faced with the danger of disaffection and even insurrection among large blocks of the population, the Patterson government instituted a system of Secure Observation Facilities. These were either Remote SOFs or Local SOFs.

A Remote Secure Observation Facility is a camp or other site where dissenters are removed from the general public and interned. The NERCC rations all resources and assigns work. These are prison camps. Internees can be remanded to a Remote SOF on the orders of a NERCC Regional Administrator, or by the finding of a Federal court, or on order of a Congressional committee.

A NERCC Regional Administrator may simply designate a specified area as a Local SOF. Barriers are erected, NERCC authority replaces local authority and registers inhabitants, and there it is. The NERCC may order people from other areas within the administrative region to relocate to a Local SOF.

A Local SOF is under martial law, enforced by NERCC troops. Inhabitants require permits to leave the area, and are restricted to travel to and from approved employment. Inhabitants remain responsible for their own consumption of resources: food, water, power, etc. All communications must pass through NERCC relay centers and are subject to censorship. In essence, the people in a Local SOF are in a ghetto in the old sense of the word, and pay NERCC for the privilege.

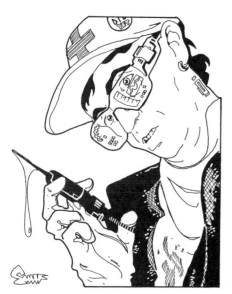

computer. When cybernetic control of the plant was assured, NERCC troopers went in. Of the 126 technicians on that shift, 14 were killed in the subsequent fighting, and many were injured. The NERCC unit commander claimed that his forces had returned the fire of armed insurgents. The NERCC used its emergency powers, which permitted it to censor news items that "endanger public confidence in the security of the United States," to suppress union counterclaims that federal troops had fired on unarmed workers. Faced with threats of internment in a Secure Observation Facility, union leadership backed down.

2020-2030: The Maelstrom Grows

The Israeli Empire

In May, 2021, the Middle East flared into war as the armies of Jordan, Syria and Iraq struck at Israel. Libya attempted to join in the attack but ended up starting a sharp border war with Egypt instead, when bungled diplomacy led to a curt Egyptian refusal to either join in the attack on Israel or to grant Libyan troops passage.

The Arab nations had suffered both plague and economic destruction, with attendant political turmoil. In 2018, a charismatic leader, Mumahd ben-Hussein, who claimed the title of Mahdi, rose from obscurity preaching a strict and fiercely militant reform movement in the Islamic nations. As civil authority disintegrated, the Moslem peoples turned to the unifying authority of their religion. The new Mahdi gained the support of more and more religious leaders in the region. When he called for a jihad against the continued existence of Israel, the ragged armies of the region responded.

Israel, fighting for its life, met the disorganized attackers with state-of-the-art military hardware and terrible determination. Surgical strikes on hostile airfields coupled with advanced combat avionics gave Israel air supremacy early in the conflict. Hi-42 attack choppers, supplied by the CIS, dispatched the obsolete Arab armor. Outnumbered, but far from outgunned, the Israelis first stopped, then threw back the desperate horde that opposed them.

At the same time, the Israelis sent private communiques to the governments of Iran and the nations of the Arabian peninsula. Stripped of diplomatic double-talk, these boiled down to promises that if they intervened on behalf of the jihad, their principal cities would be destroyed by nuclear weapons. Despite intense pressure on their eastern front, the Israeli high command dispatched air strikes to bolster the Egyptians when the Libyans broke through the Egyptian southern flank and began pressing forward.

By September, the invasion had broken, and the remains of the governments in the attacking countries toppled. Israel found itself the uneasy conqueror of Syria, Jordan and Lebanon, as well as the western half of Iraq.

Mumahd ben-Hussein fled to the CAF, where he remains to this day, as head of Justice of God, a terrorist organization.

The Russo-Japanese Economic Union

Russia and Japan formalized their increased cooperation in 2023, when the governments of both nations entered into a joint agreement. The resulting politico-economic organization, the Russo-Japanese Economic Union, merged the strongest aspects of both economies, and established the "rubyen" as an ecu (see sidebar, p. 60).

Extremely liberal regulations encouraged korps under joint Russian and Japanese management. The resulting keiretsu span Eurasia, and are among the most powerful in the world today.

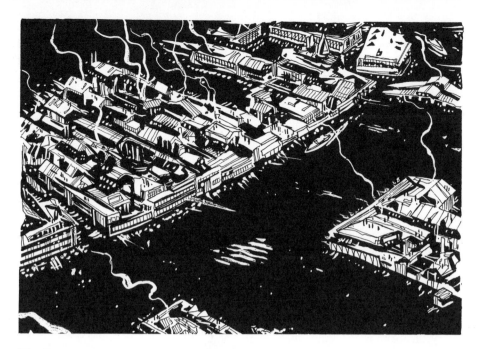

The Permanent Emergency and ProGov

In the summer of 2024, American cities erupted in flash riots, with looting, arson and terror. President Patterson ordered in federal troops and activated National Guard units, which he placed under the command of regional NERCC officers. Local authorities were ordered to give all possible assistance to federal forces. Those who resisted were summarily removed from office. Those who continued to resist were shot.

It is unclear just when the massive federal response to unrest began to look like something else. Martial law was declared in virtually every U.S. city with a population over 500,000. There were several incidents of National Guard units mutinying when ordered to fire on neighbors, leading to sharp urban firefights between National Guardsmen and NERCC troops. Indeed, in Alaska the National Guard and local citizens managed to defeat federal troops, leaving the state virtually independent. Occupied with events in the lower 48, Washington was powerless to react.

Rumors ran rampant. The President was a prisoner of the Pentagon. The NERCC had gunned down the Joint Chiefs and was running the military. The President and Joint Chiefs had taken over the NERCC.

At no time was the simple truth discovered: the Patterson administration was, by design, taking over the country piecemeal, in a coup d'etat designed to replace the constitutional government of the United States with a dictatorship. The rioting that gave Patterson his excuse for the coup was carefully provoked, but quickly got out of hand. In a sense, this saved the Patterson government's plan, since the obvious and genuine emergency drew support for the strong federal measures from authorities that might otherwise have opposed the takeover. By the time civil order was restored, it was too late for opposition.

The summer dragged on in a bloody cycle of deadly riots and brutal government response. In September the President announced that, in view of the profound state of emergency, he was suspending the Constitution of the United States, and that November elections would be postponed until no later than 2026. This order was supported by resolutions in both houses of Congress, and endorsed by statements from many state, city and corporate leaders. A challenge raised by the Supreme Court was dealt with by a NERCC task force, which took the justices and their staffs into custody. Shortly thereafter, federal courts at all levels were placed under NERCC supervision. Judges who failed to cooperate with the emergency regime were impeached by executive order.

The World in 2043

After the sharp drop in population at the turn of the century, humanity has again bred itself to crisis levels. Global numbers in 2040 were estimated at 6.4 billion.

In the opening months of 2043, there are seven brushfire wars and four violent revolutions under way, along with countless border skirmishes, terrorist operations and covert intercorporate clashes.

The average life expectancy in a firstworld country is 73.7 years. In a lastworld country, 48.2 is average. For comparison, in 1993 the average life expectancy in a developed nation was 75.9 years, and 50.2 in the most backward ones. Things have gotten a bit riskier since then.

The worldwide tech level is *early* TL8. This means that most countries are struggling along with the same old TL7 tech from yesteryear, but the firstworld countries have working TL8 technology, even though it's reserved for the very wealthy or the well-connected. See the *Technology* chapter for a thorough discussion of the availability and level of tech on the Edge.

A World on the Edge

The Greenhouse on the Edge

Hurricane Abner was an early indication that the global warming model was valid. Patterns of drought in formerly fertile regions was another, which made serious inroads on farmlands all through the first decades of the one-and-twenty. Most farmland in the newly warm northern regions lacked the same richness of soil as the drought-stricken areas, and failed to make up the difference, though Canada's rich central plains benefited both from a lengthened growing season and improved rainfall patterns. The provinces and republics of the New Confederation are the world's largest producers of wheat.

Average world temperature has risen 10°F since 1950. Increased icecap melting has raised the coastal sea levels by about 12 feet. This has had severe effects on major coastal cities.

Venice, Italy, is virtually abandoned, and most of its older buildings have collapsed as flooding destroyed their foundations. A system of levees protects downtown Washington, D.C., from flooding during high tides, and most of the East Coast megasprawl has similar problems. In most cases, the areas prone to flooding are null zones – slums where the inhabitants get along as best they can, written off by the rest of society.

As the use of fossil fuel declines, the level of greenhouse-causing gases in the atmosphere seems to be holding steady.

On what would have been Inauguration Day, 2025, Adam Hammond, Chief Commissioner of the NERCC, administered the oath of the Provisional President of the United States to Patterson.

Elections were postponed in 2026 and again 2028. Patterson died in 2031, of natural causes to all appearances. ProCon, the Provisional Congress, elected Adam Hammond to succeed Patterson as Provisional President. In his inaugural address Hammond coined the phrase "the Permanent Emergency" to define the ongoing tribulations that made it impossible for ProGov to lay aside its mandate from Congress and the people and restore free elections, "until we have once again secured the blessings of liberty and the fruits of industry that are its natural companion, across the length and breadth of America."

The permanence of the state of emergency seemed pretty well established, since elections were again postponed in 2032, 2036 and 2040. Nobody seriously expects a 2044 election.

Drug Wars

The old term "War on Drugs," coined by a U.S. administration in the 20th century, has been literal truth since 2029. The Chavez cartel in Bolivia developed a mutant strain of coca in the mid-2020s, from which a whole series of powerful designer drugs can be refined. These began to flood the United States. ProGov increased financial and military aid to Bolivia in return for suppression of the neococa trade. U.S. military advisers and ordnance were sent to Bolivia in increasing numbers as well.

The cartels initially fought the Bolivian forces with mercenaries, armed with the best weapons drug money could buy. In 2031, the cartel established a revolutionary party, the People's Will Triumphant (PWT). Many campesinos, estranged from the admittedly corrupt regime in La Paz, threw in their lot with the PWT. Bolivia's ruling junta, perhaps seeing the ghost of Che Guevara stalking the heights of the Altiplano, yelled to Washington for help.

For the past decade, Bolivia has been a battlefield between the U.S.-backed La Paz government and the PWT. Besides backing from the 'traffs (*narcotraficantes* – see p. 70), the PWT's stance as defenders of South American sovereignty from the *norteamericanos* has attracted support from nationalistic factions in Brazil and Chilentina. About 15,000 U.S. troops are stationed in Bolivia's capital cities, La Paz and Sucre, with PWT strength concentrated in rural mountain areas in the country's north, and in the lush rain forest in its eastern lowlands.

2030-2040: The Hammer Falls

The Australian Plague

On May 16, 2037, broadcasts from Melbourne, Australia reported the outbreak of a previously unknown disease. The principal symptoms were high fever and respiratory distress, with both increasing until death ensued from either brain damage, caused by the fever, or respiratory collapse. Origin: unknown. Vector: unknown. Virulence: extreme.

Communications with Melbourne ceased on May 22, 2037. No one answered any attempts to raise the city. Medical authorities at Melbourne's hastily organized Epidemic Control Center reported incidence of the disease within their own numbers during the last recorded contact, at 11:55 p.m. local time, on May 21.

By then, of course, medical experts all over the world were able to get additional information from their colleagues in Sydney, Adelaide, Perth and every other major city on the continent – until September 3, 2037.

After that date, as far as we know, everyone on the continent of Australia was dead.

CAMPAIGNS AND CHARACTERS 2

The Edge is a big, scary place, paryeni. Plenty of trouble to get into, whether you're looking for it or not. Also plenty of goodies to pick through, if the breetva is sharp enough.

This chapter gives some of the different character and campaign ideas most suited to *GURPS Cyberworld.*

Campaign Types

So you're on the Edge . . . now what? Where you gonna go? Whatcha gonna do? And why're you hanging around with those other driggin' goons?

Once the GM has his PCs lined up and ready to go, he needs to bring them together and send them somewhere. Below are a few ways to pull a team together and get them out on the streets.

Freelancers

This is the default setting for any *Cyberpunk* campaign. The PCs are a mixed bag of mercenaries and professionals in various less-than-savory fields. No need to sweat the background much. How did the team find each other? By keeping an ear tuned to the word on the street. Where are they going to go, and what are they going to do? Wherever the money is, and whatever the client wants.

Depending on the morals and tactics of the team members, adventures can range from the quasi-legal through the criminal all the way to the terroristic. This is the most popular and open-ended cyberpunk campaign type, but it can also be the most familiar and predictable, if the GM doesn't watch it.

Korporates

The team is an elite squad of corporate troubleshooters, jetting around the globe looking out for the keiretsu's interests. Korporate special missions teams look a lot like freelancers, only their hair is combed and their pants are pressed.

If the team wants to buy the korp as a patron, that can provide some degree of insurance against drigging up (as long as the mess isn't *too* dirty), but there will be a corresponding loss of autonomy. On the other hand, some squads are almost completely autonomous – "Get this done by this date and we don't *ever* want to find out how you did it." In this case the team is free to do anything that doesn't cost the korp in money or good repute. But there won't be any backup available, unless the PCs can convince the zeks that it's in the best interests of the keiretsu to increase their investment and up their risk factor – and even if help is essential, asking for it won't do the team's career prospects any good. The korps expect this kind of team to work autonomously, with no excuses.

Subversives

So there's the ProGov, sitting up there in Washington, talking about a "return to normalcy" while they're tightening their stranglehold on the citizens, promising prosperity while they're lining their own pockets, and talking about "defending the ideals of liberty" while the nerks are out shaking down the low-Cs just for living.

Those fat cats are *begging* for it.

The PCs are members of a subversive organization dedicated to bringing down the government. Their eventual goals can be re-democratization, putting themselves in power, or just blessed anarchy for its own lovely sake (maybe all of the above in the same team – revolution makes strange bedfellows). Missions might include intelligence gathering, terrorist strikes on government facilities, recruitment (a highly risky activity when you're never sure if that likely prospect is a nerk sleeper), or negotiating deals for funding or support with foreign powers or other criminal or revolutionary organizations.

A subversives campaign doesn't have to use the ProGov as the big enemy, of course – the campaign might be set in South America, with the team going after the narcotraficantes. Or the organization might be out to break up the multinational keiretsu for reasons of its own. Or the party might be vigilantes, working outside the law to bring down MafInc.

Spooks

On the other side of the fence, the team might be working for the government (or *a* government). This can be a futuristic *Espionage* campaign, with the PCs working intelligence-gathering or counterintelligence operations. Or it might be something a little less subtle, with the team as *agents provocateurs* or out-and-out chillers, disrupting the government's enemies or taking them out of the picture entirely.

Fugitives

The only thing the PCs have in common at the start of the campaign is that the same group is trying to kill all of them. Circumstances throw them together, and they team up because, hey, they need all the help they can get.

The bad guys might be the NERCC, the mob or a major korp. The individual fugitives might or might not have really done whatever the bad guys are after them for (and they might or might not *know* what the bad guys are after them for).

Eventually, the team will probably straighten out whatever got them into this mess, at which time the campaign can shift to one of the other types (maybe they'll become freelancers working for the same bunch that was formerly trying to kill them).

Low-C

This is a tough one. The PCs are only 100-point characters, and they all start out as either C-4s or nullos. Recommended options include no Wealth advantages (or even mandatory Poverty disadvantages) and no cyberwear to start the campaign – not even the groddy street stuff.

The goals are to survive and to get out, hopefully in that order. Again, if the party does make it off the mean streets, the campaign can shift to one of the types above.

Character Types

Any of the character types from *GURPS Cyberpunk* Chapter 1 can be found on the Edge. Below are some of the more common or notorious variations found in the one-and-twenty.

Assassin

Your basic assassin (chiller, hitter, zeroman) comes in a variety of different flavors on the Edge.

The *government chiller* is a professional. He specializes in efficiency and discretion. You probably wouldn't look twice at him if you saw him at a party. You wouldn't have *time* to look twice at him if you were his target.

The *korporate adjuster* is a myth. The law-abiding keiretsu of the world would never stoop to tactics like murder merely to protect their business interests.

Yeah, right.

A korp chiller is a lot like a government man, only more so – the korps require even more discretion, and they pay better. In fact, some korps regard the national governments as their farm teams.

Hitters are the mob's killers; they work on the other side of the law from the chillers. A good hitter has to understand discretion, but he also has to know how to make a noise, safely, when the client wants to make an example.

The *MafInc hitter's* tactics haven't changed significantly since prohibition. Pick your spot, move in quick, get out quick leaving the corpse behind. No muss, no fuss, no fancy variations. They aren't elegant, but they're good at what they do.

Triad hitters, on the other hand, have the streetrep of being a little crazy. Triads like the big, bloody show, and they reward reckless courage. The Triads are famous for sending agents out unarmed, to take down their target with nothing but martial arts skills. But there are those who say that this flashy stuff is all smoke screen, strictly small-time stuff. When secrecy *really* matters, the Triads can be just as hush-hush as anybody.

Russo-Yak zeromen are the best of the best, the most feared figures in the international underworld. As with everything else, the Russki-Yak take their pattern in assassins from big business, and there's only one difference between a top-flight korp chiller and a Russki-Yak zeroman – the Russki-Yak is better.

Bodyguard

Korporate shield: If a breetva wants to go legit, this is the life of choice – follow some nice, quiet nak-nik around and make sure he doesn't bump his head or stub his toesies. Of course, if your zek does get snatched or hit, that pretty much does it for your career advancement opportunities.

Protective services agent: This is a completely different breed from the basic shield. The P.S. lifeguard is a specialist, trained to deal with crisis situations. You don't use a PSA when you're snug at home and everything's sunny; you call him in when you *have* to go down into the sprawl, and you *know* there's a $1,000,000 price on your head in hard ecus.

PSAs usually work in teams of specialists: besides the actual "blockers" – the guys who intercept and neutralize physical threats – there're intelligence analysts, advance scouts, drivers and pilots, med techs, couriers and even professional decoys, all working together to see that the client doesn't get hit or snatched, or if he does that he stays alive or gets sprung.

The person who puts it all together is the team coordinator. One of these guys can do it all. They either come from the military, the korps, or both. If a successful TC decides to leave the PSA and go freelance, he can write his own job description and name his own price.

Broker

Your basic broker is the *fixer.* He's a sort of matchmaker, arranging meetings between folks who need to get to know each other, locating hard-to-find merchandise that a client might have an eye for, and seeing that certain events are planned so that they come off with a minimum of stress and unpleasantness. Fixers usually wear several hats, though, and there are a number of specialties, including the "tapper," who specializes in acquiring and distributing information, and the "shy," who can be either a lawyer (short for "shyster") or a loan shark (short for "shylock"). Bookies are also often fixers. And if the local oddsmaker isn't a fixer himself, he can definitely put you in touch with one, for a reasonable price – which makes him a fixer right there, doesn't it?

Celebrity

Even on the Edge, folks still need their heroes. Athletes, rockers and holostars all get their share of adulation. A couple of celebrity types are unique to the Edge.

A Gladiator is an athlete specializing in combat deathsports. A top-rank gladiator will combine combat skills at the upper edge of human capability with the slickest, chromiest SOTA cyberwear to be found (cyberkorps often outfit world-rank gladiators for free with their hottest new stuff – it's good advertising).

There're also the raw-meat gladiators, who don't use cybermods. This is a connoisseur's sport, without the money and recognition that goes to the samurai rumblers, but a good raw-meat killmatcher is still nobody to mess with.

The newest flavor of public celebrity is the sensostar (see "The Sensies," p. 85). Like any other kind of artistic genius, the best sensostars (or "feelers," or "headsets") are known for being a little bit bizarre, maybe a little crazy. But there's another side to the sensostars – an awful lot of them, in their sordid past, were ace deckers. It seems that both netrunning and headsetting require a similar talent for losing oneself in virtual reality and becoming one with a machine.

Cops

The most common species of cop include:

The Nerk: NERCC officers and enforcers are described in detail starting on p. 29. In the NERCC, being too smart for the job is just as dangerous as incompetence – nerks aren't recruited for their brains, and the brass gets nervous when the troops get too clever for their own good.

The Metrocop: Yeah, Officer O'Leary is still out pounding the beat. He's better armored than his grandpappy (a little), and he doesn't have nearly the patient and forgiving nature of the kindly cops of the 1990s, but he's still overworked, underpaid and risking his neck for a job that's flat-out impossible. It's no wonder most metrocops are open to business propositions of the "be somewhere else at 19:30" variety.

Korpkops are clean and polite – *scary* clean and polite. "Excuse me, sir, but if you do not remove your vehicle from this area in the next five seconds, we are authorized to begin shelling. Five, four . . . " They're also usually highly trained and enthusiastic about their jobs. One good thing about korpkops, they remember who they're there to protect – a korpkop will happily drill a vagrant or protester on korp property, but he'll not so much as lay a hand on a sarariman from his own keiretsu – at least, not until the zeks give the order.

Rentacops can be anything from highly-trained, spit-and-polish professionals to fat old Uncle Gus the watchman. It all depends on how much you're willing to pay.

Korporates

Suits fall into distinct strata.

The *top zeks* are like the old medieval dukes. As long as they pay their tribute to the king (the CEO and the board), they can do pretty much what they want with their feudal underlings – not to mention the pathetic serfs that live outside the castle. A top zek is Wealthy or Filthy Rich, and has Status 5 or 6. Don't mess around with them.

Mid zeks are Comfortable and have Status 3 or 4. They don't have the godlike power of the top zeks, but they usually have their own turf within the korp where they're top dog – and if that turf happens to be something like physical or data security, or R&D, they can be very tough nuts to crack – or very tempting targets.

Line zeks have status 1 and Comfortable Wealth. These guys are riding the tiger and they know it – they're part of a crowd of newcomers, all hungry for the job of some mid zek who probably doesn't want to be replaced. Because of this, line zeks will sometimes take crazy chances, putting everything on the line for that one big score that will either make them the fair-haired boy of the top zeks or send them back into the gutter.

Finally there's *Mr. and Mrs. Suit,* Status 0, Average Wealth. The salt-of-the-earth types who keep the keiretsu rollin' along. The thing that the streetfolk just don't get about the shaikujin is that they're really serious about this "duty to the company" line that the keiretsu feeds them every day. The korp is mommy and daddy to these folks. It's *home*. The smart guys say everybody has his price, and maybe they're right, but there are plenty of sararimen out there who'd sooner swallow a hot poker than betray the korp, and if their supervisor told them they'd been transferred to hell, they'd buy a case of sunscreen at the korp store and start packing.

Cyberprep

You don't have to be a vicious little git just because you're the child of a rich korporate or high-C family – but it helps.

Rich kids hit the streets all the time, looking to trade in the security and monotony of their homes for the excitement and danger of life on the Edge. Most of the time it's just for the night – a bunch of bored shaikujin-larva out slumming, or worse, out wilding. Gangs of high-C teens like to go out at night on thrill hunts for any C-4s or nullos who are dumb enough or unlucky enough to be caught out in the open.

Sometimes a kid will get a bellyful of respectability and bolt. Most of these runaways go crying back to daddy in a few days. The ones that don't are about evenly divided between those who get reeled back in by the korpkops or nerks (who don't mind roughing up a few low-Cs to find the little lost lamb) and those who end up dead or something worse – finding a soft, young korpbaby all hungry and alone is like Christmas for your average pimp. Of course, there are always the kids who somehow manage to get out, stay out and find their own spot on the Edge – most of the best outlaw netrunners are korpbabies. There's just no place else to get outfitted and trained for full cybernetic interface.

Drifter

There aren't a lot of drifters in the one-and-twenty. Not in the U.S., anyway. ProGov likes its low-Cs to stay nicely in their assigned ghettos until the NERCC, in its infinite wisdom, orders them to pack up and leave. If you want to travel, you need a pass, and if you want a pass, you need some clout.

So the only real drifters left are the nullos, the zeros, the blanks – those few lucky or pathetic souls who don't exist in the National Data Banks.

Most nullos got that way for a reason – their official identities got too hot, so they managed to flush them away forever. It's not easy to get that hot without getting caught, and getting zeroed takes plenty of clout all by itself. Consequently, nullos are not people you want to mess around with.

Mercenary

Most mercs are korporates – they belong to a special unit of keiretsu security. Korp merc units tend to look an awful lot like the police SWAT teams of the last century. They're sharp, shiny and well-trained, often with a standard package of combat cyber that goes with the job. Most korp units fight only in the interests of the keiretsu, but some are for rent to national governments or other korps who might need a little extra firepower.

There are still freelancers, of course. Most of them are pretty grotty – random agglomerations of combat-trained desperadoes. Some can really fight, others are less reliable, but either way when a freelance merc is off duty, he's a dangerous fellow to be around. Most work for freelance units is in lastworld countries.

There is a small elite of freelance mercenaries – highly-trained corps of troops every bit as sharp as the best company mercs. There aren't many these, and they're not cheap.

Military

Wars, and consequently armies, have gotten smaller in the one-and-twenty. Because of the return to conventional small-unit tactics, soldiers tend to be more intensively combat-trained than they were in the 20th century. A line soldier will not only know how to shoot, he'll also be trained in hand-to-hand, knife work and night fighting, along with other disciplines that were mostly the preserve of special ops during the world wars.

These days, "special ops" usually means "cybered ops." The elite forces of the 21st century are heavily enhanced with combat cyberwear. Most of the street samurais are veterans of special-ops units.

A new sort of military unit is the Metro Militias – urban strike forces that grew out of the SWAT teams of the last century. Depending on the city, urban militias can be anything from crack troops to paid thugs. They're mostly used for riot control and hostage situations. Most urban militias are a mix of professional troopers and on-call weekend warriors, the exact ratio depending on how hot a particular city is.

Mobster

The major criminal organizations are detailed on pp. 66-74. Few criminal organizations will give their soldiers an excuse to run with non-mob freelancers on a regular basis. If the party isn't all mobsters, a mobster PC will probably be a renegade, and therefore a very hot property. The mobs occasionally allow a member to retire, but not to resign . . .

Netrunner

Netrunning is an art in its infancy, so it's no surprise that netrunners are mostly infants.

There are two broad groups of netrunners. The original crop was trained during the data wars of the early '30s, and some of these grizzled veterans are now pushing 40! Only a few vets are still active on the net; most of those aren't outlaws, they're nice sararimen for the Korps, working data analysis or data security.

Then there are the young Turks. Like the teen-age hackers of the 1980s, these are kids who are out to conquer the net just because it's there. Most netrunners start out as cyberpreps. The keiretsu gives them their interface jacks and initial training, so that when the time comes for them to pick up their briefcase and go to work, they'll already be at the cutting edge of tech. As long as they stay nice and snug in the arms of the keiretsu, the korps turn a blind eye to a certain amount of snooping – after all, kids will be kids, and tracking these intruders is useful in revealing security holes. Of course credit theft, data piracy and data tampering are not tolerated.

Sometimes these kids take off and go renegade, though, and this is a korp's worst nightmare. A trained netrunner can always find someone on the street to stake him for a rig and to pay him for his services – the trick is getting a deck and a clientele without having to sell his soul to whoever's paying for his gear.

Private Investigator

In the information-based economy of the one-and-twenty, private investigation is a growth industry. The best gumshoes on the edge usually have some stealth and electronic surveillance cyberwear.

A private eye needs a working knowledge of Law, plus skill in Criminology, Stealth or Shadowing, or Research. Lip Reading is awfully handy.

A new kind of investigator is the freelance data analyst. The difference between an FDA and a hacker is that the analyst works (nominally) on the right side of the law, combing through public information sources for potentially valuable or lucrative information that might not be obvious to the casual reader. An FDA is a lot like a prospector, shifting through tons of random data searching for the odd gold nugget.

The FDA isn't a tapper – the tapper is the person the FDA sells his gleanings to. Newskorps also hire FDAs to dig up confirmation on hot stories.

A freelance data analyst needs high skill in Research and Computer Operations. Merchant skill is also useful, to let him negotiate fair value for his information.

Splicer

It's a dirty job, but somebody's gotta do it. A splicer makes his living scavenging raw material for the body banks. There are lots of names for splicers out on the street – bodtech, medico, mixmaster, vatdoc.

Some splicers are legit, cleaning up after accidents and firefights, only taking parts that the original owner has no more use for. A few are real humanitarians, taking care of streetfolk, and only selling spare parts to subsidize their medical practice.

Most splicers, though, are tough customers. They're not above giving a patient a little nudge in the direction of salability. Some don't even care if the "donor" is sick or injured – healthy parts are worth more. Drig, some splicers don't even care if the donor is *conscious* or not.

A splicer needs skill in Physician and Surgery.

Street Op

There are basically two ways to go on the street, solo or in packs.

The packs are either gangers or tribals. A gang is a business concern – the gangers are out to acquire cred, through whatever means present themselves. Tribals are more of a cultural thing – tribes are less interested in making cred than in defending their territory from outsiders. This sounds fine, except that most tribes are a little bit crazy, and most of them are violently bigoted, against other races or just other tribes.

Tribes usually have flashy colors and easily-identifiable characteristics. Some gangs follow this example, but smart ones try to blend into the surroundings.

There are two basic types of solo street op. A solo thugger is just hired muscle. The only reason he's not working for the mob or some other organization is probably that he's not worth keeping on the payroll. A ronin is a completely different matter. A ronin is a specialist – a professional – who for reasons of his own doesn't want to be tied down to any individual or organization. Ronins are some of the most feared and respected livewires on the street, but that doesn't do anything to improve their remarkably short life expectancies.

Terrorist

This is another growth industry on the Edge, and specialists are in high demand. Not all terrorist are wild-eyed bomb-chucking fanatics, but they're still out there too, and some of them are good at what they do.

A freelance terrorist will need good combat skills, as well as Stealth, Demolition, Traps and Psychology.

There are also specialized data terrorists – hackers from hell who specialize in crashing systems and eliminating data. The only skill needed is Computer Hacking, but they have to be good at it.

Advantages

Literacy
See p. B17; 5 points

Public education on the Edge is not what it used to be. Most citizens can write their names and read simple, step-by-step instructions and ProGov directives, but they're not trained to extract abstract information from a written text, or to reason using written notes. Therefore, full literacy – the degree of literacy expected of a 20th-century high-school graduate – is a five-point advantage.

Default Literacy costs zero points, but only gives someone a very basic reading ability, approximately equal to that of a 20th-century sixth grader. Full *Illiteracy* is a 5-point disadvantage (see below).

Patron, Unusual Background
See pp. B23-24

If a PC wants to start the game with rare or state-of-the-art cyberwear, the GM should require him to take one of these advantages.

Wealth
See p. B16

There aren't a lot of idle rich in the one-and-twenty. Most of the old money dried up and blew away during the Grand Slam. Consequently, the notes about how many hours each week rich folks need to work (or rather, don't need to work) can be ignored. Top zeks and mob bosses might be Filthy Rich, but they don't work any shorter hours than their underlings.

As with Patron or Unusual Background, above, characters who buy Wealthy or Filthy Rich at creation may also be allowed to start the game with SOTA cyberwear.

New Advantages

Fashion Sense
5 points

You're never caught by surprise when fashions change; your look is always one step ahead of the crowd. You have the ability to create a fashion statement out of the cheapest and most nondescript materials. A person with this advantage and the Artist skill has the potential to be a successful fashion designer.

Fashion Sense gives you a +1 to all reaction rolls in social situations where you have a chance to plan your attire in advance.

Sensie Talent
2 points per level

You have a natural ability to communicate your sensory inputs to a sensie recorder so that your eventual audience will find them particularly pleasant or intense. Note that Sensie Talent does the character no good unless he also buys at least half a point in the Sensie Interface skill (below).

Disadvantages

Addiction
See p. B30.

With a new wave of narcotics comes a new wave of addictions. All of the new designer drugs refined from cocanova are highly addictive. A daily dose of most of these drugs costs between $21 and $100. All of the old standby drugs – heroin, opium, marijuana – are still available, and in some ways easier to acquire.

A relatively new group of addicts, but one that's growing rapidly, are the Senseheads – people who do nothing but plug in

Sensie chips and lie on the couch. Sensies are legal, but fairly expensive, so this disadvantage works out to -15 points.

Illiteracy
See p. B17; -5 points

Since Literacy in a *GURPS Cyberworld* campaign comes out as a 5-point advantage, then being Illiterate – not being able to read *at all* – is a -5-point disadvantage.

New Disadvantage

Non-Iconographic
-10 points

The computer-age equivalent of Illiteracy. Your brain is unable to process abstract symbols and images. Maps, graphical user interfaces and non-verbal signs (like the little silhouettes used to distinguish the men's room from the women's room) are completely meaningless to you. You cannot use any computer interface except an old-fashioned text interface or full environmental virtual reality.

New Skills

Cyberaxe *Mental/Hard*
Defaults to equivalent
conventional Musical Instrument-4

This is the ability to play a musical instrument with a cybernetic interface. The capabilities of a cyberaxe are explained on p. 86. Musical Talent modifies Cyberaxe skill normally.

Musical Instrument skill also defaults to Cyberaxe at -4.

Sensie Interface *Mental/Hard*
Defaults to Computer
Operation/TL8 (Cyberdeck)-3

This is the skill of interfacing with a sensie recorder to create trip chips and other works of sensie art. Sensie Interface is modified by the Sensie Talent advantage.

Job Table

The Job Table lists common occupations for the Edge. Most have skill or advantage prerequisites. At least half a point must have been spent on a skill prerequisite. Default values are not permitted. "LJ" stands for Lost Job, the "d" indicates dice of damage and an "i" indicates the loss of a single month's income. When two entries are separated by a "/," the second result is only used when a natural 18 is rolled.

Job (Prerequisites), Monthly Income	Success Roll	Critical Failure
Poor Jobs		
Solo Thugger* (Brawling or Weapons skills), $400	PR	Arrested/3d
Tribal (Streetwise 12+, Brawling or Weapons skills, Area Knowledge), $300	worst PR	arrested/-2d
Struggling Jobs		
Ganger (any Combat or Thief/Spy skills), $50×PR	PR	arrested/-2d
Rentacop (Guns 12+), $750	vision roll	LJ/-3d
Ronin* (Any Combat skill 15+), $800	PR	-2d, arrested/-6d
Terrorist: fanatic (Demolitions, Psychology, Traps 12+), $500	Worst PR	-2d/-5d, arrested
Average Jobs		
Data analyst (Research 12+), $100 per point of Research	PR	-1i/-3i
Korpkop (IQ 11+, Guns 12+), $1,000 + $75 per year of service	IQ	-3d/LJ
Korp merc (any 3 Combat skills 13+), $100 × worst PR	Worst PR	-5d/LJ
Line military (Enlisted) (Guns 14+, Karate 12+, Knife 12+), $1,000	Guns	-2i/-4d
MafInc soldier (Streetwise 11+, Guns 12+),	$1,200	Worst PR-2d/LJ, -3d
Metrocop (Streetwise 12+, Guns 12+), $1,100	Worst PR	LJ/-5d
NERCC (Guns 13+, Brawling 13+), $1,200	Worst PR	LJ/-4d
Sarariman (any Professional Skill 12+), $800 + $100 per year of service	PR	-1i/LJ
Special ops (Guns 15+, Karate 14+), $1,500	Worst PR	-2i/-6d
Triad hitter* (Any combat skill 15+), $1,250	PR	-3d/arrested
Comfortable Jobs		
Gladiator* (any Combat skill 15+), $9,000	PR	-3d/-1i, disqualified
Line zek (Administration 12+), $2,500	PR	demoted to sarariman/LJ
Military officer (Leadership 12+, Administration 12+), $1,000 + $1,000 per level of Rank	Worst PR	demoted 1 Rank/LJ
NERCC officer (Administration 11+), $3,000	PR	-3d/LJ
Wealthy Jobs		
Broker (Accountant 13+, Streetwise 14+), $10,000	Worst PR	arrested/-1i, -4d
Corporate assassin (Stealth 15+, any Weapon skill 15+), $15,000	Worst PR	-1i, arrested/-6d
Government assassin (Stealth 13+, any Weapon skill 13+), $10,000	Worst PR	-2i/-6d
Netrunner (korp) (Cyberdeck Operation 14+), $1,000 × level of skill	PR	-2i/LJ
Protective services project coordinator (Administration 15+, Leadership 13+), $1,500 × worst PR	Worst PR	-4d/LJ
Russki-Yak assassin (Stealth 15+, any two weapon skills 17+), $20,000	worst PR	-3d/-6d, arrested
Sensostar* (Sensie Interface 12+), $10,000	PR	-3i/-6i
Splicer (Surgery 11+), $5,000	PR	-1i/arrested
Terrorist* (Demolitions 14+, Traps 14+, Psychology 13+), $150 × worst PR	PR	arrested/-6d

*Indicates Freelance Job

3 THE UNITED STATES

Face it. Most adventures on the Edge will be in the battered old U.S. of A. Even with all its troubles, the U.S. is one of the happening places on planet Earth. There's valuta to D/L to the right credcards, and the biz is sharp – sharp enough to slice a paryen who doesn't keep his needler cold and his cyber hot.

ProGov, the Provisional Government, grabbed what was left of control almost 20 years ago. It's been trying to maintain its grip ever since. The Feds are strongest in the Megasprawl, the jungle-bundle of cityplexes and walled-in 'burbs that runs from Maine to Georgia. ProGov keeps a high profile in the other big urban complexes as well. They figure they have to keep a tight rein on the cityproles and street ops, make it safe for the shaikujin in the fortified suburbs and condos. The rest of the country will toe the line with a visit from the nerks, as needed. So outside the metroplexes, except for the resource reservations, government control drops 'way off. Local control can be tough, or weak, or not there at all.

The Provisional Government

On paper, the same three branches that ran the U.S. government run ProGov, but in practice, the executive branch runs the show. The Provisional Congress, ProCon, is a debating society that gives people the illusion of a representative government. It makes cushy jobs for people who do major good things for ProGov, too. The courts make decisions that uphold ProGov decrees. They enforce the Uniform Code, and scare the faex out of dissenters with sentences to killing prisons.

What keeps ProGov in power? A simple answer is that old villain called "the military-industrial complex." President Patterson stacked the deck to favor the multinational keiretsu, the korps. Even before the Coup of 2024, Patterson and his supporting coalition profited from korp favor: tidy, quiet contributions to folks in public office, with nice slots as lobbyists or "consultants" waiting when they left office. It made for a cozy relationship between the politicians and the korpocrats.

At the same time, the beefed-up U.S. military was digging out from under 20 years of cutbacks. The politicos and their corporate allies groomed officers that could be depended upon to see where their best interests lay. As for the grunts in the ranks, the military was the only home that many of them knew, their only way out of starving cities and dying farms. When the officers ordered them to point their guns at crazed mobs, it was as though they faced people from Mars, not their family or friends. Or themselves. Pull the trigger? No problem.

But is that all? The U.S. submits to ProGov because it has most of the guns and money? Most citizens are scared of the chaos of life without government. They've seen it up close and personal, and they have every right to be terrified of it. So when ProGov comes along, banners waving (and bayonets gleaming, you bet) and promises they'll put food on the table and keep street ops out of taxpayers' neighborhoods, it looks like a good deal. It isn't just fear of ProGov that keeps people in line; it's fear of what they'll have to deal with if ProGov isn't around.

Neofeudalism: Two Views

"Since the geographic centralization of authority under the Provisional Government, and the concomitant return of local control in unpoliced zones to popular will, we have observed an exciting new political experiment being carried out by the American people.

"True, in some areas apparent lawlessness reigns. The popular will has not yet achieved a stable level, demonstrating the anarchic condition from which Provisional President Patterson saved the country in 2024. However, in many regions, civil authority has coalesced around what we may call nodes of natural authority: local corporate presence, residents possessed of the resources to provide for the common safety, even power groups which might have been perceived as criminal before achieving a responsible position of local authority.

"These are the neofeudal enclaves. The natural power, expressing the desire of lawful citizens for order, responsibly wielded, is vested in the local authority by the consent of the governed, *de facto* or *de jure,* to follow the direction of local authority, just as, on the larger scale, the responsible exercise of freedom under the Provisional Government . . . "

– From *Our United States: A Patriot's View* by Arthur Overhill, Ph.D.

"Neofeudalism. Tchort! That's a driggin' fancy word for lettin' the wolves take care of the sheep, paryeni. The proggies let some minshy crook with a dozen goons on the payroll scare the folks in his zone into line. As long as the proggies get their cut, and the local boss spouts the official line of faex, he's a little king. So they call it neofeudalism.

"Doesn't matter a drig if yer out inna boonies or middle of some 'plex. Rules're all the same. Walk through a high-control zone, you don't even breathe wrong or the mileetsya's all over you. Laws're run tight, no rhythm unless yer a high-C. Out inna null zones, where the cops 'n' nerks don't go, law's what ya pack inna holster.

"In 'tween, ya got the nee-yo-foo-dal zones. Korp's gotta local factory, got the guns to keep it safe, maybe a 'burb-fort for the shaikujin? Hey, they get a prize, get to run the whole zone. Local gangbangers cut a deal with the nerk goons? Good boys, they get to call the tune for everyone inna 'hood.

"But ya wanna see yer taxbux in action? Let some poor low-C shlubs arm up an' try to take care of themselves, an' they'll have nerks and proggies all over 'em like flies on faex. Strong-arm barons and korp kings, ProGov'll kiss 'em like long-lost malchikis, fatted calf an' all. Cits with guns make 'em real nervous . . ."

– From a subversive pirate Netcast intercepted by federal authorities.

Talkin' One-and-Twenty

C-1: A "Scale One Citizen." The elite class of U.S. citizens according to the Citizenship Scale instituted by ProGov.

C-2: The "middle class" scale of U.S. citizenship under ProGov.

C-3: The working or lower class scale of U.S. citizenship under ProGov.

C-4: The underclass: outcasts, political dissidents and the like form this, the lowest scale of U.S citizenship under ProGov.

Cred: Money, specifically money as a function of the world financial network, i.e., electronic funds.

D/L: "Download." Anything that moves data from the Net to a local datastore, including financial transactions.

Echeverista: A member of the Cuban revolutionary movement, headed by Rafael Echeveria, devoted to releasing Cuba from U.S. control.

Faex: Excrement. A common expletive.

Low C: Insulting slang term for someone with a lower Citizenship Scale than the person using it.

The Low Six: The six Reserved states created after the U.S. annexed Mexico.

Neofeudalism: A fancy name for local rule by the strongest faction.

Null zone: Any area where local law does not apply.

Nullo: A U.S resident who doesn't have a Citizenship Scale rating – i.e., a Zero, whose identity does not exist in the National Data Banks (see p. C21).

Prog, proggie: Agents or officials of the Provisional Government.

ProGov: The Provisional Government of the United States.

Tchort: (Russ.) Literally "Devil." A common expletive.

Valuta: (Russ.) literally "foreign currency." Refers to any hard currency, either electronic or scrip.

Adam Hammond, Provisional President

ProPresident (or ProPres, or colloquially, ProPrexy) Hammond is the head of ProGov. He is the dictator of the United States.

Born to well-to-do parents in 1977, Hammond attended excellent universities and became a highly competent design engineer. However, his real genius lay in a sure-fire instinct for spotting trends in technological development and relating them to market requirements. In 1997, he started his own firm, North American Technologies. NAT stayed on the cutting edge of pivotal developments and holds patents on many key processes and systems.

NAT's success made Hammond both wealthy and powerful. He used his money and influence to steer U.S. politics in the direction he thought they should go. He favored an increasingly conservative stance that surrendered most controls over corporate power, that rewarded individual initiative used to support social needs, that was ruthless in excising budgetary waste, and that enforced the law rigorously. Hammond's support helped Patterson win the vice-presidency in 2008; he continued to support Patterson's later campaigns.

When the NERCC was established in 2017, President Patterson nominated his long-time supporter as its head. The media widely praised Hammond for leaving his position as CEO of NAT to become one of the administration's "dollar-a-year" men. The nerks and nerk-commanded police and military used draconian measures to suppress anything they interpreted as insurrection. Even so, many citizens viewed Hammond's early performance as Executive Commissioner of the NERCC favorably, as he devoted his undeniable organizational skills to keeping vital resources flowing, especially in the devastated inner cities.

When Patterson established the Provisional Government, Hammond was one of the advisers who designed the new regime. NERCC communication channels carried the most sensitive information involved in the coup. NERCC personnel coordinated the capture of key sites during the fighting. If rumor can be trusted, NERCC agents also handled the removal, by arrest or assassination, of officials who might have opposed the birth of ProGov.

Hammond's efficiency in this central role confirmed Patterson's regard for his abilities. Over the remaining years of the first ProPresident's life, more and more authority passed into the hands of Hammond and the NERCC.

Patterson's death in 2031 created a "constitutional" crisis. The last Vice-President had died just before ProGov came to power. The aging Patterson had adamantly refused to name his successor, or to enable any legislation on presidential succession. The 25th Amendment, and related legislation, were not considered to be in force, since Executive Order P-23-1 suspended the Constitution.

A consortium of Cabinet members and ProCon leaders, led by Hammond, drafted a decree enabling ProCon to "elect" a new Provisional President. The decree limited the eligibility of candidates to senior executive appointees or members of ProCon. To no one's great surprise, Hammond himself was chosen as the new Provisional President.

Under ProPresident Hammond, the NERCC's authority has increased dramatically. Hammond is also the NERCC's Supreme Commissioner, an *ex officio* position, comparable to his rank as Commander-in-Chief of the armed forces. The Cabinet-level office of Executive Commissioner still exists, and is charged with day-to-day operation of the Commission.

Hammond instituted the National Recovery Plan as an index of "domestic tranquility and economic stability," and has said on more than one occasion that the plan will indicate when the Provisional Government can step down and restore free elections. He is, however, vague about the precise indicators in the plan which would trigger this event, and the actual parameters of the National Recovery Plan are highly classified.

The Cabinet

The ProPres hires and fires cabinet members. Congress doesn't get to say anything about it. Cabinet members are *not* automatically in line for the President's job. In fact, Hammond, like Patterson, has no designated successor.

In theory, cabinet members are in complete charge of their departments and the resources in those departments. In reality, cabinet powers are limited by a couple of things.

First, Hammond is well aware that the most dangerous challenge to his authority is likely to come from his immediate underlings. In order to keep any one person in the cabinet from getting too powerful, Hammond switches his favor from one member to another unpredictably. One week, the ProPres will support Secretary of State Barton's policies against all opposition. The next, Barton can't do anything right, and Secretary of Business Dennison has the presidential ear.

Second, it is almost impossible for a cabinet-level department to do anything without getting into a turf fight. A resource-exploitation program run by the Department of Business may run afoul of a regulatory agency over at Agriculture, or Industry, or, of course, the NERCC.

And this is the third factor that complicates cabinet infighting. The NERCC has a finger in almost every government pie.

All of this tends to make the top levels of ProGov more concerned with power plays and butt-covering than with the efficient operation of their departments. The attitude trickles down the organizational tree, so that at "street-level," the local bureaucrats play the same dominance games as their bosses. For example, during the Chicago Food Riots of 2037, the Department of Agriculture diverted emergency stocks of food to the city. The NERCC district commissioner was fighting over priority scheduling with his counterpart in Agriculture and refused to authorize transport to carry the rations from their warehouses to the starving parts of the Windy City. After the third day of rioting, of course, it didn't matter much, since the mobs had set fire to the warehouse district and destroyed the stockpiled relief rations.

The Provisional Congress

When ProGov came to power in 2024, members of Congress fell into two categories: the quick and the dead. The former were quick either to support ProGov (65 senators and 273 representatives did so), or to get out of Washington and drop out of public view. Sixteen senators and 83 representatives managed to survive the coup without actively supporting Patterson's takeover. The rest were either arrested for treason or reported "missing in urban disorders, presumed killed."

The role of Congress was defined in Executive Order P-24-13: "The Provisional Congress of the United States is established to provide the long-suffering citizens of this great, embattled nation with personal representation within the structure of the Provisional Government."

ProCon has a Senate and a House of Representatives, just as Congress did under the Constitution. The resemblance pretty much ends there. Senators are elected, one to a state, and serve for life, or until they retire. Actually, the law states that " . . . Senators shall serve for the duration of the state of emergency now obtaining." As that state evolved into the Permanent Emergency, amendments to Executive Order P-24-13 allowed for senatorial retirements and succession. Representatives serve 2-year terms. Senators and representatives have C-1 status (see p. 31) during their terms of office.

Adam Hammond, Provisional President of the United States

Age 66; 6'1", 180 lbs.; gray hair, gray eyes.

ST 11, DX 10, IQ 14, HT 10.

Basic Speed 5, Move 5.

Dodge 5.

No armor or encumbrance.

Advantages: Charisma +2; Literacy; Status 7; Wealth (Filthy Rich).

Disadvantages: Age; Compulsive Behavior (record-keeping); Overconfidence; Stubbornness.

Quirks: Loves gardening, public displays of piety, and conservative morality; Secretive; Workaholic.

Skills: Accounting-14; Administration-14; Bard-16; Botany/TL8-16; Computer Operation/TL7-14; Detect Lies-15; Diplomacy-13; Economics-15; Electronics/TL8-15; Guns (Pistol)-9; Politics-15; Research-16; Savoir-Faire-15.

Languages: French-14; German-10; Japanese-10; Russian-13.

Hammond talks the talk of a sincere and dedicated elected official, but he doesn't walk the walk. He is aware that his word is law, at least in areas where the NERCC, or military loyal to ProGov, maintain control. Hammond has an uncanny ability to gauge what his administration can get away with, as well as a highly-developed sense of public mood. When a ProGov official gets caught in a scandal, the ProPresident usually expresses horror at this abuse of trust, and the scapegoat finds himself in a starring role in a videorendum treason trial or a thrillvid ordeal show.

Hammond's personality is engaging, a mixture of forceful, decisive executive and folksy politician.

The U.S. Cabinet

Agriculture (Secretary: Brad Winston): Coordinating food production in the U.S., as well as the import and export of foodstuffs, Agriculture is often involved in turf fights with NERCC.

Business (Secretary: William Carlton): Managing U.S. relations with business, specifically Big Business, it has a role similar to that of the State Department in dealing with the multinational, semi-autonomous korps.

Defense (Secretary: Anthony Riccio): Management of the Armed Forces is its province.

Energy (Secretary: James Tarleton): Responsible for implementing energy policy, it oversees safety and emission standards, the national power grid and federal power generation programs.

Enforcement (Enforcer General: Arthur Williams): The Department of Justice was renamed the Department of Enforcement during Patterson's first term. The Attorney General was similarly renamed the Enforcer General, in accordance with the President's premise that ". . . an *attorney* general sends the wrong message to the criminal scum oppressing all Americans. Swift and sure *enforcement* of the law is needed, to guarantee the safety of decent men and women in this great country. Only the honest man deserves justice."

The Department coordinates federal courts, penal establishments, the FBI and other federal law-enforcement organizations and programs.

Health (Surgeon General: Margarita Esteves): This department is charged with all public health programs, oversight of medical research and correlation of medical records on all citizens.

Continued on next page . . .

Elections

Senatorial elections are held as needed. Elections for representatives are held every two years, in November. A voter does not need to wait for election day to go to the polls, however. He doesn't even have to go to the polls. At any time during a campaign, a voter can "pre-approve" his vote, registering it in the National Data Banks. Once it is in, it cannot be changed, and stands even if the voter dies before the election.

ProGov shows a keen appreciation of the political wisdom of William Marcy ("Boss") Tweed. "Let 'em vote for anyone they like, as long as I get to make the nominations." The state government nominates senators, subject to federal approval. Usually, governors and state legislatures are given a list, or simply a name, to place in nomination.

A seat in the Senate is one of the principal prizes offered to korp execs, military commanders, local officials and other very senior figures who contribute to ProGov's authority.

Congressional elections are livelier. Nominations are made according to state laws. After all, folks, these are *your* personal representatives. Generally, the states require that nominees be at least Scale 2 citizens (see p. 32). Winning candidates are typically sponsored either by ProGov, by one or more major korps, or both. A typical campaign rally for a mainstream candidate resembles a cross between a traveling circus and a Roman Saturnalia. Free food and booze, legalized drug distribution, entertainers, prizes, korp recruiting stations . . . all reward the faithful for their pre-assigned ballots.

Fringe candidates were a common feature in the first few sets of elections. That was before folks noticed that anyone who ran on a platform that ProGov didn't like wasn't around to run again two years later. It wasn't the crazies that disappeared – any candidate who might pose a real threat to ProGov was in grave danger.

If a candidate who doesn't toe the ProGov line still shows signs of winning a congressional race . . . well, the votes are tabulated in the National Data Banks. Another of Boss Tweed's gems of political wisdom says "As long as *I* count the votes, what are *you* going to do about it?"

The Videorendum

When the Provisional Government began to stabilize the national communications network, and to centralize government data processing functions, it used them to offer a direct voice in government to citizens. Numerous referendums were called, inviting citizens to vote through their home terminals and interactive vidphones. Any citizen with at least Scale 3 standing is eligible to vote in a *videorendum.*

On the average, voting takes place on at least one national videorendum each week, on one or more issues. Input is open from 0600-1800, local time. Terminals with full multimedia capability can also display pertinent documentation in the cases. This may explain the surge of concerned citizens who seem to vote any time a juicy, and graphically documented, sex scandal is on the issues menu.

A citizen simply inserts his citcard (see p. 35) in a terminal connected to the National Data Banks, calls up the issues menu, and enters his vote. This automatically triggers a low-level card check.

Some cynics, just aching for a C-4/D rating (see p. 33), have pointed out that the issues settled by videorendum are always trivial, even when they are sensational. For example, when federal courts found the ringleaders of the Chicago Food Riots guilty of treason, sentencing was fixed by a videorendum of Chicago citizens. The vote was *not* over their guilt or innocence, but whether the accused were to be executed, and if so, how, or whether they were to receive life sentences in a penal facility.

Trials by videorendum have become increasingly violent, with the victims condemned to gladiatorial combats, manhunts and similar entertainments by the impartial vote of their fellow citizens.

Some of the more subversive elements who contaminate society have even suggested that, since ProGov computers tally the votes, the usual result of a videorendum, upholding the government's position, is a sign that the figures are being falsified somewhere along the way.

Of course, ever since the issue was put to a videorendum on March 27, 2038, it has been a Class C Felony to assert publicly that videorendum tallies are falsified.

ProCon Functions

The Provisional Government ruled by executive decrees from its inception in 2024 until 2032. In 2032, with much fanfare, newly "elected" Provisional President Hammond redefined the relationship between the executive and legislative branches of ProGov.

The ProPresident retains the authority to issue Executive Orders. These have the force of law but must be for a specified period of time (90 to 180 days is the typical length). The Executive Orders issued prior to 2032 remain in force as they were originally specified, for the duration of the "state of emergency." Executive Orders that are not ratified by ProCon by the end of the specified period lapse. ProCon cannot countermand an Executive Order during its effective period.

Moreover, ProCon gained the right, which it did not originally have, of passing bills for Presidential approval. However, if he vetoes a bill, it cannot override him.

These sops of authority thrown to ProCon by Hammond, surprisingly, were sufficient to consolidate his authority with a large majority of senators and representatives. Since ProCon members would have had neither perquisites nor power without the continued presence of the Provisional Government, Hammond could buy legislative support fairly cheaply.

The NERCC

President Patterson established the National Emergency Resource Control Commission in 2017 to coordinate national distribution of vital resources during the Grand Slam chaos. The Commission has authority to deal with anything affecting resource manufacture, transport or distribution. Since the NERCC itself decides what is or is not a vital resource, the "nerks" swiftly got into the business of watching everything and everyone.

After Patterson created the Provisional Government, the NERCC was given an increasing role in all areas of security and enforcement. When ProPres Patterson died, Adam Hammond, the NERCC head, succeeded him, and the Commission became even more powerful.

In a campaign context, the nerks are designed to be "bad guys." They are the secret police, the faceless bureaucracy and the power-behind-the-throne, all rolled into one. In any campaign based on revolution against America's one-and-twenty ruling clique, the nerks will be the PCs' principal opponents.

As an alternative, the PCs can *be* nerks. A campaign like this will involve lost of backstabbing and political maneuvering – with plenty of mindless violence along the way.

Industry (Secretary: Jennifer Brookes): Overseeing all matters of industrial production subject to federal control, it arbitrates labor disputes, reviews safety standards and measures productivity.

Information (Secretary: William Chang): Operating and maintaining the National Data Banks, it is in charge of producing, distributing and validating citizen cards (see p. 35). It also oversees U.S. communications media and education programs.

Interior (Secretary: Otis Jordan): Charged with proper management of U.S. natural resources, it issues mining licenses, oversees timber production, properly engineers water courses and so on. It also manages the Reserved Access Parklands: two-year waiting list for a visitor's permit for a C-2. You're a C-3? Forget it, citizen.

National Emergency Resource Coordinating Commission: See *The NERCC*, p. 29.

State (Secretary: Carlos DiVincenzo): It handles U.S. relations with other governments.

Treasury (Secretary: Philip Morton): It governs the U.S. money supply and maintains the National Credit System.

Urban Planning (Secretary: Cynthia Washington): Also called the Department of Bread and Circuses, Urban Planning maintains federal programs designed to prevent disorder in the cities.

U.S. Political Parties

Yes, the U.S. has lost a lot, but it still has political parties: lots and lots of political parties. The two-party system blew up after disastrous campaigns in the late 1990s, resulting in a mess of splinter groups and special-interest parties. The U.S. had to learn how to handle coalition politics, and judging by the first third of the one-and-twenty, it looks like it didn't do its homework.

After ProGov took over, it outlawed the most militant fringe parties, especially the ones left of center. They formed the nucleus for most of the revolutsiya simmering around the country since the 2030s.

Conservative parties that back ProGov and centrist parties that play loyal (read: ineffective) opposition continue to operate legally. They put up candidates in ProCon elections, and use their influence to advance their agendas in federal and local government.

The major parties are profiled here.

Archconservative

Committed to domestic economic growth by minimizing government interference in business policy, it advocates a strict law-and-order regime. It often opposes NERCC policies which seem to regulate the korps, though it favors most ProGov programs designed to keep the urban population docile.

Allied: Efficiency Party, God's Own Party, Meritocrats, True Americans.

Opposed: Centrist Democrats, Globalists, Technolibertarians.

Centrist Democrat

A moderate coalition, the Centrist Democrats push for an increase in civil liberties and in federal programs to improve the lot of disadvantaged citizens. They are viewed as ineffective reformers by the powers-that-be within ProGov.

Allied: Globalists, Light Of Wisdom, Technolibertarians.

Opposed: Archconservatives, God's Own Party, True Americans.

Efficiency Party

Dedicated to running the government as if it were a successful business, it is strongly supported by U.S. business for its protectionist stance. The Efficiency Party was one of the strongest proponents of the expansion of toxic industrial production in Mexico.

Allied: Archconservatives, Meritocrats, Technolibertarians.

Opposed: God's Own Party, Light of Wisdom.

Continued on next page . . .

NERCC Organization

The Commission is strictly hierarchical. Much like the military's Pentagon, its national headquarters in Washington is the nerve center of all operations.

The U.S. is divided into nine administrative regions: Northeastern, Middle Atlantic, Southeastern, Caribbean, South Central, North Central, Northwestern, Southwestern and Pacific. Two additional "Special Administrative Regions" exist, one for Alaska and one for the Mexican states.

Each region is divided into a number of districts. Each state is a district. In addition, every major urban area with a population of 500,000 or more is a district. Within each district, a number of local NERCC offices operate.

For example, New York state is part of the Northeastern Region. The New York District covers the entire state, except for the Greater New York Metroplex District, which controls New York City and its environs.

Industrial Regulation

In 2020, the functions of the EPA, OSHA, NRC and other bureaus concerned with industrial conditions, pollution standards and safety controls were shifted to the NERCC. In President Patterson's words, this was intended to "rationalize the regulatory atmosphere in our industries, and move forward in the task of reconstruction with the greatest speed concomitant with the health and safety of the public."

This laudable plan has been implemented in a number of ways. Pollution and dumping regulations were eased even further. Highly toxic processes were moved to Mexican sites. Disclosure laws and requirements for impact statements, which had already been weakened by relaxed enforcement regulations, were suspended for an indefinite period.

Immigration

The NERCC is charged with ensuring the orderly flow of citizens seeking to move from the Reserved states to the rest of the U.S. This translates into making sure that when the Upper 48 needs bodies in the labor force, enough Mexican C-3s arrive to take the wages management wants to pay.

Labor pool management companies handle recruiting drives for U.S. employers in the Reserved states, under franchises awarded by the nerks. Organized crime reputedly runs most of these operations (see p. 66).

Security

The NERCC directly controls all internal security in the U.S., and its enforcement arm requires full cooperation from federal and local law-enforcement agencies in any matter of security. The NERCC does not deal with other criminal matters, with the exception of crimes that interfere with, or impede, the rationing system or interstate commerce.

In theory, other federal law-enforcement agencies, such as the FBI, the Secret Service and the U.S. Marshal's office, continue to carry out their original functions, with the exception of matters concerning U.S. security. In practice, the NERCC can take over any investigation at any time, though agents and other resources from the office that originally had jurisdiction may be seconded to NERCC control.

Students of 20th-century history may recognize certain similarities between the operations of the NERCC and the KGB in the old Soviet Union. Of course, students of history would legally require Class 2 library-system access to study such material in any detail.

U.S. Citizenship

In 2027, ProGov instituted the U.S. Citizenship Scale. The privileges and civil rights of citizens were adjusted according to " . . . the contribution of the individual to the national recovery effort." Initially, the NERCC administered the program. In 2036, the Bureau of Citizen Evaluation was created to handle the program, under the direction of the Department of Information.

Citizenship is rated from One to Four.

Scale One Citizen

A C-1 is a member of the U.S. ruling elite. Officially, his status reflects outstanding contributions to national recovery, U.S. security, or some similar accomplishment. Effectively, C-1 status goes to the very rich, upper-level corporate managers, high government officials, leading scientists, sports figures, major media stars and the like. C-1s have a Status of 3 or higher. Three percent of the population are C-1s.

Scale One citizens pay lower taxes, enjoy more generous rations and luxury bonuses, and have access to legal free markets. C-1s have access to higher tech than other citizens, especially medical tech. Practically speaking, C-1s usually have enough influence to avoid prosecution for minor, and sometimes major, crimes. The bureaucracy defers to them, unless they are known to be out of favor, and lower-rated citizens who know the score are well advised not to cross them, since C-1s usually have contacts that can make a "low C" regret that he ever irritated his betters, or even that he was ever born.

C-1s enjoy most of the protections under the law that all U.S. citizens had, at least in theory, prior to the establishment of the ProGov. See p. 15 for details.

Globalist

A small minority, dedicated to a more cooperative role for the U.S. in international affairs. Free trade is a high priority.

Allied: Centrist Democrats, Light of Wisdom.

Opposed: Archconservatives, True Americans.

God's Own Party

This party proposes that ProGov adopt a blatantly theocratic stance, ruling the U.S. by the narrowest interpretation of conservative Christian doctrines.

Allied: Archconservatives, True Americans.

Opposed: Centrist Democrats, Efficiency Party, Light of Wisdom, Technolibertarians.

Light Of Wisdom

According to its critics, this is the "Granola" party: all the nuts and flakes are in it. Light of Wisdom supports ProGov as the "karmic adjustment" for generations of U.S. "gluttony." They are aggressively "Green," and reliably support any policy, no matter how repressive, which makes a case for preserving the environment.

Allied: Centrist Democrats, Globalists.

Opposed: Efficiency Party, God's Own Party, Technolibertarians.

Meritocrat

The Meritocrats propose a social hierarchy based on their definition of "merit." This is a combination of updated social Darwinism, technocracy and a caste system based on education and productivity.

Allied: Archconservatives, Efficiency Party.

Opposed: Centrist Democrats, Light of Wisdom.

Technolibertarian

They suggest that the U.S. will be best served by unhampered research in new technologies. The Technolibertarians are the most outspoken opponents of the NERCC in ProCon, and are viewed with the greatest suspicion by the administration.

Allied: Centrist Democrats, Efficiency Party.

Opposed: Archconservatives, God's Own Party, Light of Wisdom.

True Americans

Somewhat to the right of the Archconservatives, they strongly support military intervention to protect American interests. Overtly racist, they propose relocation of minorities to the Low Six. The True American party is pushing hard for the use of tactical nuclear weapons in Cuba.

Allied: Archconservatives, God's Own Party.

Opposed: Centrist Democrats, Globalists.

Northeastern Region: Boston Urban Complex District, Connecticut District, Delaware District, Greater New York Metroplex District, Maine District, Massachusetts District, New Hampshire District, New Jersey District, New York District, Pennsylvania District, Philadelphia Metroplex District, Rhode Island District, Vermont District, West Virginia District.

Middle Atlantic Region: Federal Capital District, Maryland District, North Carolina District, South Carolina District, Virginia District.

Southeastern Region: Alabama District, Atlanta Urban Constellation District, Florida District, Georgia District, Miami Urban District, Mississippi District, Tennessee District.

North Central Region: Chicago Megaplex District, Detroit Urban Complex District, Illinois District, Indiana District, Iowa District, Michigan District, Minnesota District, Nebraska District, North Dakota District, Ohio District, South Dakota District, Wisconsin District.

South Central Region: Arkansas District, Dallas/Fort Worth Urban Constellation District, Houston Urban District, Kansas District, Kansas City Urban District, Kentucky District, Louisiana District, Missouri District, New Orleans Urban District, Oklahoma District, Texas District.

Northwestern Region: Idaho District, Montana District, Oregon District, Seattle/Tacoma Metroplex District, Washington District, Wyoming District.

Southwestern Region: Arizona District, Colorado District, Denver Urban District, Joint Southwestern Water Control District-Southwestern Authority, Las Vegas Special Coordinating District, Nevada District, New Mexico District, Utah District.

Pacific Region: Bay Area Metro District, California District, Greater Los Angeles Metropolitan District, Hawaii District, Joint Southwestern Water Control District-Pacific Authority.

Caribbean Region: Cuba District, Puerto Rico District, Virgin Islands District.

Mexican Special Administration Region: Baja District, Central Industrial Coordination District, Ciudad Juarez District, Guadalajara District, Juarez District, Mexico City District, New Tejas District, Tenochtitlan District, Veracruz District.

Alaskan Special Administrative Region.

Scale Two Citizen

The upper middle-class are C-2s. Professionals and skilled workers are usually C-2s, and have a Status of 0 to 4, though the majority will have a Status of 1 to 3. The population is about 33% C-2s.

The life of a C-2 would be, in some respects, familiar to a middle-class resident of 20th-century America: go to work, raise a family, pay taxes and go about your business. Of course, in the one-and-twenty, there are a few additional concerns: urban terrorist strikes on C-2 neighborhoods (security there is much easier to penetrate than in C-1 enclaves), the interest of a NERCC review board, a korporate readjustment sideswipe, and so on.

Scale Two Citizens pay the highest taxes in the U.S. today. Still, most C-2s express satisfaction with their lot, and praise the efforts of ProGov and the nerks . . . excuse me, a slip of the tongue . . . NERCC, to maintain order and put the country back on its feet.

Scale Three Citizens

C-3 is the classification of most U.S. citizens: white- and blue-collar workers, low-level labor and unemployed citizens who stay out of trouble and cooperate with work-subsistence programs. Retirees on fixed pension incomes, without disposable wealth from investments and the like, are often downgraded to C-3 after a working life spent at C-2. C-3s with a regular income pay taxes at the same rate as a C-2. C-3s can have a Status of -1 to 2. They make up 52% of the population.

The nature of ProGov's America is such that most immigrants are assigned to Scale Three, as are many non-white citizens who are not in the upper brackets of the economy. A middle-class job that would win a white a C-2 rating will leave a black, Oriental, or Hispanic citizen at C-3.

Being a C-3 carries a -5 point Social Stigma when dealing with anyone of a higher Citizenship Scale.

Scale Four Citizens

C-4s are convicted felons, welfare recipients, inhabitants of Secure Observation Facilities, those on probation or parole and unemployed citizens who do not cooperate with NERCC work-subsistence programs and similar uplifting agendas. Citizens classified as Scale 4 for economic reasons will almost always have negative Status.

A citizen can be downgraded to C-4 for political reasons: dissidents, "religious dissenters" such as Quakers and Wiccans, people assigned to reside in a Secure Observation Facility, are all Scale 4 citizens, without regard to their economic standing in society. At least 12% of the U.S. population are C-4s.

All C-4s have an assigned subcode (see below), indicating the specific reason for their classification and the kind of official scrutiny they are likely to be under. C-4s also suffer a Social Stigma when dealing with higher Scale citizens.

C-4s have extremely limited civil rights under the Uniform Code (see p. 34).

Scale Four Subcodes

Only C-4s receive Citizen Scale subcodes to indicate why they have been relegated to the bottom rung of American society. Being a C-4 is a Social Stigma all by itself; the subcode determines just how badly their classification affects their social interactions. "Poor-but-honest" C-4s and, ironically, paroled felons are subject to the least amount of social prejudice. Political dissidents, religious offenders, and other threats to national tranquility suffer a more severe loss of standing.

C: Convict. Ex-convict, actually. The C-4/C served time for a felony. Social Stigma value: -10.

D: Dissident. The United States is a free society, and citizens have the right to espouse views that disagree with ProGov policy. However, when such citizens, in exercising their rights, impede the legal mandate of the Recovery, society may properly impose sanctions such as a C-4/D classification for its own protection. Social Stigma value: -15. The C-4/D is an outsider in his own country.

I: Inmate. The C-4/I is incarcerated in a prison, rehabilitation center or similar penal program. A C-4/I may also be in a mobile penal surveillance program (see *House Arrest*, p. 00). Upon release, the C-4/I is usually reclassified C-4/C or C-4/P, unless his offense was political, in which case a C-4/D is usual. Social Stigma value is -15 when dealing with non-prisoners.

M: Medical. This usually implies a certified mental condition, but can also apply to registered drug addicts, or others whose condition causes them to be classified as Scale Four. Social Stigma value: -5.

P: Parole/Probation. The C-4/P is on parole, on probation, or under a suspended sentence. Social Stigma value: -5.

R: Religious dissenter. The C-4/R is a member of a religion ruled invalid by ProCon: a Wiccan, a Quaker, a Scientologist, a Unitarian, etc. Social Stigma value: -10.

S: SOF inmate. The C-4/S is assigned to a Secure Observation Facility, either remote or localized (see p. 14). Upon release from the SOF, a C-4/S is usually reclassified a C-4/D. Most other citizens, even other C-4s, are reluctant to be openly friendly to a C-4/S, since the NERCC is fond of the concept of guilt-by-association, and you never know when they are watching. Social Stigma value: -15.

W: Welfare dependent. The C-4/W is assigned for long-term presence on the welfare rolls, to hardcore unemployables, unlike unemployed C-3s, who are considered at least a potential member of the labor force. Often, the difference between an unemployed C-3 and a C-4/W is the personal favor (or enmity) of the local NERCC or Bureau of Citizen Classification administrator. This is the largest category of Scale Four citizens. Social Stigma value: -5.

NERCC Enforcer

ST 11, DX 11, IQ 9, HT 12.
Basic Speed 5.75, Move 5.
Dodge 5, Parry 6.

Armor includes dress uniforms and fatigues (PD 0, DR 0); standard duty uniform light monocrys (PD 2, DR 8); combat uniform medium monocrys (PD 2, DR 16). (See p. C49 for details on monocrys.) The Emergency Response Squads, the equivalent of SWAT teams, wear full TL8 Combat Infantry Dress when going into action (see p. C50). All uniforms are matte black.

Standard, combat and combat infantry uniforms require a helmet. This is a TL8 Combat Infantry Helmet (see p. CP50), equipped with HUD, short-range communicator and a multi-view visor providing light-intensification, anti-glare and thermal-imaging capability. The NERCC-issue helmet is the same matte black as their uniforms. The visor is one-way plastic, which hides the wearer's face behind a featureless shield of dully reflective black. This look gives rise to the commonest (printable) nicknames for the Enforcers on the street: flatblacks, blacktops, etc.

Advantages: Legal Enforcement Powers; Military Rank (Private 0, NCO 1, Senior NCO 2)

Disadvantages: Duty (to NERCC); plus at least 10 points worth of Disadvantages drawn from: Bad Temper; Bully; Greed; Intolerance (Anyone lower than Scale 2 Citizen); Lecherousness; Sadism.

Skills: Area Knowledge-11; Beam Weapons/TL8-14; Brawling-13; Driving (Car)-13; Gunner/TL8-12; Guns/TL8-14; Interrogation-9; Shadowing-12; Stealth-12; Streetwise-10.

Typical specialist skills include Demolitions, Leadership (for NCOs), Tactics (for NCOs), possibly Diplomacy or Politics, or technical skills such as Computer Operation, Armoury, etc.

Weapons: NATArm M-19 submachine guns, 3d damage; FE Rakete-P gyroc pistols, usually with APEX rounds (see p. C44). The standard-issue shotgun is the NATArm UCW, 5d damage. Enforcers expecting heavy combat carry M-23 assault rifles, 7d damage, and may be issued heavier weaponry (machine guns, mortars, grenade launchers, etc.).

All NERCC weapons are equipped with HUD targeting displays, routed to the HUD units in the helmet.

The typical NERCC Enforcer is a goon, plain and simple. Usually recruited from the lower ranks of C-3s at age 16 or so, the Enforcers are trained in NERCC camps, and conditioned to give total loyalty to the Commission. After an 8-month basic training course, Enforcers are placed in active duty.

A typical Enforcer is venal, corrupt, and cruel. He, or she, knows that as long as he keeps the street scum in line, and kisses any boots above him on the ladder, he'll do fine. Enforcers are usually susceptible to bribery, if they think no one is watching.

NERCC Elite Enforcer

ST 12, DX 13, IQ 10, HT 13.
Basic Speed 6.5, Move 6.
Dodge 6, Parry 7.

Armor includes dress, fatigues, and standard issue uniforms as for regular Enforcers (see p. 33). Combat uniform is full TL8 Combat Infantry Dress (see p. C50), with the standard issue helmet.

Advantages: Legal Enforcement Powers; Military Rank (Private 0, NCO 1, Senior NCO 2).

Disadvantages: Duty (to NERCC); plus at least 20 points worth of disadvantages drawn from: Bad Temper; Bully; Greed; Intolerance (Anyone lower than Scale 2 Citizen); Lecherousness; Sadism.

Skills: Beam Weapons/TL8-15; Brawling-14; Demolitions/TL8-13; Driving (Car)-14; Gunner/TL8-14; Guns/TL8-15; Interrogation-12; Shadowing-12; Stealth-12; Streetwise-12; Tactics-11.

Weapons: NATArms M-23 assault rifles, 7d damage; in many cases, also NATArms Sunbeam laser weapons: PL-5 pistol, 2d damage; RL-5 rifle, 2d damage. Elite units in regional or higher commands are always armed with lasers.

All NERCC weapons are equipped with HUD targeting displays, routed to the HUD units in the helmet. Lasers are also equipped with a laser-keyed anti-theft system and a D-tag (see pp. C46-47).

Elite Enforcers are assigned as members of Emergency Response units, bodyguards for high-ranking officials, guards at high-security installations and other sensitive positions. Often, an Elite non-com will be leading a squad of regular Enforcers.

Elites are given wide latitude in carrying out orders. As long as the body count isn't *too* high, and is limited to C-3s or lower, disciplinary action is rare. The Elites aren't called in unless a situation is already dangerous or secret, and most Elites are arrogant about their status.

Nullos

Officially, only social misfits, criminals by virtue of their very existence, reject the Citizenship Scale and fail to register for their legal scale rating and the perquisites and duties that go with it.

The government calls them "Unregistered Non-Citizens." The common slang for such folks is "Nullos," or "C-Zeros."

A nullo has no rights under U.S. law. If he is apprehended in commission of a crime, the arresting authority can dispose of the case as it sees fit. Of course, laws exist for dealing with nullo criminals who are processed into the system. They are assigned a rating of Scale Four-C, and immediately subject to charges of Unregistered Resource Consumption, a Class B felony. This is in addition to whatever charges accompany the crime for which they were apprehended.

However, if the arresting officer prefers to shoot first and request identification later, he is not subject to federal penalties, though local regulations may apply.

Moreover, unless extraordinary circumstances apply, no rated citizen of Scale Two or better is subject to penalties for assaulting, or even killing, a nullo. Thrill-seeking gangs of high Cs are often found in the null zones of the cities or countryside, hunting for nullos. C-3s and C-4s may be subject to investigation for unprovoked attacks on nullos – not out of concern for the nonexistent rights of the nullos, but because the authorities view any sign of violence among low Cs with suspicion. However, a C-3 or C-4 who kills a nullo in self-defense, or when the nullo was committing a crime, will usually be cleared in an official inquiry (though the incident becomes part of his permanent record).

The Uniform Code

In 2028, ProGov introduced a greatly streamlined code of criminal and civil justice. Martial law had prevailed since the outbreak of civil unrest in 2023, and the Uniform Code was touted as a regularization of the conflict between martial law in the troubled regions of the country, and the surviving shreds of civil law enforced elsewhere. It imposed a single legal code on the United States, and accommodated ProGov and NERCC controls, as well as the then-new Citizenship Scale.

The Uniform Code has been modified many times since its introduction as the ProGov tightens or loosens pressure on the reins of government. Why does a dictatorship like the Provisional Government bother with dotting the i's and crossing the t's of the legal code? Because, like many fascist governments, ProGov worships loudly and publicly at the altar of legality. The government may be brutal, repressive and violent, but it will play the game by the rules it has rigged, if at all possible. ProGov depends on the acquiescence of the majority in its rule. The present rulers of the United States believe that as long as resistance can be blamed on a "criminal minority," they can prosper. Also, even though it may *seem* omnipresent, the resources of ProGov and the nerks remain finite. Keeping the rules clear and explicit allows the ProGov to automate the process a little bit, turning over bread-and-butter enforcement to other agencies, and leaving the NERCC in a supervisory capacity.

Control Ratings

Control Ratings, defined on p. C110, provide a quick method of measuring the overall level of legal control that a government exercises on its citizens.

The overall CR in ProGov's U.S. is 5 (Repressive). However, different CRs apply to different situations – specifically Weapons, Cyberwear and Tech.

The Weapon CR is used as specified on p. C111.

The Tech CR governs the availability and use of non-cybernetic equipment at

TL7 or higher. See the *Technology* chapter for individual item descriptions. Control Ratings are different for each piece of equipment, cyberwear, etc., and will be mentioned in the item's description.

Control Ratings applied to C-1s should be reduced by one point. For example, in a situation where a lower-scale citizen would be under a Control Rating of 5, a C-1 is under a Control Rating of 4. This modification does *not* apply in cases involving subversion, treason and the like. A C-1 teenager who empties a machine pistol into a low-C crowd may be displaying "youthful high spirits." That same teenager using a cyberdeck to broadcast anti-ProGov messages on the Net is "an unregenerate punk, deserving the full weight of the law."

C-2s and C-3s in the U.S. are subject to unmodified Control Ratings regarding weapon laws, cyberwear and other matters.

Add +1 to Control Ratings applied to C-4s.

Zone Ratings

In a monolithic social order with a tight system of control, a country's CR would be constant everywhere. George Orwell's *1984* presents a picture of such a society. The U.S., however, is a highly fragmented, almost splintered society, and governmental control varies from place to place.

A *high control zone* is an area where CRs apply at their full value. These are usually areas where ProGov directly enforces the law. Less rigorously policed areas will have a rating, a Control Modifier of 1 to 4. GMs should *reduce* the Control Rating in such areas by the Control Modifier.

At the other extreme are the *null zones,* where the rule of law does not extend under normal circumstances. Null zones are effectively anarchistic, with a zone CR of 0. This is not the theoretical ideal of an enlightened anarchist, but an area where the only thing that protects anyone from the depredations of others is his own ability to defend himself.

Citcards

In 2043, the law requires all U.S. citizens to carry *citcards*. Citcards use "smartcard" technology, with a powerful onboard computer chip. Most transactions use the card's built-in memory, which can be updated from the National Data Banks at any time, during an online "card check."

Card Checks

Physically, a citcard is the size of a 20th-century credit card, 1/4 inch thick, and weighs about 2 ounces. It is somewhat flexible: a person can carry one in his hip pocket and sit on it without damaging the card. Immersion in water will destroy the card's circuitry. A citcard can be powered for one year on a AA battery.

The front of the card carries a holopicture of the bearer, a small printout screen which displays various data when the card is accessed, a contact point for data wands used in local card checks, and a thumbprint pad for verifying the bearer's identity.

It also has three mini-LED readouts. The authenticity LED displays green or red, depending on whether identity checks verify the bearer's identity. For example, if a citizen presses the thumbprint pad of someone else's citcard, the authenticity LED will flash red. If he presses the pad of his own card, it will flash green.

The self-check LED detects failures in the card's circuits, either logical or physical. Under normal circumstances it burns green at all times. It turns red if the card's circuits fail a self-test. It goes out (as do all other powered elements) if the citcard's battery is removed or runs down. It is a Class D misdemeanor to leave a citcard without power by deliberately removing the battery or failing to replace an

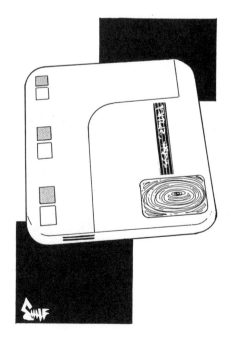

NERCC Officers (Continued)

Snot-Nosed Officer:
ST 11, DX 12, IQ 12, HT 12.
Basic Speed 6, Move 6.
Dodge 6, Parry 6.
Advantages: Legal Enforcement Powers; Literacy; Military Rank (Level 3 or 4). Typical additional advantages might include: Appearance; Charisma; Intuition; Language Talent; Strong Will; Wealth.
Disadvantages: Duty (to NERCC); plus 30 points of disadvantages drawn from: Addiction; Alcoholism; Bad Temper; Bloodlust; Bully; Cowardice; Fanaticism; Gluttony; Greed; Impulsiveness; Intolerance (Anyone lower than Scale 2 Citizen); Lecherousness; Overconfidence; Sadism.
Skills: Administration-13; Beam Weapons/TL8-14; Brawling-12; Computer Operation/TL8-14; Diplomacy-12; Guns/TL8-13; Law (U.S.)-12; Leadership-12; Politics-14; Interrogation-14; Stealth-10; Streetwise-10.

This fellow is a NERCC officer for one of several reasons. He might be a C-2, or even a C-1, who needed a job but wasn't good at anything important. He might be in it for power, planning a career in ProGov. He might be a true patriot (yes, they do exist), convinced that this is his duty to his country, and that the survival of America depends on using maximum force to keep the gutter-scum in line.

If a veteran NERCC officer can be compared to a career KGB agent, using the system for his own survival, the snot-nosed NERCC officer is often more akin to the haughty young Aryans of the Gestapo and SS Elite during WWII – corrupt, charming when it suits him, well aware of the privileges of his position and always looking for a way to use that to his own profit.

Weapons: PL-5 laser sidearms, 2d damage, at all times. Officer uniform helmets carry additional comm circuitry allowing them to track the D-tags on their troops' weapons. Otherwise, armor and weapons are the same as those of regular Enforcers.

exhausted battery. The self-check LED will start to blink green when the battery begins to run low, 1d+1 days before the battery becomes completely exhausted.

The third LED is the tamper-alarm circuit. Green under normal circumstances, it burns red if the card's self-test detects deliberate tampering with the card's circuits, either physically or via illegal reprogramming. The owner of a citcard with a dark or red tamper alarm is subject to immediate arrest. If accidental damage activates the circuit, the citizen is required to present himself at the nearest NERCC, FBI, or Department of Information office immediately to get the error corrected and undergo a full, online card check. False tamper alarms become part of a citizen's permanent record.

Deliberately tampering with a citcard is a Class C felony, apart from any other criminal charges that might result from that tampering. For example, someone who loads fake credit into his citcard would be charged with felony card tampering as well as credit fraud for using nonexistent funds.

Citcard Security Checks

There are four levels of card check.

A *visual check* is just that. The holopic of the card's owner is compared to his face, he may be asked to touch his thumb to the card's built-in print verifier, and the color of the built-in tamper-check LED is noted. When a faked citcard undergoes a visual check, roll vs. Forgery/TL8. If the test fails, the forgery has been spotted.

A *local check* interrogates the card's onboard memory, checks it for tampering and verifies credit and ration balances presently on the card. This is the most common type of card check. A faked citcard must pass a second roll when it is tested electronically. It will fail this check unless it has onboard validation or can do a "double-shuffle" (see p. 38). If the forgery has these features, roll vs. the skill that was used to install the electronic forgery (usually either Electronics/TL8 or Computer Programming/TL8).

Network checks compare the card to data in the National Data Banks. The card check calls up the citizen's file and checks the card's onboard data store against it.

The only really safe way to fool a network check is with an Alternate Identity or Temporary Identity (see p. C19), which creates identity files in the National Data Banks that correspond to the forged citcard.

A *low-level network check* does a very cursory data comparison, to minimize demands on the government network. For this reason, it can be defeated by a "double-shuffle." A faked citcard that cannot do a "double-shuffle" will automatically fail a low-level network check! If the card does have this feature, roll vs. the Computer Programming/TL8 skill that was used to install it, to see if it successfully passes the card check. If the citcard is backed up by a file (real or fake) in the National Data Banks, then it will automatically *pass* a low-level network check.

A *high-level network check* is a more lengthy, detailed comparison, and can *only* be defeated by a card that has a corresponding file in the National Data Banks. If the file is "real," placed there by an official input source, then the card passes the check automatically. As far as the network is concerned, it is a perfectly valid citcard.

If the file was placed by a hacker, then roll vs. his Computer Hacking skill, to see if the cross-references and other safeguards are fooled.

Personal ID

The citcard verifies the bearer's identity and, depending on the level of card check carried out, displays any licenses, endorsements, privileges or restrictions that apply to the bearer. For example, a weapon license would be encoded on his citcard.

Citcards are equipped with a touchpad, programmed to respond to thumb-prints. The legitimate bearer's thumb on the pad produces a verification signal. Anyone else's thumbprint causes a rejection signal. Thumbprint parameters, and additional ID parameters used in higher card checks, are stored in onboard memory.

Medical Records

A citcard stores the bearer's medical history, allergies and of course his Medical Resource Allowance (i.e., what treatments he is entitled to) in onboard memory. All legal cyber modifications are registered in the medical record; possession of an unregistered modification is a Class C Felony under the Uniform Code.

Cashcard

A citizen carries out his principal banking through his personal Treasury Account. His citcard allows him to transfer funds, pay bills, accept payments and download verified credit to the card's onboard memory, which he can then use to pay for things without going through a low-level card check every time he orders rations from the local, licensed Resource Vendor.

A C-1's card can download pretty much any amount of onboard credit. A C-2 will be validated for an amount from $1,000 to $10,000, depending on his standing as a reliable citizen. C-3s and C-4s are limited to $100 in onboard credit.

The citcard also stores the bearer's current ration standings. Thus it verifies not only whether one can afford something, but whether one is allowed to buy it in the first place.

Credit Transfers

For citcard transactions, most merchants keep a hand-held scanner, about the size of a large blow-dryer. In order to buy something with a citcard, the customer presents his card to the merchant, who inserts it into a slot in the scanner. The merchant then scans a coded area on the goods; if the buyer's credit is good and his access to such merchandise is unrestricted, it's his.

If there's a problem, a one-line readout screen on the scanner displays a message ranging from a simple "transaction denied," to "unlawful activity detected; stand-by for contact by federal authorities; do not leave the area," with innumerable bureaucratic requests for additional information or authorization in between.

A citcard transaction between two individuals is a bit more involved. The two must carry out their transaction at a public data terminal. This requires a successful Computer Operations roll, and the individuals must answer several questions about the nature of the goods or services at hand. Most citizens have no desire to go to this much trouble when, for instance, buying some used video games from a co-worker, so scrip or outright barter is usually preferred for such transactions. However, it is illegal to exchange any sort of controlled substances or merchandise except through credcard transfer.

Fake Citcards

Forging a citcard is difficult, since the card operates on two levels. It must be a decent physical copy of a legitimate card and it must fool various cybernetic tests as well. Forgery skill alone is not enough.

As specified on p. B65, Forgery/TL skill is used to make a fake document, in this case a citcard, *and* the skill is rolled again whenever the card is checked. In addition, since citcards have to stand up to electronic inspection too, skills besides Forgery/TL8 are needed. These skills, like Forgery, may be rolled again when the card is examined, depending on the type of card check involved (see p. 36).

NERCC Commander

ST 11, DX 12, IQ 12, HT 12.
Basic Speed 6, Move 6.
Dodge 6, Parry 6.

Advantages: Legal Enforcement Powers; Literacy; Military Rank (Level 5 or 6). Typical additional advantages might include: Appearance; Charisma; Intuition; Language Talent; Strong Will; Wealth.

Typical Disadvantages: Duty (to NERCC); plus 30 points of disadvantages based on: Addiction; Alcoholism; Bad Temper; Bloodlust; Bully; Cowardice; Fanaticism; Gluttony; Greed; Impulsiveness; Intolerance (Anyone lower than Scale 2 Citizen); Lecherousness; Overconfidence; Sadism.

Skills: Administration-14; Beam Weapons/TL8-14; Brawling-12; Computer Operation/TL8-14; Diplomacy-13; Guns/TL8-13; Law (U.S.)-12; Leadership-14; Politics-14; Interrogation-14; Research-12; Tactics-14; Writing-13.

A NERCC regional or district commander is in charge of enforcement in a large area, though he is subject to "requests" from the commissioner in charge of the NERCC's civil operations his area. In most cases, the commander defers to the commissioner, unless the military and civil arms of the local NERCC are engaged in an active "turf war," which often happens.

Most commanders are intensely aware that headquarters will blame *them* for any foul-ups in their jurisdiction. Most NERCC commanders respond to even minor disturbances with brutal force, not to mention running covert operations with maximum deniability and using other techniques to cover their behinds when something untoward does happen.

Most commanders are desk officers, and rarely join in field operations. There are a few rare birds who hold their rank through military prowess rather than political acumen, and are likely to lead their troops from the front. When in the field, commanders are armed like the troops under their command, though they have the same enhanced helmet communications as other officers (see p. 35).

The United States

NERCC Field Agent

ST 13, DX 14, IQ 12, HT 13.
Basic Speed 6.75, Move 6.
Dodge 6, Parry 10.

Advantages: Alertness; Combat Reflexes; Law Enforcement Powers; Literacy; Patron (NERCC Official).

Disadvantages: Extremely Hazardous Duty (to NERCC); 20 points drawn from Bad Temper; Bloodlust; Bully; Enemies; Fanaticism; Greed; Impulsiveness; Intolerance; Lecherousness; Paranoia; Sadism; Sense of Duty.

Skills: Acting-16; Area Knowledge (of area they usually operate in)-14; Armoury-12; Beam Weapons/TL8-16; Computer Operation/TL8-14; Computer Hacking/TL8-14; Demolition/TL8-13; Detect Lies-12; Diplomacy-12; Driving (Car)-14; Electronics Operation/TL8-13; Escape-12; Fast-Draw (Pistol)-14; First Aid/TL8-13; Forensics/TL8-12; Forgery/TL8-12; Guns/TL8-16; Interrogation-15; Judo-15; Karate-15; Law (U.S.)-12; Leadership-13; Lockpicking/TL7-14; Photography/TL7-12; Poisons-13; Politics-12; Research-14; Shadowing-15; Traps/TL8-13.

Languages: Any two, at skill 13.

Equipment: Pretty much anything they want in terms of personal weapons, armor, technological gizmos, and the like. Field agents can also be equipped with up to 30 points worth of cyberwear.

The creme de la creme of NERCC enforcement personnel, field agents are concerned with domestic U.S. security. Undercover investigation, covert ops, black projects and wet work are their specialties. Most field agents are attached to the staff of a relatively high-ranking NERCC official: a regional commander or commissioner, or higher, who acts as their Patron. There is an elite squad of field agents, reporting directly to President Hammond, who are often assigned to ferret out possible subversion in the upper reaches of ProGov and to counter it. Permanently.

A field agent has wide authority, including a license to kill in most circumstances. Their credentials are a "get-out-of-jail-free" card, requiring assistance from all local governments and law enforcement agencies.

Making a visually authentic citcard takes three days per attempt. The forger needs, at a minimum, portable Engineer and Electronics tool kits (see p. C52). A card which will pass visual inspection costs $2,000 at typical street prices.

A forged citcard can also have *onboard validation.* The card's internal circuitry will provide realistic data if subjected to a local card check (see p. 36). A citcard without onboard validation will *automatically fail* a local card check.

Adding onboard validation to a forged card takes two days and adds $5,000 to its street price. The forger needs a ROM-burner, a 1-gig chip and access to a Complexity 2 computer, as well as the other resources listed above. A successful roll vs. Electronics/TL8-3 or Computer Programming/TL8 is needed to program the validation.

A forged card can also do a "double-shuffle." This is a sophisticated form of onboard validation that will fool a low-level network check by altering its onboard validation to match the inquiries from the network. The electronics and programming for a "double-shuffle" citcard adds $10,000 to the cost of the forgery and takes 3 days to install. The forger requires Computer Programming/TL8 to make a "double-shuffle," and his roll is at -2.

Faked Identity Files

The best forgery is a citcard that actually corresponds to a citizen file in the National Data Banks. The physical card in this case is simply a card with onboard validation. Since it will pass a high-level network test *for real,* the scores used to make it are almost irrelevant. However, getting the file into the data banks requires action by someone in the NERCC (a Patron, or someone taking a bribe) or action by a hacker. Most spies and security agents working undercover will have this kind of identification provided. Street prices vary enormously, but the average is $100,000, divided by the Citizenship Scale of the faked ID. A false identity with a C-1 rating would cost the full $100,000. A faked C-4 identity can be had for a mere $25,000.

U.S. Territory

The 48 continental states and Hawaii are directly controlled, in theory, by the Provisional Government based in Washington, D.C. Puerto Rico was admitted to statehood in 2002. The U.S. Virgin Islands were made part of Puerto Rico in 2027, as part of a plan by ProGov to regularize U.S. territorial administration in the Caribbean. Alaska Free State is nominally part of the U.S., but is virtually a separate nation (see below).

In addition, there are seven "Reserved" states, created in 2027. Six of them (the "Low Six") are in Mexico; the seventh is Cuba. Despite the savage guerrilla war now being fought on that sad and battered island, ProGov still counts the island as a state, and thus the American flag in 2043 shows 58 stars.

In the Pacific, the U.S. still controls Guam and such uninhabited possessions as Midway and Wake Islands. The inhabited possessions in the Pacific (American Samoa, the Marianas, and the Marshall and Caroline Islands) petitioned the U.N. to recognize the dissolution of the various compacts and articles which bound them to the U.S. shortly after ProGov came to power. The U.N. took no action, and the islands remain under U.S. control, despite frequent flareups of nationalist violence.

Alaska Free State

Alaska was the only state to wrench free of ProGov's grasp at the beginning of the regime. Discontent had been growing in the state ever since the creation of the NERCC in 2017. Alaska's tremendous wealth of natural resources drew NERCC bureaucrats in droves. The arrogant use of emergency powers to exploit the state, without any concern for the environment or individual rights, was guaranteed to enrage the traditionally independent Alaskans.

In 2024, when federal units in Alaska attempted to establish ProGov control, National Guardsmen, along with disaffected regular troops and a large contingent of armed civilians, attacked and destroyed or captured virtually all the federal forces. Rather to their own surprise, the Alaskans found themselves, for a time, the perpetrators of a successful counterrevolution.

Governor Adele Hawkins had run for office on a platform which opposed the most intrusive NERCC practices in the state. She remained at the head of the state government after the uprising. Hawkins quickly established trade relationships with other Pacific Rim governments, notably her nearest neighbors, the Federated Provinces of Columbia and Alberta and the flourishing Russo-Japanese trade community.

When the U.S. government got around to dealing with the Alaskan question in 2026, they were confronted with these international relationships. In addition, the Alaskan government informed Washington that many of the valuable resource areas, the wealth that ProGov was so hungry for, were mined with low-yield nuclear devices. "If the regime now ruling the U.S. tries to take

Alaska by force," Governor Hawkins said in a widely televised address, "they will spend their soldiers and their wealth to win a burned-out corpse. Alaska will live in freedom, or die for it."

A delicate dance of negotiation, threat and counter-threat now began. The Alaskans were not eager to commit suicide, after all. ProGov was anxious both to legitimize its rule and to ensure continued access to Alaskan resources. Eventually, an arrangement was hammered out that, predictably, satisfied neither side.

Alaska has complete home rule, though it remains, nominally, one of the United States. Alaskan members of the Provisional Congress have almost diplomatic status, including immunity from most U.S. prosecutions. Of course, they are also excluded from most of the insider wheeling and dealing in Washington.

A given amount of essential resources, notably oil, is delivered to ProGov, more or less for free, and in return Alaska can conduct trade with U.S.-based companies, access the National Data Banks, and enjoy other benefits of statehood.

Alaska completely rejects the Citizenship Scale (see p. 31). Ordinary Alaskan citizens are treated as Scale Two citizens when traveling elsewhere in the U.S. State officials are accorded C-1 status by federal authorities.

All of this has made Alaska a mecca for refugees from the ProGov regime, as well as a hotbed of activity by would-be rebels. This puts Juneau in a delicate position. The state cannot absorb an unlimited number of refugees. Moreover, if

Black-Box Citcards

A forger can build a black box that will pass local and network card checks, depending on its programming, that does not actually look like a citcard. Thus, the gizmo will fool remote testing devices, but won't pass a visual inspection by a human being under any circumstances.

Skip all Forgery tests when building a black box citcard. Reduce the price for such units by 20%. A black box citcard is usually housed in a casing the same size and basic configuration as a real citcard, but without any external markings. Clumsier units, weighing about ½ pound and trailing ribbon cables, hooked up to the standard I/O strips and slots of a citcard, are also available, and reduce the price of the forgery by 50%.

Alaskan Special Operations (AlSOF) Troops

ST 11, DX 12, IQ 11, HT 13.
Basic Speed 6.25, Move 6.
Dodge 6, Parry 7.
TL8 Combat Infantry Dress (see p. C50); Light encumbrance.

Advantages: Military Rank; Reputation (Elite Unit, Anti-ProGov).

Disadvantages: Code of Honor; Enemy (NERCC); Extremely Hazardous Duty; Fanaticism (Alaska Free State); Intolerance (ProGov/NERCC); Sense of Duty (U.S. Citizens).

See *GURPS Special Ops,* pp. 45-50, for a fuller discussion of generating an elite forces character.

Skills: Acting-13; Armoury/TL8 (Guns)-13; Armoury/TL8 (Beam Weapons)-13; Beam Weapons/TL8-14; Boating-12; Brawling-14; Camouflage-12; Climbing-13; Demolition/TL8-12; Driving (Tracked Vehicles)-11; Driving (Wheeled Vehicles)-11; Electronics Operation/TL8-12; First Aid/TL8-10; Forward Observer/TL8-12; Gunner/TL8 (Electromagnetic Grenade Launchers)-12; Gunner/TL8 (Electromagnetic Mortars)-12; Guns/TL8 (Assault Rifle)-15; Guns/TL8 (AT Weapon)-13; Guns/TL8 (Machine Gun)-15; Guns/TL8 (Pistol)-13; Interrogation-10; Jumping-12; Knife-12; Leadership-11; Navigation/TL7-11; Parachuting-12; Savoir-Faire-11; Scrounging-11; Scuba-12; Skiing-13; Survival (Arctic)-14; Survival (Mountain)-13; Stealth-12; Streetwise-13; Swimming-13; Tactics-11; Teaching-11; Thrown Weapons (Grenades)-14; Traps/TL8-12.

Cyberwear: All AlSOF troops are equipped with 25 points worth of SOTA cyberwear. There is no standard configuration, but the implants must make sense in a special-operations context.

Weapons: Full combat gear: AK-107V assault rifle, 6d+1 damage; close combat: NATArms M-19 SMG, 3d damage, or the FE ACAW, 5d damage; support weapons (medium MGs and FE PEMG grenade launchers). In the recent anti-terrorist strike at the Ketchikan fusion plant, units were equipped with Koroshi Laser Personal Arms, 1d+2 damage.

Continued on next page . . .

Alaska is directly implicated in attempts to overthrow ProGov, the U.S. administration might decide the free state is too dangerous to continue to exist and risk an invasion.

Accordingly, while the Alaskan administration's unofficial stance to anti-ProGov organizations is one of "benign neglect," anyone involving the state in anything outrageous may be arrested by Alaskan law enforcement and extradited to ProGov territory.

The Alaskan Special Operations Force

In the fall of 2024, the 2nd Force Recon company, USMC, was moved into the Prudhoe Bay area, ostensibly for training in sub-arctic conditions. The local NERCC commander attempted to place the Marines under his command in order to secure the pumping station at the head of the Trans-Alaska pipeline.

The next communication from the administrative facility at Prudhoe Bay came from the Marine company commander, addressed to NERCC Northwest Regional HQ. "Pipeline secured for the people of the United States. Will defend from all enemies, foreign or domestic. Try us, nerk."

No subsequent reports were received, then or ever, from the NERCC detachment at the installation.

Stricken from USMC records as mutineers, 2nd Force Recon formed the cadre around which the elite Alaskan Special Operations Force was built.

The Cuban Revolution

On August 17, 2041, explosions ripped through the NERCC headquarters in Havana, killing the district commissioner and most of his staff. Simultaneously, troops attacked key ProGov centers on the island, killing or capturing most of the administrative personnel.

Pirate broadcasts, injected into the networks from satellites and via hacked access to cable-feed systems, were seen all over the U.S. A man identifying himself as Major Rafael Echeveria, a NERCC officer of Cuban descent, proclaimed Cuban independence from ProGov. Echeveria implored the people of the United States and the world to support Cuban independence and a montage of footage showing brutal atrocities by ProGov forces ran for several minutes before frantic technicians could get the pirate signals off the net.

ProGov spent a week trying to sort through the conflicting reports from the disrupted U.S. forces still on the island. Elements of the 3rd Rapid Urban Response regiment, stationed at Guantanamo, were deployed to Havana on August 19, but their copters met ferocious SAM bombardment, and after suffering heavy casualties, retreated to their base. ProGov mobilized for war.

Operation Cuba Libre began on September 3, with a series of bombing raids on Havana. The bombardment continued for almost four weeks. On September 29 an air-sea assault landed almost unopposed. Most of Havana lay in ruins, but Echeveria and his forces had withdrawn to the mountainous interior, where they continue to wage a lethal guerrilla war against the occupying U.S. troops.

Support for Cuba

Weapons captured from Echeverista rebels provide two contradictory clues about the Cuban uprising. Not counting captured U.S. ordnance, the arms come from a wide variety of sources: SAMs from China, Indonesian small arms, Mosk-Arms grenade launchers and mortars, combat uniforms and other equipment from a score of sources. Echeverista equipment seems to be uniformly good quality TL7 and TL8 materiel.

Someone is paying heavy cred to arm the Echeveristas. The burning question in Washington is *who?* Rumor attributes Echeverista backing to the Chilentinans, the South American narcotics cartels, the Chinese, the Russians, or some combination of the above.

GURPS Cyberworld does not specify just who is backing the Cuban revolution. The GM is free to decide what faction, or combination of factions, is providing funds and ordnance to the Echeveristas.

Support from political entities opposed to U.S. policies, such as Chilentina, would be a straightforward matter. Anything that embarrasses *el giganto del norte* in the Western hemisphere, and weakens its influence over the South American nations, is considered a good thing by Chilentina.

If the support is coming from the 'traffs (see p. 70) it does not necessarily mean that the rebellion is a pawn of the criminal syndicates. The Echeveristas would deal with the Devil himself to free their country.

Support from countries that are publicly neutral (e.g., China) or even "friendly" to ProGov would involve more complicated politics. The Cuban situation might be part of a plan to undermine the U.S. dictatorship for idealistic reasons, or simply to weaken U.S. power regardless of who is in charge.

Alaska has an immense amount of influence and wealth to dispose of; it might very well take the dangerous step of covertly underwriting a challenge to ProGov half a world away.

The rebels, even Echeveria himself, may not *know* who is supporting their cause.

Mexico

Since annexation, Mexico has been treated as a vassal state. The partitioning of the United Mexican States into six Reserved states, nominally members of the United States, was not accomplished without bloody military action. NERCC district commanders in each Mexican state are given a free hand in maintaining order.

Mexican Society

U.S. and korp enclaves function at high TL7, and some production facilities are actually TL8, although they often produce more pollution than one would expect from a TL8 factory.

Alaskan Special Operations (AlSOF) Troops (Continued)

Equipment: Auxiliary equipment usually includes various communications and detection gear and counter-detection gear.

The Alaskan Special Operations Force trooper is an elite, and he knows it. His typical missions are counter-terrorism and hostage rescues. For further discussion of such missions and the soldiers who tackle them, see *GURPS Special Ops*. In the event of a ProGov invasion, AlSOF intends to spearhead partisan actions against U.S. forces.

AlSOF troops have extremely high esprit de corps. They are also motivated by an abiding hatred of ProGov and the nerks. An AlSOF's favorite mission is one that puts him up against covert NERCC operations in Alaska, maybe some of those drigging field agents. Of course, officially, the NERCC is not involved. Why would the nerks engage in covert ops in Alaska, a loyal jurisdiction of the United States, after all? But there have been incidents. On one occasion, a package with a Fairbanks postmark arrived at NERCC HQ in Washington, D.C. It contained the carefully freeze-dried head of a nerk field agent who had no further use for it.

The United States

Echeverista Guerrilla

ST 12, DX 11, IQ 10, HT 9.
Basic Speed 5, Move 5.
Dodge 5, Parry 6.

Irregular troops: civilian clothes (PD 0, DR 0), no encumbrance; Regulars: Combat Infantry Dress (p. C50), Light encumbrance.

Advantages: 15 points worth of the following: Absolute Direction; Acute Hearing; Acute Vision; Alertness; Combat Reflexes; Danger Sense; High Pain Threshold; Rapid Healing; Toughness.

Disadvantages: Enemies (U.S. Forces, Often); Intolerance (Norteamericanos); Sense of Duty (Cubans); Wealth (Struggling).

Skills: Acting-10; Area Knowledge (Cuban Interior)-14; Brawling-13; Camouflage-12; Demolitions/TL7-11; First Aid/TL7-10; Gunner/TL8 (Machine Gun)-10; Gunner/TL8 (Rocket Launcher)-10; Guns/TL8 (Pistol)-13; Guns/TL8 (Rifle)-13; Guns/TL8 (Submachine Gun)-13; Stealth-13; Tracking-11.

Weapons: Echeverista rebels among the general population are armed with perhaps a pistol or a demolition pack concealed among their meager belongings. Hunting rifles, shotguns, maybe a TL7 or even TL6 military rifle may be hidden in homes and vehicles along with improvised weapons such as Molotov cocktails.

Echeverista regulars are equipped with captured U.S. weapons, or the steady trickle of materiel that flows into Cuba from Echeveria's unknown backers. A mix of assault rifles, machine guns, and other military weapons from pp. 101-106, are typical in Echeverista troops. Some are knockoffs of weapons produced in the firstworld, from lastworld arms companies. others are the real thing. All of them work just fine, as U.S. troops in Operation Cuba Libre are all too aware.

Mexico's population is 102 million, and almost 21 million people live in the massive sprawl of Mexico City, still the most populous urban area in the world.

One percent of Mexico's native population is rated C-1 on the U.S. Citizenship Scale. These are mainly officials of the former Mexican government who cooperated in the annexation of their country, or top officials of the present administration of the region – senators and representatives of the Mexican states and the scions of the "old wealth" who have always been an important factor in Mexican society.

Eighteen percent of the population – its top educators, technical specialists and other professionals who have not drawn unfavorable attention from ProGov – are C-2s.

C-1s can travel freely anywhere in the U.S., and C-2s can obtain travel permits with minimal difficulty. Thus, many high-C Mexicans use their status to escape from their ravaged birthplace. Indeed, the passport that admits many members of the professional class to Scale Two is an offer of employment at a korp facility in the Upper 48.

Fifty-seven percent of the Mexican population is rated C-3, and the remaining 24% are rated C-4, almost double the average percentage of C-4s in the Upper 48. Many citizens in the Low Six live in terrible poverty, depending on state and federal relief programs for their subsistence. They are classified C-4/W. Moreover, virtual exile to the Mexican states is a common tactic when ProGov wants to get rid of particularly irritating C-4/Ds whom it is not politic to simply eliminate.

Since C-3s and C-4s cannot legally travel from the Low Six to the rest of the United States without difficult-to-obtain permits, once a C-3 or C-4 passes south of the Line, he is stuck in the Low Six unless he cares to try his luck against the NERCC patrols who guard that border.

The NERCC In Mexico

Mexican Regional Commissioner: Rowena Jenkins
Mexican Regional Commander: Hector Ortiz
Mexico City District Commissioner: Frederick W. Mathers
Mexico City District Commander: Martin DiAgostino

Mexico is a separate administrative region in the NERCC structure. Each of the six Reserved states is a District, as are the swarming urban centers of Mexico City, Guadalajara, Monterrey, Ciudad Juarez, Puebla de Zaragoza and Leon.

The NERCC in Mexico has concerns above and beyond its charter elsewhere in the United States. The nerks in the north oversee the flow of people from the Low Six to the rest of the country. The District authorities in Baja and New Tejas, working with their counterparts in the Southwestern Region, maintain heavy patrols along the border, much as the Immigration Service did when the United States and Mexico were separate nations.

The teeming border cities of Tijuana, Nogales and the El Paso/Juarez sprawl are home to a thriving "coyote" industry, smuggling Mexican C-3s into the Upper 48. Scenes at the border checkpoints in these areas bring back memories of Berlin before the Germans tore down the Wall.

Numerous industrial zones in the Low Six are almost uniformly devoted to essential manufacturing that is too toxic to be allowed in the north. The nerks keep these plants productive. Oh yeah, and minimize environmental impact, absolutely. Can't forget about the environment, no sir.

Social rehabilitation and industrial efficiency meet in the Federal Penal Enclave in the state of Guadalajara. About 200 miles north of the urban center of the arid state, the prison/factory complex produces essential components for use in power cells, microtronics and other technologies that involve highly toxic processes. Its nickname is *El Infierno,* and the average lifespan of its prisoners is 5.3 years.

The six Reserved states, their state capitals and the original Mexican states that compose them, are:

Baja: (Capital: Mazatlan) Baja California Norte, Baja California Sur, Sonora, Sinaloa.

Juarez: (Capital: Ciudad Juarez) Chihuahua, Durango.

New Tejas: (Capital: Monterrey) Coahuila, Nuevo Leon, Tamaulipas.

Guadalajara: (Capital: Guadalajara) Aguascalientes, Colima, Guanajuato, Jalisco, Nayarit, San Luis Potosi, Zacatecas.

Tenochtitlan: (Capital: Mexico City) Guerrero, Hidalgo, Mexico, Michoacan, Morelos, Queretaro, Tlaxcala.

Veracruz: (Capital: Veracruz) Oaxaca, Puebla, Veracruz.

The remaining states of Mexico form Mexico Libre ("Free Mexico").

Mexico Libre

The southern region of Mexico was never completely pacified by U.S. troops. The thick jungles of the Yucatan peninsula are tailor-made for guerrilla warfare. The rebels included insurgent elements of the Mexican armed forces, vengeful refugees from the destruction in the northern part of the country and outright bandits and *narcotraficantes* who were displaced by the invasion of organized U.S. criminals in the wake of ProGov's troops.

When ProCon passed the Mexican Statehood Act of 2027, the five southernmost states of old Mexico exploded into open rebellion. The rebels declared Oaxaca, Tabasco, Campeche, Yucatan and Quintana Roo to be an independent Mexican republic. U.S. troops were sent to Veracruz and Acapulco. An amphibious force landed in the resort city of Cancun, which was devastated in vicious house-to-house fighting.

The U.S. and Mexico Libre fought a sluggish and inconclusive campaign from 2027 to 2029. The numerically superior U.S. forces were unable to force a decisive confrontation with the elusive Mexican guerrillas. At the same time, an equally tantalizing diplomatic battle was going on in the U.N. and OAS. In February, 2030, the OAS finally defied ProGov's saber-rattling and recognized Mexico Libre's government. Troop buildups in the Central American nations were noted. Chilentina started stationing rapid deployment forces into Guatemala. World opinion was heavily in favor of Mexico Libre and pressure on ProGov mounted.

The U.S. decided against pursuing a campaign that promised to be expensive, both militarily and politically. However, ProGov refused to recognize the government of Mexico Libre directly. Since the insurgent government had petitioned for membership in the Union of Central American States, Washington's dealings with Mexico Libre were conducted through the UCAS.

Under the treaty of Oaxaca, signed in 2032, the U.S. recognized Mexico Libre as an autonomous region of the UCAS. Cancun was declared an open city, controlled by a commission whose members were appointed by the U.S., OAS and UCAS.

The United States

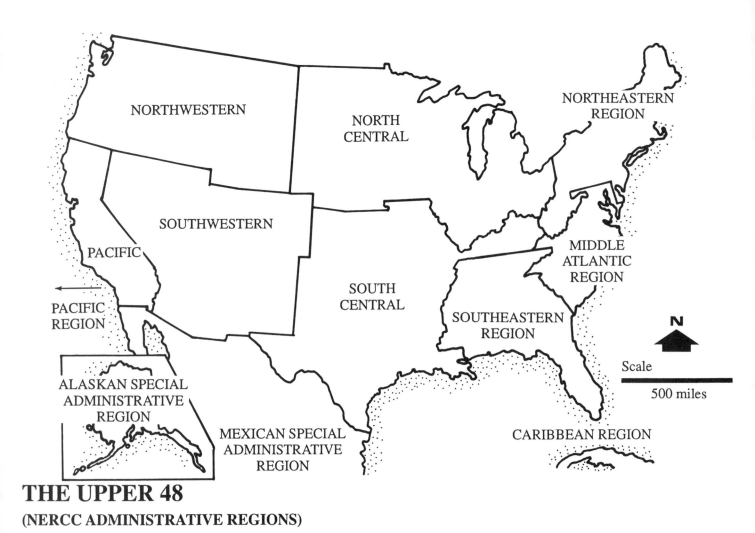

THE UPPER 48
(NERCC ADMINISTRATIVE REGIONS)

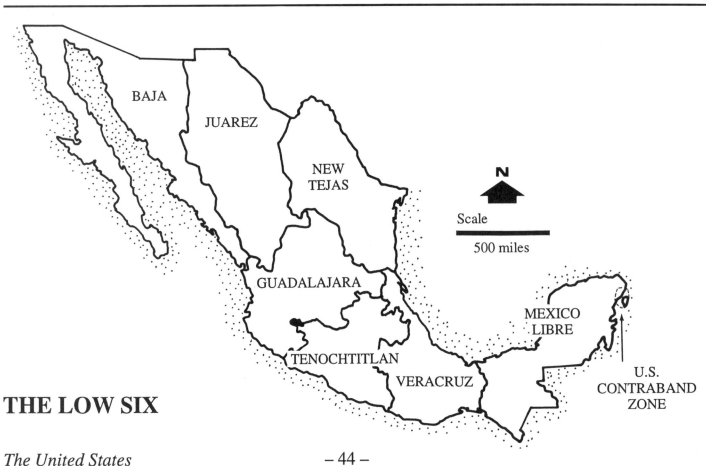

THE LOW SIX

GEOPOLITICS

4

It's a big planet. Not as big as it used to be, maybe, but it'll do. It's ironic that at the same time information technology makes the virtual world so small, there are still a lot of barriers between different cultures. Perhaps the threat of being sucked into one big, homogenous society triggers a defense mechanism somewhere in the part of our brains labeled "cultural identity."

Talkin' One-and-Twenty

Breetva: (Russ.) Razor. Anyone with combat-oriented cyberwear.

Cred: Electronic funds.

Dengi: (Russ.) Money. Colloquially, "soft money." Unstable national currencies or korp scrips. "Trash dengi" refers to currency that is subject to runaway inflation.

Fold: Actual currency, in hardcopy scrip; bills, folding money. Still around, you bet. Too useful to die.

K-mark: Keiretsu mark, or korp mark. Currency issued by a multinational corporation.

Keiretsu: A corporation, cartel, or conglomerate.

Korp: Slang for a keiretsu, from the Russian "korporahtseeya."

Korpo: A korp employee.

Loco: A local company, an independent business with no korp connection.

Nak-nik: from *nachal'nik* (Russ.). Supervisor, boss. A low-or mid-level manager.

Shaikujin: Lit. "honest citizen." A korp employee, a "suit."

Suit: A straight citizen, usually a korp or government employee.

Ten-Tan: Slang for Kosmozavot Tenno Tanjo, the Russo-Japanese orbital facility.

Zek: An executive.

Some patterns are the same over most of the planet. Unfortunately, they aren't the ones that do folks much good: polarization between the have-lots and have-nots; rule by force, either military or economic; alienation verging on paranoia as social norms break down. People everywhere dance with these dangerous partners as they struggle to keep their balance on the Edge.

North America

The only other countries in North America are the three nations formed by the Canadian provinces after the dissolution of the Confederation in 2010.

Communaute d'Atlantique Quebeçois

The "Quebec Community of the Atlantic" consists of Quebec, New Brunswick, Nova Scotia, Newfoundland and Prince Edward Island. The Communaute controls access to eastern Canada by sea. Originally united in 2022, as the Atlantic Community, the smaller member states have fallen under the economic domination of Quebec.

Quebec is the most populous member of the Communaute, with more than 66% of the population. Quebec has significant economic ties with France, one of the Community's most important trading partners. Increasingly aggressive factions in the Quebeçois government are taking more and more advantage of their position.

In 2036, Quebec rammed legislation through the Chamber of Deputies, formally renaming the Community and imposing deadlines over the next decade by which other members must phase in stringent bilingual regulations. (These were similar to those imposed on Canada before its dissolution.) In Quebec itself, almost all legal transactions must be in French. Display or use of English in most business is subject to a rigid code defining size of signs, validity of documents, and even accepted forms to use when answering business phone calls.

NORTH AND CENTRAL AMERICA

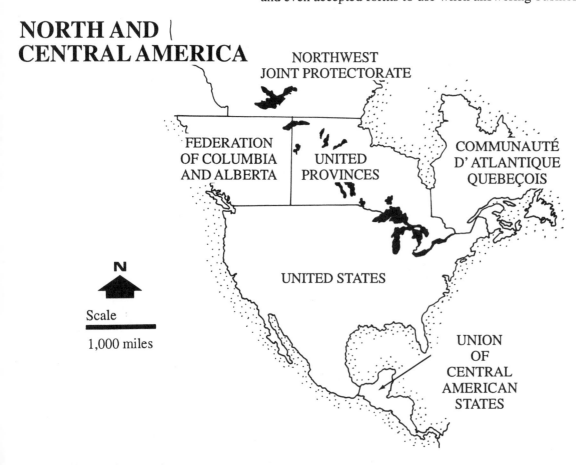

NORTHWEST JOINT PROTECTORATE

FEDERATION OF COLUMBIA AND ALBERTA

UNITED PROVINCES

COMMUNAUTÉ D'ATLANTIQUE QUEBEÇOIS

UNITED STATES

UNION OF CENTRAL AMERICAN STATES

N

Scale

1,000 miles

The Quebec-Montreal sprawl is the urban center of the country, with a population of over 5.5 million. No other city in the Communaute even comes close. Halifax, provincial capital of Nova Scotia and the second most populous city in the country, has a population of barely 300,000.

The United Provinces

Upon the dissolution of the Confederation, the provinces of Ontario, Manitoba and Saskatchewan almost immediately combined their resources into a confederation little different from the larger one that had just collapsed. The United Provinces, like the Federated Provinces of Columbia and Alberta, are an active member of the British Commonwealth of Nations. Unlike their western neighbor, they still recognize the king of England as their sovereign, though this is a ceremonial title only.

The United Provinces are the most heavily industrialized of the Canadian nations. They also share the north-central plains of the continent with The Federated Provinces of Columbia and Alberta, producing surplus grain for export.

The Federated Provinces of Columbia and Alberta

Alberta and Columbia, having raised what they felt were significant issues during the dissolution of the Confederation of Canada, did not accept Ottawa's invitation to join the new United Provinces. While "Col-Bert" also accepted membership in the Commonwealth of Nations, they keep Britain at arm's length.

The Federated Provinces trade extensively with Japan and the U.S., exporting grain, meat, oil and lumber products. Vancouver is the gateway to the western half of Canada. The Federated Provinces also enjoy a close alliance with Alaska.

A "pipeline" for anti-ProGov immigrants to Alaska runs through Columbia, and often feeds rebel infiltrators and equipment in the opposite direction, into the Seattle metroplex or across the border into the sparsely-populated northern states.

The Northwest Protectorate

One agreement, ratified by all the provinces, that allowed the Confederation to dissolve with minimal bloodshed prescribed the administration of the sparsely populated Northwest Territory's massive resources.

The resolution impanelled a Joint Commission, with one commissioner appointed by each of the former provinces. A simple majority makes decisions; annual resource exploitation and price-setting budgets are voted on annually.

As the provinces formed new associations, each local government retained its seat on the Joint Commission, which has led to an interesting balance of power. The Communaute d'Atlantique holds four seats, the United Provinces three, and the Federated Provinces two. As long as the western governments act in concert, they control the commission. But when they do not act in concert, Quebec's four votes control Commission decisions.

While Quebeçois appointees are under tight governmental control, members from the other governments are more independent. The politicking can get intense, since one non-Quebeçois commissioner's vote can hand a decision to the Communaute. Alternatively, when the Federated and United Provinces are at odds, both ardently pursue the Communaute's decisive bloc of votes.

Union of Central American States

The governments of Central America formed the UCAS in 2027. Their economies were in complete collapse, the U.S. was making noises about expanding its "protective" sphere from Mexico to Panama, korp wheeler-dealers were buying up the countries piecemeal . . . Sacrificing some autonomy seemed a small price to pay for resisting further erosion.

Regional Consolidation

The defining trend of 21st-century geopolitics has been regional consolidation. Small countries have been merging with their neighbors into strongly-tied confederations, or even totally new countries. Despite a few notable exceptions (the disintegration of South Africa), there are fewer countries now than there were 50 years ago, and the countries that exist are larger.

The optimistic call this a sign of the new globalism – a trend toward harmony and cooperation that will eventually result in an enlightened and peaceful one-world government. Others compare it to playground toughs choosing up sides before the big fight.

By some standards, the one-and-twenty has been a peaceful era (though you wouldn't know it to walk down a Moskva back-alley after midnight). Wars have been short and local. The closest thing to a real international war this century was the Israeli war, over 20 years ago. By 20th-century standards, that would barely have qualified as a bush war.

Again, there are those who take this as a sign that humanity is finally getting smarter. Others point out that TD and the Grand Slam put civilization in a position where it couldn't afford to squander healthy lives on the battlefield – they had to stay home and concentrate on producing food and other essentials. These cynics – or realists, take your pick – predict that if present trends continue, many countries will be enthusiastically back in the invasion-and-conquest business within the next decade.

International Law

As of 2043, there is no international law as such. The last serious attempt at a global forum, the United Nations, saw its influence decline rapidly after the Gulf War of 1991, when attempted U.N. actions to pacify the former Soviet Republics – notably Bosnia-Herzegovina – fell through with no meaningful action taken. By the time the Patterson administration commandeered the former U.N. building in 2023, to serve as the NERCC's administrative headquarters, the organization was almost totally moribund. Fewer than 25% of the member nations were even bothering to send representatives to the General Assembly, and fewer than half of those nations were paying any part of their dues. When the U.S. took over U.N. headquarters, no serious attempt was made to reconvene the organization elsewhere.

There have been only two times so far in the 21st century when the nations of the world adopted anything remotely resembling a global accord. The first was when the Russo-Japanese Alliance rammed through the International Rain Forest Protection Pact (see p. 50), and the second was the international scientific conference convened to react to the Australian plague (see p. 16).

However, the international scene is not quite as anarchic as one might expect. The reason is the multinational corporations. The korps may not have a formal, public deliberative body like the U.N., but they can and do meet together to set trade policies, and even international political policy. And once the korps agree on a certain course of action, they have the clout to bring the national governments into line. The rain forest pact is the most dramatic example of this new balance of power – it was the Russo-Japanese multinationals who decided that the pact was needed, and it was corporate economic pressure that brought the other countries into line. The actual governments of Japan and the CIS were nothing more than mouthpieces for the korps on the rain forest pact.

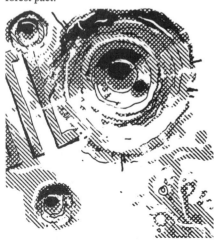

The states that make up the UCAS include Belize, Costa Rica, El Salvador, Guatemala, Honduras, Mexico Libre, Nicaragua and Panama. Each remains an independent nation, with its own laws and government. However, the individual states have handed over to the UCAS the power to make treaties, to regulate imports and exports and to maintain a combined military force.

There's still more than enough poverty and oppression to go around in Central America – it will take decades more before the region is fully recovered from the aftereffects of the Grand Slam – but in general, the UCAS has been good for the region. Central America has been growing steadily more prosperous and less corrupt since 2027.

The UCAS walks a fine line with its big neighbor to the north. On the one hand, it's completely essential to the UCAS economy that trading channels to the U.S. remain open. On the other hand, the UCAS knows that ProGov has its eye on extending its power at least as far as the Isthmus of Panama. In order to keep the U.S. at arm's length, the UCAS has cultivated strong economic and political alliances with Chilentina and the Russo-Japanese alliance, both of whom have a vested interest in keeping the U.S. from spreading – the Russo-Japanese because they don't want the ProGov in control of the Panama Canal, and the Chilentinans because they just don't want them any closer to South America.

South America

South America suffered chaos in the Collapse. In several northern countries, the vast resources of the narcotraficantes (traffs) make the criminal cartels the effective government. In others, power is the prize for which half a dozen viciously contending political factions squabble, usually violently.

U.S. intervention in South American politics continues, though overt military interventions are much rarer. Chilentina is actively trying to restore order in the more vexed nations.

Chilentina

In the 2040s, Chilentina has become the principal source of technology in the New World. Although it can't approach the Russo-Japanese korps in terms of quantity, in most fields the quality of its products equals Eurasian standards. Chilentina is also becoming more and more a source of new ideas and innovations, beating the Japanese to the punch on several key developments of the last decade, sometimes by as much as two years. It's no wonder that Chilentina has become known as "the Japan of the West."

In 2025, when the rest of South America was at an all-time low ebb, Chile and Argentina quietly merged into a single nation, and re-formed their government into an efficient parliamentary democracy set up along Japanese lines. The architect of this change was Emilio Arellano, a Chilean businessman, who has been hailed as the most effective political reformer since Mahatma Gandhi. Arellano never held political office, but he campaigned tirelessly for unification from 2018 on. He died late in 2023, of an undetectable brain hemorrhage, only 16 months before his dream became a reality. There are those who say that Arellano's death was a remarkably efficient high-tech assassination perpetrated by agents of the U.S., Japan or even a faction of the Chilean or Argentine government. These claims are generally dismissed as mere conspiracy theory.

SOUTH AMERICA

Data havens are the international cottage industry of the one-and-twenty. Virtually every microscopic lastworld state too small to support a real industrial base has taken a stab at setting itself up as an international data haven. Less than a double handful of these establishments are really taken seriously by the multinationals – or by computer criminals.

Zurich-Orbital (see p. 51) is in a class by itself as far as off-line security is concerned. The top earthbound havens are listed below, in approximate order of reliability.

Switzerland: The international data-storage business effectively originated in Switzerland, where it was a logical outgrowth of the Swiss banking industry. The main national data banks are located deep in the Alps (most top-rank data havens are located on remote islands or under mountains), about 30 miles southwest of Leicht. Although most of the richest clients of the Swiss transferred to Zurich-Orbital when it went up in the late '20s, the groundside banks are still maintained with state-of-the-art-plus security and confidentiality, for those who aren't quite rich enough or paranoid enough to patronize Z-O. Where Z-O prices are astronomical, prices for Leicht are merely unbelievable.

The Andes: Chilentina maintains an excellent haven in the mountains about 20 miles northeast of Rancaqua. This is the newest major data haven, opening for international business in 2039. Security is top-rank and prices are reasonable (compared to the Swiss, anyway). Business at the Andes facility has been modest, however. U.S. and Russo-Japanese korps aren't wild about sending their data to Chilentina for safekeeping, and Chilentinan korps generally prefer someplace farther from home for their offsite backups. So far the biggest customers of the Andes facility are drug lords from the northern countries, which hasn't done much for the facility's PR image.

Andorra: Andorra has a data haven much as Monte Carlo has a casino – the haven entirely supports this tiny country's economy (see p. 52). Andorra is probably the best value in international data storage, balancing security and cost concerns.

Mauritius: This small island in the Indian ocean was annexed by Madagascar when the French government collapsed. It's been a data haven for more than 25 years, and has acquired an excellent international reputation. Many large multinationals divide their data storage between Andorra and Mauritius, so as to avoid putting all their eggs in one geographical basket.

Continued on next page . . .

Data Havens (Continued)

Malta: The biggest problem with the Malta facility is that it's overpriced. It's more expensive than either Mauritius or Andorra, and it offers no better security. There are also unsubstantiated but persistent rumors that the German government has access to Malta's data banks.

Vatneyrl: This facility, in Iceland, is very affordable, and the integrity of the staff and administration is unquestioned, but its technology is less than state-of-the-art, and its security is rather low-key. Most international clients prefer beefier security for their data.

Singapore: The technology and security at the Singapore data haven are at least as casual as the Vatneyrl facility, and Singapore lacks Iceland's advantage of geographic isolation. The prices, however, are very reasonable – Singapore is the only international data haven that's affordable by small businesses and wealthy individuals, as opposed to mega-korps and national governments.

Fiji: Fiji's haven has sophisticated tech, excellent security and an ideal location. It would definitely be one of the top five global data havens except for one thing – the facility was heavily subsidized by the U.S. government, and the word has been out for years, "If it's something you don't want to share with the NERCC, don't send it to Fiji."

The Chiletinan government makes no bones about the fact that its primary function is to foster big business. Productive members of society are offered useful work, a comfortable lifestyle and guaranteed health care for life. However, dissidents, troublemakers and ne'er-do-wells are not tolerated. The Chilentinan justice system is harsh, particularly against violent crime. Convicted criminals are usually conscripted into work gangs that handle much of the manual labor throughout the country. The government will not hesitate to pacify difficult prisoners through narcotics or cybernetic implants – and if the treatment happens to fry some or all of their brains in the process, no great loss – better to be a drone for society than a parasite against it.

Criminal penalties for "white collar" crime, on the other hand, are almost ridiculously light – critics of the Chilentinan legal system like to point out that the criminal penalty for loitering (one to three years hard labor) is more severe than the penalty for embezzlement (up to one year house arrest, and repayment of embezzled funds, plus penalties of up to 200% of the amount stolen). However, the government also gives the corporations a great deal of latitude in disciplining their own employees, and corporate "justice" often makes those sentenced to labor gangs look like the lucky ones.

Political dissidence is tolerated – to a point. Chilentina maintains a free press, and citizens are allowed to voice opposition to the government, either vocally or in print. Known malcontents are placed under almost constant observation by the government, and will be slapped down hard if they step the least bit out of line (and there are those who say that if a dissident goes long enough without stepping out of line, the government's not above giving him a little push).

ProGov is quite vocal on the subject of the "chilis" and the threat they pose to the United States' proper position as arbiter of the Western Hemisphere. The main reason for U.S. opposition to Chilentina – other than a simple desire to be the biggest goldfish in the bowl – is an ongoing "brain drain," in which politically liberal or moderate U.S. citizens who can get out of the country seek political asylum in Chilentina (which may not be a freethinker's paradise, but is still infinitely better than the U.S.).

The Chilentinan government is traditionally eager to honor such petitions for asylum, if the refugee is educated – particularly in technology or finance. In the last few years U.S. pressure has forced Chilentina to back off sharply on its immigration policies, but there are still more top-rank professionals leaving the U.S. for Chilentina than ProGov likes.

Brazil

The rain forests of the Amazon Basin produce more oxygen than any other area on the earth, but throughout the 20th century they were being clear-cut and burned out at a rate of up to 50 million acres a year.

In this century, with global warming going from a theory to an imminent threat and eco-catastrophe looming on the horizon, this had to stop.

Brazil was hit hard in the Tolliver's Disease pandemic. This slowed the deforestation somewhat simply because there were no longer enough people to cut the trees and man the ranches and plantations. But by 2030, the progress of deforestation was accelerating again, and the earth was in no shape to tolerate further depletion of her oxygen reserves.

The solution was the International Rain Forest Protection Pact of 2031. This international treaty was pushed upon the international community by the Russo-Japanese, using tactics that ranged from friendly lobbying to outright economic blackmail. Even the United States went along, after being brutally threatened with a 100% import/export embargo from both the Russo-Japanese and Chilentina. No firstworld country could ignore the pact.

The pact created an ecological reservation throughout the Amazon Basin. Millions of square miles – including the most productive and profitable farm and ranch land in Brazil – were set aside for rain forest. All economic and agricultural exploitation of these reserved lands is strictly forbidden. (A few small indigenous tribes have the only exceptions to this, and their population and rights to exploit the land are rigidly regulated.)

The pact is enforced by the International Ecological Protective Agency, an independent organization staffed by personnel from all the pact's signatory countries. The Agency breaks down into two bureaus. Bureau A is made up of about 700 scientists – ecologists, botanists, zoologists – dedicated to expanding the rain forest and maximizing its global ecological impact. Bureau B consists of about 3,000 crack ranger troops that serve as game wardens, patrolling the Basin and enforcing the pact.

In return for outlawing exploitation of the rain forests, Brazil receives an annual stipend from each of the pact countries. Any country that doesn't pay is subjected to crippling economic sanctions from the other signatory nations, including Chilentina, the Russo-Japanese and (reluctantly) the U.S.

Still underpopulated from Tolliver's Disease, this stipend is enough to provide a slender but adequate income for every Brazilian citizen. The pact rigorously limits Brazilian industry and agriculture, the former mainstays of the Brazilian economy. Now the major part of Brazil's economy comes from the pact stipend, with tourism the major local industry. Brazil is working to rebuild its economy along environmentally sound lines (so as to preserve its pact stipend). Plans include promoting an international entertainment industry, and encouraging high-tech light industry after the Chilentinan model.

As might be expected, the pact is not universally popular. However it's virtually the only global policy (along with the UCAS) that the Chilentinans and Russo-Japanese completely support. Consequently, these two powers have been able to strong-arm international enforcement of the pact. Most international analysts predict that if there's any political or economic weakening whatsoever of either Russo-Japan or Chilentina, the International Rain Forest Protection Pact will be the first thing to crumble. Even in Brazil, there are nationalist groups who charge that the pact is an affront to national honor and traditional masculine values, and these groups have been known to make their points violently.

United Europe

The Maastricht accords of 1991 laid the foundation for United Europe. Economic union in 1993 was followed by a united military establishment and a supranational security/police structure in 1995, ratification of supranational powers to the European Assembly (formerly the European Congress) in Brussels in 1997, and the formal act of union in 2000.

National governments retain significant power, but foreign policy, certain areas of trade and military concerns are largely the domain of the Assembly.

Zurich-Orbital

Zurich-Orbital is a space platform in Earth orbit on which various data files are maintained that are either backups of hot data on Earth, or too hot to store on Earth. Sensitive monetary transactions, transfers of stolen data, dossiers too dangerous to leave accessible on Earth and similar materials are the commodities handled by Z-O.

Absolute data security is promised by the consortium that manages Z-O. The platform is armed with state-of-the-art missile defenses, the comm-laser links to the Net are guarded by the most ferocious security software ever devised (but "black ice" is a myth – *sure* it is), and the station personnel are able to wipe the massive databanks in seconds as a last-ditch defense. Rumor has it that the platform is also rigged to self-destruct on the receipt of a command from its Earth-based HQ, in the event that it is captured.

Using Z-O is not cheap. The cost to store a gigabyte of data on Z-O for a year is about equal to the cost to purchase a square foot of land in the heart of the Moskva business district – which is more than the annual incomes of about 92% of the families on earth.

The Korp World

As governments totter on the Edge, a lot of the real power has passed into the hands of the big korps. The multinationals and the politicos dance a tight little dance, and nobody, maybe not even the dancers themselves, can tell you who's leading.

The most formal, polite name for the multinationals is *keiretsu*. It's a Japanese word meaning a corporation that's autonomous and self-contained. *Shaikujin,* the people who work there, get security from cradle to grave, as long as they do their bushido-biz duty to the keiretsu and don't drig up too bad. They live in korp housing, shop at korp stores using korp cred, sing the korp hymn every day at start of shift . . .

If you live on the Edge (and don't we all), you're *going* to cross paths with the korps. Netrunners who want the hottest data gotta hack it out of korp databases. The samurai, the breetva, muscle-boys 'n' girls on the street, are gonna find korp valuta behind lots of the jobs the fixers find for them. Korps like a lot of deniability when they have to do wetwork, or even slightly damp work. Gentlecrooks too, when a korp needs someone for a spot of "competitive R&D," or soft extractions . . . sorry, make that "intercorporate executive recruitment." Even rebels, trying to pry ProGov's fingers off America's throat, will find their politics can make for korp bedfellows, no matter how strange they may be.

All told, there are maybe 100 korps worldwide that qualify as real international keiretsu. There are also plenty of smaller national and regional companies left, though most of them make their cred subcontracting for the keiretsu, rather than marketing goods or services directly to the consumer. The smaller korps usually serve as "farm teams" for the keiretsu. If a national or regional concern is consistently successful and innovative, it will eventually be absorbed by one of the multinationals. And whether or not it *wants* to be absorbed is not really an issue – the best an independent can hope for when it comes time to join the big leagues is a choice of deals or parent companies.

Non-Korp Business

There's no such thing as a "small business" on the Edge. There are plenty of entrepreneurs, and freelancers all over the place, but the really successful freelancers take their contracts from the korps, and the serious entrepreneurs are looking to make their fortunes by selling out to the korps. In general, any business larger than Mom & Pop's hot dog stand can be assumed to be either owned outright or directly controlled by some korp with a net worth of $100 million or more.

Currently there are two main power groups in the U.E. The most powerful is the militant nationalist faction led by Germany and Italy, but a moderate faction dominated by the Iberian Federation, the Scandinavian states and England has so far managed to restrain it. The Benelux retains its traditional neutrality in political struggles.

Andorra

Andorra (a tiny state between France and the Iberian Federation) has become a haven for data of questionable origins and dubious legality (see sidebar, p. 49). Backed by unidentified (but major) concerns, a large hole was blasted in the Pyrenees and loaded with computers to store all manner of material, no questions asked. Andorra is not the only tiny state to establish a national data haven – others include Monte Carlo, Gibraltar and several Pacific islands – but Andorra has the best reputation of any of the "second tier" data havens. It's regarded as having security and confidentiality that approach Swiss standards, at less than half the price of the Swiss haven.

The Prince-Bishop of Seo de Urgel, in the Iberian Federation, is nominal ruler of the principality, but actual authority rests in the Council of Syndics, a self-perpetuating oligarchy committed to maintenance of the data haven. France relinquished all claim to Andorra during the displacements earlier in the century.

The Benelux

United Europe centers its government in Belgium, the Netherlands and Luxembourg, with the European Assembly in Brussels, the Supreme Tribunal in The Hague, the Bourse Centrale in Luxembourg, and many other U.E. departments and functions in the region.

As a result, the Benelux is also a hotbed of international espionage, intrigue, korp activities, etc.

Eire

Britain withdrew from Northern Ireland in the face of increasing agitation to eliminate "foreign entanglements" during the economic depression of the mid-90s. An Act of Union between Ulster and Eire was engineered as part of this withdrawal, but the terms (limited autonomy for the North, guarantees of representation for Protestants in the Seanad – the Senate) displeased IRA extremists, just as the union itself infuriated hard-line Ulster factions. Terrorism and internecine strife are still frequent occurrences in the Republic. Perhaps the strangest twist in the conflict is the Ulster Liberation League, whose bomb raids on U.K. sites have the avowed purpose of forcing Britain to "recognize its historical debt to Ulster and restore our rights as British citizens."

France

France's central government was formally divested of power in the Tax Revolutions of 1998; the Multipartite Republic was established in 2012. Paris is home to a debating-society legislature and a figurehead premiere, while real power rests in the autonomous departmental governments.

Germany

Germany is presently the leading power in the European Union. It's second only to the Russo-Japanese alliance in cutting-edge tech.

Germany, under increasing competitive pressure from Chilentina and others and hungry for resources, has become more overtly nationalistic in recent years. This is making its U.E. neighbors nervous. While the European Defense Force is theoretically commanded by the Union, rather than any member nation, the German contingent of the EDF constitutes just over 50% of its total strength. The Germans' most committed political ally in the U.E. is Italy.

Increased activity by neofascist factions is another destabilizing element in German politics.

The Iberian Federation

Spain and Portugal united in 2000, in conjunction with the U.E. Act of Union. Portugal and the former Spanish province of Catalunya maintain a constitutionally mandated degree of political and cultural autonomy, but for all practical purposes the three are one country. Iberia is the leader of the moderate coalition within the U.E. that opposes Germany's more militant proposals.

With a stable, growing economy and a peaceful, educated population, many analysts are predicting that Iberia will supplant Germany as the dominant power in the U.E. within 10 years.

The Commonwealth of Independent States

Established by the declarations in Minsk and Alma-ata in 1991, the Commonwealth replaced the Soviet Union, which was formally dissolved at midnight, Jan. 1, 1992. The Commonwealth is presently composed of the Federated Russian Republic, Ukraine, Byelorussia, Latvia, Georgia, Moldavia, Azerbaijan and Armenia. The central Asian republics seceded from the Commonwealth following violent ethnic confrontations in the mid-90s.

Together with the Japanese, their firm economic allies, the Commonwealth reigns unchallenged as the dominant world power of the 21st century. The combination of CIS resources with Japanese efficiency and expertise is unstoppable. Nobody surpasses Russo-Japanese tech in terms of quality *or* quantity.

Money talks, and the Russo-Japanese alliance's status as the richest entity on the earth also makes it the most politically powerful entity on the earth. Its most

The Bolshy Ten

The Bolshy Ten are the most powerful korps on the Edge. Each has assets in excess of $1 trillion. Each is involved in, and often controls, key industries central to life in the one-and-twenty.

Fabrique Europa

Fabrique Europa is Europe's largest conglomerate, formed in 2022 when a number of firms that had been working more and more cooperatively formalized their connections in a series of mergers, with one or two takeovers to deal with those reluctant to admit the benefits of consolidation.

It's well-known that FE products are at least as high in quality as the Russo-Japanese can produce, but not as cheap.

Han-Rhee Ltd.

Han-Rhee is Korea's largest korp. It began its climb to the top rank in 2018, when it forged effective trading ties with the Central Asian Federation in the early one-and-twenty. Japanese and Western firms tended to react poorly to the almost tribal patterns of worker-management relations in places like Uzbekistan, not to mention the invidiously embedded system of *nomenklatura*, or semi-official corruption.

The Seoul-based firms of Sun Rhee Associates and Dae Han Ltd. chartered a new venture to move production facilities into the area and to develop a workable corporate culture on the ruins of the old Soviet mind-set.

It wasn't fast, it certainly wasn't easy, but 20 years later, Han-Rhee finally hit the big leagues of the Bolshy Ten. Besides the CAF, most of its business comes from the Arab Nations and India, but it's making strong inroads into the U.S., where doing business with the Russo-Japanese korps is quietly frowned upon by the ProGov.

Han-Rhee's products aren't of outstanding quality or outstanding value, but it keeps its place at the top by skillfully exploiting those markets that other korps ignore.

Continued on next page . . .

Geopolitics

North American Technologies

This conglomerate was formed as part of a deliberate effort by ProGov to produce a competitor for the Russo-Japanese. With vigorous NERCC "encouragement," 17 major U.S. companies were shoved together (not necessarily with their consent), under the nominal auspices of the original NAT founded by Adam Hammond. Surprisingly, it worked.

NAT products are of average quality and (thanks to the NERCC's union-busting policies) competitive price. Besides dominating most U.S. markets, NAT does good business in Canada and Central America, with growing influence in Europe and Asia.

Rio Largo Manufacturing

Rio Largo is the flagship of the upstart Chilentinan korps (the only one in the Bolshy Ten, although three more Chilentinan companies are in the top 20 and coming up fast). Rio Largo's quality and cost equal and often better the Japanese. Only the difficulty in cracking new markets keeps Rio Largo and the other Chilentinan companies from mounting a serious challenge to Russo-Japanese dominance of the international market.

The Russo-Japanese Korps

Six of the Bolshy Ten are Russo-Japanese keiretsu. It doesn't matter if the corporate name is Russian or Japanese: either way the company is headquartered in Tokyo with production facilities in the CIS. And the rest of the name shouldn't be taken too seriously either – Hiromatsu Power Systems has just as much interest in communications industries as Ishido Communications does, and vice versa – all the Russo-Japanese keiretsu have their fingers in *all* the pies.

To the rest of the world, the Russo-Japanese mega-korps are pretty much indistinguishable. They fight furiously among themselves over new subsidiaries and markets, but they call off their feuds and present a unified front when some upstart outsider threatens to erode Russo-Japanese economic power anywhere in the world.

The Russo-Japanese contingent of the Bolshy Ten includes: Hiromatsu Power Systems, Ishido Communications, Korsakov-Shimadzu, Kosmozavot Tenno Tanjo Ltd., Shinowara Integrated Industries, Todai Technosystems. For what it's worth, Shinowara is normally considered the most stable and politically influential of the korps, though in terms of net profit it's down near the bottom of the Bolshy Ten. Right at the moment Kosmozavot is the richest korp on the planet, but that could change literally overnight.

audacious political move so far has been to force international compliance with the International Rain Forest Protection Pact to halt the destruction of the Brazilian rain forest. The Russo-Japanese are not normally known for being environmentally enlightened, but they do listen to their scientists, and when the best projections available said that continued destruction of the rain forests would make Earth uninhabitable in three centuries, they took action.

Minsk, the capital of the Commonwealth, is in most respects a fairly unremarkable city (unless you happen to be a diplomat, spy or international lobbyist). The real action is in the great sprawls of St. Petersburg and Moscow. Neon on the Moskva is the theme there, and the wheelers and dealers of this world on the Edge migrate there like hajji to Mecca.

In general, the mines, factories and refineries of the Russo-Japanese alliance are in the CIS, while the korp headquarters, top universities and R&D labs are in Japan. There are already several small nationalist groups within the CIS who want to break away from Japanese influence. These movements are strictly on the lunatic fringe so far – both Japan and the CIS are still getting too much out of their alliance for a split to seem attractive to anybody but the most dedicated bigot. But as the CIS becomes more and more prosperous and educated, resentment against the Japanese monopoly on management and research is sure to grow.

The Central Asian Federation

The member nations of the CAF – the former Soviet republics of Kazakhstan, Uzbekistan, Tadzhikstan, Turkmenistan and Kyrgyzstan – originally united with other former members of the USSR in the Commonwealth. But following a nationalistic surge in the Slavic states, which met terrible riots in the central Asian states, the governments of the CAF seceded from the CIS. A cache of nukes held by extreme elements in Kazakhstan persuaded the Commonwealth to accept the central Asian resolution peacefully.

If there is a "bad guy" in the world, in the old Cold War sense, it is the CAF. The CAF is constantly stirring up the Islamic League, extending puppet strings into eastern Asia, competing with Chinese industry, etc.

The government of the CAF is nominally a socialist republic, but actually it's a byzantine, self-perpetuating oligarchy, much like the central committee of the old USSR.

The racist and fascistic elements in Soviet culture, disgusted with the globalism of the CIS, have settled in the CAF. Consequently, there are constant armed struggles between various ethnic and political factions. This internal struggle tends to limit the CAF's effectiveness as a global player. Islamic fundamentalists also form a potent power bloc.

Although the socialist government of the CAF is technically diametrically opposed to the ProGov of the U.S., the two regimes have a great deal in common politically, and often form an unofficial alliance against the Russo-Japanese.

The Middle East

A bizarre combination of factors led to Israel controlling or occupying virtually all of Jordan, Syria, Lebanon and eastern portions of Iraq (see p. 14). At the moment, Israel is badly in need of friends. For several years Israel has been making blatant overtures to the Russo-Japanese alliance, hoping to become a junior partner in the alliance. The Russo-Japanese response has been generally positive, but they've always stopped short of fully enfranchising Israel as part of their hegemony. In the meantime, the U.S., traditionally Israel's strongest political ally, is becoming increasingly alienated by Israel's growing relationship with the CIS.

On the Arabian peninsula, the oil sheikdoms have largely returned to pre-WWII conditions (in some cases, pre-WWI conditions). Oil is still a useful resource, but it's no longer the lifeblood of technical civilization (the importance of oil in the mid-21st century can be compared to that of coal in the late 20th). This loss of economic clout among the Arabs is one of the main reasons Israel is able to continue to survive.

After the Israeli war, Iran absorbed western Iraq, but immediately became enmeshed in bickering with the Saudis for top slot in the Islamic League. It still finds time to fight covert actions with Israel and back Islamic terrorist organizations, etc. It is known to be receiving funds from the CAF.

Africa

Africa has deteriorated in the 21st century. In most regions, the population lives no better than it did 200 years ago.

Africa's troubles started in the mid-1990s, when a breakdown in South African racial reforms led to a bloody race war. By 1998, the white minority in South Africa was either fled (mostly to South America) or dead. With the whites all gone, the black coalition that had purged the country immediately broke up into battling factions, and South Africa rapidly disintegrated into a mire of tiny, squabbling tribal states.

When the TD plague came along, Africa was hit harder than any other part of the world, with fatality rates exceeding 75% in most areas. Over most of the continent civilization was effectively abandoned, as people reverted to tribal society. Technically, national governments still exist, but in most places they're little more than a political fiction. A few metropolitan areas remain, but they are filthy, dangerous places ruled by whatever local tyrant can grab the reins of power.

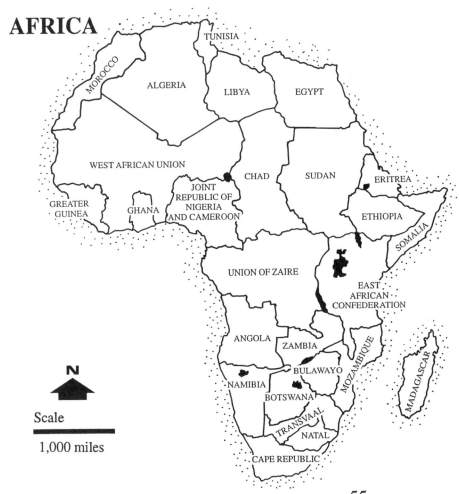

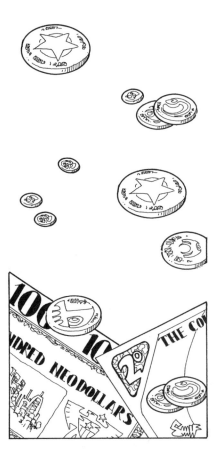

Conversion Factor

The Conversion Factor (CF) for a currency measures how much local money it takes to equal $1.

To convert a figure in ecus into another currency, multiply the figure in ecus by the CF for the currency. For example, the Swiss franc has a CF of 2.1. $1 equals 2.1 Swiss francs. An item that costs $100 costs 210 Swiss francs.

To convert a figure in local currency into ecus, divide it by the CF. For example, if a fancy personal computer crafted by the techno-gnomes of Lucerne costs 3,200 Swiss francs, it costs 3,200 divided by 2.1, or $1,524.

The three ecu currencies, the neodollar, eurotaler and rubyen, all have a CF of 1.00. But not all ecus are created equal, and they have different rates of flux.

Conversion Factors aren't essential. They are included for background color. In game terms, all that matters is the real value of the transaction in ecus. But when a fixer has to lug a barrel of Serbian balkis (1,200 balkis = $1) to a meet in Krusevac, it makes life a little more interesting.

The only exceptions to the rule of non-civilization are Egypt, which goes along as it has for 6,000 years, and Madagascar, which has managed to maintain a poor but functional government. When France crumbled, Madagascar seized control of the islands of Mauritius and Réunion, and has recently established a successful data haven on Mauritius. Of all the other putative nations of Africa, those nations in the northwest seem to be making the most tangible progress toward reorganization.

At the moment, the only foreign aid to the African mainland comes from the Russo-Japanese Alliance, which has its eye on eventual control and exploitation of the natural resources of the African continent. The Russo-Japanese plan is to give the Africans just enough aid to make them grateful, without giving them enough to make them independent. The CAF has made overtures, particularly in Northwest Africa, but so far hasn't offered more than token help.

India

India has changed little in the last 100 years. Theoretically, the TD pandemic should have offered at least temporary relief from the Indian subcontinent's chronic problem of overpopulation. But the combined effects of the TD and the Grand Slam so devastated India's industrial base that even with far fewer people, the general population remained as hungry as ever. What wealth exists there is controlled by a small rich elite.

For the last 25 years, India and Pakistan have been actively negotiating with an eye towards eventual reunification, but little real progress has been made. The Arabs and the CAF want to control Pakistan themselves; China is worried that if Pakistan returns to India, Nepal, Bangladesh and Bhutan will follow, depriving China of three valuable buffer states. So far, all this foreign pressure has been enough to forestall reunification.

China

China has returned to its status as the Forbidden Kingdom. Its border states and clients are largely independent, acting as buffers against impertinent intrusions.

China is the leading power in genetic research. Under the brilliant direction of Dr. Chou Jen-Jhai (1977-2034), Chinese genetic science leaped ahead of the rest of the world. However, the tightening of the Bamboo Curtain cut off the exchange of scientific information between Chinese researchers and the rest of the world in 2032.

The Australian Plague of 2036 is generally assumed to have been caused by a Chinese military virus that was released (accidentally or deliberately) by a rogue Chinese intelligence agent. However, while an outraged world imposed economic sanctions on China as a result, fear of devastating biological retaliation has, so far, forestalled any active military response.

Shanghai and Hong Kong have been completely under the control of the Chinese government since the turn of the century, and were closed off along with the rest of the country in 2032.

Eastern Asia

The countries on the Asian Pacific Rim are the up-and-coming players on the global stage of the one-and-twenty. They're democratic, progressive and fiercely capitalistic. The tech and other goods produced by these countries is frankly second-rate, but it's cheap and easily available all over the world. And it's getting better. Economic prophets like to speculate about which of the Pacific rim coun-

Money Games
Rules for fiddling with exchange rates and the uncertainty of fiscal stability are discussed because this is a staple in many cyberpunk settings. The GM may decide this is far too much bookkeeping, and scrap the whole idea. He can also set flux rates at his own whim, without referring to dice rolls. We do recommend keeping the basic currency exchange, rather than putting the whole planet on ecus, or some other arbitrary currency. That's a lot too orderly for the Edge, livewire.

tries is poised to become the next Japan. Korea and the Philippines are the front runners, but Thailand, Vietnam and Taiwan are seen as having strong dark-horse potential. And the race is on . . .

Australia: Poisoned Treasure

Of all the tragedies and catastrophes that have marred the first half of the 21st century, the most frightening is the Australian plague of 2037. Something completely depopulated an entire continent in less than six months, and nobody's sure what it was. Most nations blame the Chinese, but the Chinese aren't talking.

There are just too many unanswered questions about the Australian plague – mainly centering on how on earth the thing is vectored. It obviously can't be spread by birds or insects, or it would certainly have spread to Indonesia or New Zealand by now. Likewise satellite photography shows the Australian ecology apparently flourishing. Herds of wild cattle and packs of wild dogs have been spotted, and the kangaroos are doing just fine, thank you. On the other hand, if the plague was only spread by humans or primates, surely the quarantine measures imposed in the summer of '37 would have saved *somebody*. Based on the little evidence available, virologists speculate that the plague was a viral infection, fatal only to primates but carried by an indeterminate number of other land mammal species, almost certainly including rodents. It's virtually certain that such a specific and devastating infection would have to be custom-designed. Most scientists think that once all the humans were dead the plague would rapidly become extinct . . . probably. A couple of the firstworld countries have airdropped teams of expendables (convicts and political prisoners), but they never survive long – just long enough to report a complete lack of human life and lots of decayed bodies everywhere. Then, after about a week, communications cease.

Right now, Australia is like a high-stakes game of Russian roulette. Whoever's the first one to pick up the gun and pull the trigger gets the prize, if he survives – only nobody knows how many of the chambers are loaded.

An international scientific conference on the Australian mystery convened in 2038. The conference agreed to wait at least 50 years before attempting any sort of expedition to the Australian mainland, and then to make the effort a joint international venture. But it's been five years with nothing new out of Australia, and some countries might be getting itchy fingers. The CIS is believed to have dropped robotic probes, similar to those used to explore the surface of Venus, into the ruins of Australian cities. The most paranoid scenario suggests that the Chinese (or whoever designed the plague) might know *exactly* how long it will remain active, and will mount a massive invasion of the continent as soon as it's safe to do so, while the rest of the world stands around with their tongues hanging out. Of course, all countries with an observation satellite in the air (which is almost all of them) have been paying special attention to their pictures of Australia. Some analysts claim to have found visual evidence of low-tech human activity in the deep outback, but this conclusion is hotly disputed. If somebody is alive out there, they must be *deliberately* trying not to be seen.

There is a nominal Australian government still active, headquartered out of Hobart, Tasmania, but it's in no position to make a serious claim for control of the mainland if one of the big boys decides to make a grab.

After the plague struck, New Guinea (completely under the control of Indonesia since the first decade of the 21st century), New Zealand and Tasmania were placed under strict quarantine restrictions, out of fear that the Australian infection would somehow jump to those islands. These restrictions were lifted in 2042, but the economic damage they caused the affected countries will take decades to correct. Consequently, these states lag far behind other countries of the Asian Pacific Rim in terms of tech and commerce.

When Not to Make Flux Rolls

As a rule, trivial transactions, less than $100, should not require flux rolls. However, the GM may decide to call for a flux roll for small purchases once in a while, just to keep players from getting entirely comfortable. Nothing like having a smartcab announce, "That will be 10 Neodollars, 8 Class-A Keiretsu Marks, or 12 U.S. dollars . . . adjustment . . . 13.50 U.S. dol . . . adjustment . . . 14.75 U.S. dollars, please."

Anyone paying in "fold," real hardcopy cash, can skip flux rolls. That applies to money printed by a government, scrip certificates from a major korp, or any kind of non-electronic currency. However, if a character converts fold into cred (deposits hardcopy currency for transfer to an electronic account), he should check the flux at that time.

Table of Tech Levels and Control Ratings

Tech Level (TL): Indicates the average Tech Level for the country. This does not mean the technology available to every inhabitant, but rather the median point.

Wealthy members of the society may have access to more advanced tech; poor members of society will be limited to significantly lower technology.

Note that TL8 means *early* TL8, and that most of the tech in that country will be TL7, with the TL8 stuff reserved for korps and the wealthy.

Control Ratings: Ratings are assigned for three areas. The General CR (Gen.) measures the presence of law enforcement, strictness of laws, and the overall level of government regulation. The Weapons CR (Wpns.) specifically governs the Legality of weapons (see p. C110). The Technology (Tech.) CR measures the Legality of cyberwear and cyberdecks, as well as government regulation of industry, medical resources, power sources, and other high-tech features of life in the one-and-twenty.

Wealth Level (W): A citizen of average Status (Level 0) will live at the Wealth Level indicated.

D	Dead Broke
P	Poor
S	Struggling
A	Average
C	Comfortable

North and Central America

Country	TL	Gen.	Wpns.	Tech.	W.
United States	8	5	5	4	A
Communaute d'Atlantique Quebeçois	8	5	4	4	S
Federated Provinces	8	3	3	3	A
United Provinces	8	3	4	3	A
Northwest Protectorate	6	2	1	0	P
Union of Central American States	7	4	3	1	D

South America

Country	TL	Gen.	Wpns.	Tech.	W.
Bolivia	8	6	6	4	P
Brazil	7	1	0	0	D
Chilentina	8	4	4	3	C
Colombia	7	3	1	0	S
Ecuador	7	6	6	6	D
Guyana	6	3	5	2	D
Paraguay	6	5	2	0	D
Peru	7	4	6	4	S
Uruguay	6	5	2	0	P
Venezuela	7	6	6	6	P

United Europe

Country	TL	Gen.	Wpns.	Tech.	W.
Albania	6	2	6	2	S
Andorra	8	4	6	0	C
Austria	8	3	6	2	C
Baltic League	7	3	4	4	A
Belgium	8	4	6	3	A
Bohemia	7	5	6	5	S
Bosnia	6	6	6	6	D
British Union	8	5	6	5	A
Bulgaria	7	3	3	3	A
Croatia	6	6	6	6	S
Cyprus	7	5	6	5	A
Denmark	8	3	6	0	C
Eire	8	4	6	2	A
Estonia	7	5	3	3	A
Finland	8	3	3	1	C
France	8	5	6	5	A
Germany	8	4	6	1	C
Greece	7	6	6	4	S
Hungary	8	4	2	0	A
Iberian Fed.	8	4	4	4	A
Iceland	6	3	1	0	A
Italy	8	4	6	5	S
Liechtenstein	8	4	4	4	C
Lithuania	6	5	5	5	S
Luxembourg	8	4	4	4	C
Macedonia	6	5	6	6	P
Malta	6	3	6	2	S
Monaco	8	3	6	0	C
Netherlands	8	4	6	3	A
Norway	8	3	6	3	A
Poland	8	3	4	3	C
Romania	7	4	6	4	S
Serbia	6	6	6	6	D
Slovakia	6	3	4	2	P
Slovenia	6	6	6	6	P
Sweden	8	4	6	2	C
Switzerland	8	3	4	2	C
Turkey	7	5	6	5	S

Commonwealth of Independent States

Country	TL	Gen.	Wpns.	Tech.	W.
Armenia	7	4	2	2	S
Azerbaijan	7	4	2	2	S
Byelorussia	8	4	4	2	A
Georgia	8	4	2	2	A
Latvia	7	4	4	4	S
Moldavia	7	4	2	2	S
Russia	8	4	4	3	C
Ukraine	8	4	4	2	C

Central Asian Federation

Country	TL	Gen.	Wpns.	Tech.	W.
Kazakhstan	8	5	3	5	A
Kyrgyzstan	7	2	2	2	S
Tajikistan	7	3	3	3	S
Turkmenistan	7	3	3	3	S
Uzbekistan	8	4	2	0	A

Middle East

Country	TL	Gen.	Wpns.	Tech.	W.
Arab Union	8	4	2	0	C
Iran	7	6	6	6	S
Israel	8	5	6	4	A
Kurdistan	6	3	1	3	D
Kuwait	8	5	6	1	C
Yemen	7	6	6	6	P

Asia

Country	TL	Gen.	Wpns.	Tech.	W.
Afghanistan	6	2	0	0	P
Bangladesh	7	4	6	2	D
Bhutan	6	5	6	5	D
China	8	6	4	6	S
India	7	6	6	5	D
Mongolia	6	3	0	0	P
Myanmar	6	6	6	6	P
Nepal	6	3	2	0	P
Pakistan	7	5	4	5	P
Philippines	7	4	6	2	S
Sri Lanka	6	3	3	3	S
Tibet	6	2	2	0	P

Pacific Rim

Country	TL	Gen.	Wpns.	Tech.	W.
Australia (Tasmania)	7	3	3	2	P
Brunei	8	3	6	0	A
Cambodia	6	0	0	0	P
Indonesia	7	5	6	4	P
Japan	8	4	6	2	C
Korea	8	4	4	2	A
Laos	6	2	2	2	A
Malaysia	7	4	3	3	S
New Zealand	7	3	6	0	S
Singapore	8	6	6	1	C
Taiwan	8	4	6	1	A
Thailand	7	3	3	3	C
Vietnam	8	4	2	2	A

Africa

Country	TL	Gen.	Wpns.	Tech.	W.
Algeria	6	3	3	3	S
Angola	7	6	6	6	P
Botswana	6	3	3	3	D
Bulawayo	6	6	3	6	S
Cape Republic	7	6	6	6	P
Chad	7	6	4	4	S
E. African Confederation	6	6	2	2	P
Egypt	8	4	5	3	A
Eritrea	6	2	2	2	D
Ethiopia	6	6	6	6	D
Ghana	6	2	2	2	D
Greater Guinea	6	4	4	0	P
Joint Republic of Nigeria and Cameroon	7	6	6	6	S
Libya	6	2	2	2	P
Madagascar	8	4	5	2	A
Morocco	7	4	2	2	S
Mozambique	6	2	2	2	D
Namibia	7	4	2	4	P
Natal	6	4	3	1	P
Seychelles	8	4	5	4	A
Somalia	6	1	1	0	D
Sudan	6	6	6	6	P
Transvaal	8	5	5	5	S
Tunisia	6	3	3	3	S
Union of Zaire	7	4	2	0	P
West African Union	6	6	6	6	S
Zambia	6	6	4	6	S

ECONOMICS

Dyadooshka used to say that "money makes the world go 'round." Today that goes "valuta gives a breetva Edge" (money gives a razor its Edge).

Doublepun talk, paryeni. All us breetvas on the street know where we get our Edge, neh? When a fixer signs you up for a hot job, make sure it's hard valuta he's slottin' into your card, not the local sloppy-soft dengi. Cred or fold, machts nichts as long as it turns into ecus nice and clean.

Cred and Fold

Most of the world's money is *cred*, electronic currency. Cred is tracked by the interlocked accounting computers of the world's banks, rising and falling by the millisecond in the unstable economy of the one-and-twenty. Legit citizens can access their funds through their ID cards or nice, traceable bank accounts that keep track of every cent as it moves from one person to another. Coded accounts and crows (escrows) let folks move cred without sustaining the irritation of legal identities.

A tiny trickle of money is *fold*, folding money, hardcopy cash, real bills. The firstworld governments keep trying to switch to a cashless society, and even the most tightly controlled ones find that they can't do it. Too many important people need money that can't be traced through the Net. No netrunner ever backtracked to its source a plastic sack stuffed with small bills.

In the firstworld, about 95% of the money supply is electronic cred. A well-behaved shaikujin can go his whole life long and never see a scrap of fold. That other 5% – trillions of ecus – flows through the gutters of the streets and in the quietest offices of the spacescrapers, oiling the secret machinery that makes society run.

In the lastworld, fold is much more common. Tchort, there are still places where the folks wouldn't know a credcard if you fed it to them! People can use cred in lastworld cities, even in some of the bigger towns. But out in the boonies, you use the local fold or start talking barter.

Valuta and Dengi

Valuta is hard money, either cred or fold. Currency backed by the strongest firstworld economies or the top korps is the best kind of valuta.

Everything else is dengi: soft currency, changing in value daily, usually for the worse. Some dengi isn't bad. You can get paid in it one week and still afford the rent the next. Most of it is trash cash; accept it at your own risk.

Ecus

Ecus, "Economic Community Units," are the hardest valuta there is. Whenever a figure in these rules is preceeded with a "$," it refers to the amount in ecus.

World economics (and the prices in this book) are based on an "ideal" ecu, with a baseline value pegged to international trade balances, gross national products, money supply and a thousand other variables.

There are real ecus – the international trading currency of the three firstworld trading communities. In the Americas, it's the *neodollar*. This is the main economic indicator in the Americas. Driven by the growing economic friction between the U.S. and the rest of the hemisphere, the Chilentinan peso shows signs of becoming the basis of a purely South American ecu. This would have a drastic effect on trade balances and international debt for both continents. The American

Payment Plans

A person's willingness to pay debts in valuta, and to accept dengi as partial payment to himself, can be a critical factor in negotiations about payment.

Most payment for criminal or hard-to-get goods or services is a mix of hard and soft currencies. Standard payments are divided into four equal blocks. One block will be in class-B valuta, two will be class-C dengi, and the fourth will be class-D dengi.

Each block can be negotiated once and once only. The appropriate skills are Merchant (for any situation) or Streetwise (for criminal goods or services). Fast-Talk *may* be suitable, if the deal has to go down in a hurry, and the player can convince the GM that he has a plausible line.

Roll a Quick Contest between buyer and seller (the person to be paid) for each block to be negotiated.

The seller can try to upgrade the flux class of a block, but this may reduce his effective skill for the Quick Contest.

Upgrading class-D to class-C . . . . -0
Upgrading class-D to class-B . . . . -2
Upgrading class-D to class-A . . . . -6
Upgrading class-C to class-B . . . . -0
Upgrading class-C to class-A . . . . -4
Upgrading class-B to class-A . . . . -2

The seller can also negotiate for a block in folding cash without any negative modifiers to his skill roll.

If the seller wins, he gets his way. If the buyer wins, he may either downgrade the block one flux class, or reduce its real value by 10%.

For example, Vin Slade needs to hire a netrunner. He offers $10,000 to Jumping Jack: $2,500 in class-B deutschmark, $5,000 in class-C U.S. dollars, and $2,500 in class-D Quebeçois francs. (Vin is the buyer; Jack is the seller.)

Jack tries to get Vin to improve the offer. They roll a Quick Contest over the deutschmark block. Jack is at -2 on his skill roll, since he is trying to get Vin to upgrade to eurotalers, a class-A currency. Vin wins and Jack is beaten down to taking $2,250 in marks.

Jack switches to an argument over the Quebeçois money. He wants to be paid in fold. Jack wins this Quick Contest.

Jack tries negotiating on the $5,000 in U.S currency, rolling once for the whole five grand, to upgrade it to Swedish krona, a class-B currency. Jack wins.

At this point, all four blocks have been negotiated. So the final deal is $2,500 in Quebeçois francs, paid in fold, the rest in electronic cred: $5,000 in krona, $2,250 in deutschmarks.

If this is too complicated for your tastes, a standard Merchant contest can be rolled. The winner gets to raise or lower the overall price by 10% or raise all the blocks one class: one class-A, two class-B, one class-C.

powers are very cautious about radically altering their financial structure, for fear of disturbing economic stability.

The United European ecu is the *eurotaler*. Pegged primarily to the German deutschmark, it is supported by the market values of the other strong European currencies. Nationalist movements in key countries defeated attempts by the early architects of European confederation to eliminate national currencies and replace them with a single currency. Some of the smaller countries have adopted the eurotaler as their only currency, but the major powers retain local money as well. Eurotalers are eagerly accepted everywhere in Europe, and it is the favored hard currency in northern Africa and the Middle East.

The hardest valuta in the world is the *rubyen,* the ecu supported by the joint economies of Russia and Japan. The economies of the CIS and large portions of the Pacific Rim are tied to the rubyen.

Ecus are nominally at par. That is, one ecu equals $1.00, whether it is a rubyen, a neodollar or a eurotaler. However, even ecus can vary from this ideal value.

Currency Tables

Flux classes and numbers are assigned using the following criteria.

A: Ecus. Strongest firstworld economies. Top 5 korp-marks.

B: Average firstworld economies. Next 5 korp-marks.

C: Weak firstworld economies. Strongest lastworld economies. Other major korp-marks.

D: Average lastworld economies. Minor K-marks.

E: Weak lastworld economies.

16: Very stable currency (dynamic economy, strong balance of trade).

14: Stable currency (growth economy, good balance of trade).

12: Unstable currency (stagnant economy, poor balance of trade).

10: Inflationary currency (economic downturn, recession).

8: Trash currency (depressed economy).

The Ecus

Currency	CF	Flux
Eurotaler ($)	1.0	14A
Neodollar ($)	1.0	12A
Rubyen ($)	1.0	16A

North American Currencies

Country	Currency	CF	Flux
Communaute d'Atlantique			
Quebeçois	Quebec francs	3.8	12C
Federated Provinces	Confed. dollars	1.8	14B
United Provinces	Confed. dollars	1.8	14B
Northwest Prot.	Confed dollars	1.8	14B
United States of America	dollars	1.2	16C

South and Central American Currencies

Country	Currency	CF	Flux
UCAS	unions	8.0	12D
Bolivia	boliviano	24.5	12D
Brazil	cruzado	820.0	14C
Chilentina	peso	40.0	12B
Colombia	peso	53.0	14C
Ecuador	sucre	30.1	12D
Guyana	guyan	2.5	10D
Paraguay	guarani	126.5	8E
Peru	inti	408.1	12E
Uruguay	peso	10.6	12E
Venezuela	bolivar	4.3	14D

Continued on next page . . .

Currency Fluctuation

The financial situation on the Edge is anything but steady. PCs should never be completely comfortable about the safety of their bankrolls. The key to playing games with the money supply is fluctuation between one currency (the one the person has) and another (the one he needs to get what he wants).

Unless characters try to make a killing by trading in currencies, this usually involves measuring the stability of money compared to the "ideal" ecu. Whenever an adventurer takes money in or pays it out, the GM can check to see if the state of the world's economy helps or hurts him.

The score that controls this is called *flux*.

Flux

Flux measures the degree by which a currency can vary from its face value. Valuta has a very low rate of flux; when it does fluctuate, it often increases in value. That's why it's valuta.

Dengi has a very high rate of flux, and it often decreases in value.

Flux is measured by two ratings: a *flux number* and a letter, the *flux class*. High flux numbers are considered good – that is, currencies with a high number are more stable. Flux classes are rated A through E. An "A" or "B" indicates very stable valuta. A "C," "D," or "E" indicates dengi. Class-E dengi is particularly unstable currency, subject to wild inflation – "trash dengi," in street jargon.

The flux number and flux class come into play whenever money changes hands. Any time an operator is involved in a significant financial transaction, the GM can require the player to make a *flux roll*.

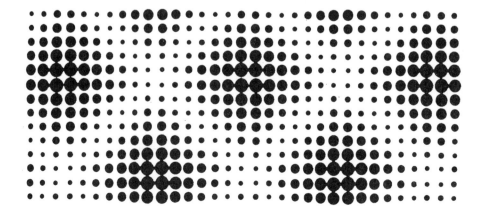

Flux Rolls

Whenever an individual is being paid, or when he buys something, the GM should roll 3d against the flux number for the currency he is using (see sidebars, p. 60-62). For example, if a character is paying in U.S. dollars, the roll is against 16, the flux number for that currency.

Treat the flux number like a skill for purposes of calculating critical successes or failures, as described on p. B86.

If the roll simply succeeds, then money changes hands at face value. Any other result changes the amount of money involved. The exact amount depends on the currency's flux class.

On a critical success, valuta is subject to *positive flux*. The player character gets a percentage of cash in his favor. If someone pays him, he gets more money than usual. If he spends money, then the price of whatever he buys is reduced. Dengi, with a flux class of C or worse, doesn't benefit from positive flux.

If the roll fails, that's *negative flux,* and the exchange rate gets worse for this transaction. The exact percentage depends on the number of points by which the roll failed. If the person is receiving money, the amount is reduced by the percentage. If he is paying someone else, his cost goes up by the same percentage.

On a critical failure, add 1d-1 to the margin of failure. That is, if a critical failure misses the flux number by 4, roll 1d-1 and add the result to 4 to measure the actual effect of the negative flux. For example, the player rolls an 18 against a currency with a flux value of 16C. This normally would reduce the money's value by 2+3% (see *Flux Class* chart below). But since 18 is a critical failure, he rolls 1d-1, adds the result to the 2 points by which the first roll missed, and adds *that* to 3%!

Effects Of Flux Classes

A: Positive flux: (2d-2)×5%. Negative flux: 1% per point by which the roll was missed.

B: Positive flux: (1d-1)×5%. Negative flux: 2% per point.

C: Positive flux: Has no effect. Negative flux: 3% per point.

D: Positive flux: Has no effect. Negative flux: 5% per point.

E: Positive flux: Has no effect. Negative flux: 7% per point.

In the sidebars (pp. 63-64) are two examples of how the GM can use flux during money exchanges in the campaign.

Walking Around the Block

So, a paryen is haggling over a deal and the flux roll comes up lousy. What can he do about it? After all, if the world monetary exchanges are as fickle as we've just described, he could maybe go out for a cup of kaff, come back in half an hour, and get a whole new deal, right?

Nice try, livewire.

There are two situations to consider here. In the first, and simplest, case, the operator has *already* agreed to the deal. Backing out is, at the least, going to give him a street rep as a weasel (either temporarily or as an out-and-out Reputation disadvantage). If he pulls it on the wrong people, he may just get killed. If he has agreed to take payment in Turkish liras, he can't change his mind when the lira takes a nosedive, and demand East African kenyattas instead. In general, this happens when the person is getting paid. The flux rolls are made when his employer pays him, whether it is a regular salary from the Jobs Table, or a one-time transaction after some irregular piece of skullduggery for a korp's "Competitive Research" office. Of course, once he's paid, he's free to sit on the payment and wait for a better exchange rate to roll around, as long as he doesn't have any bills to pay or groceries to buy in the meantime.

United European Currencies

Country	Currency	CF	Flux
Albania	balki	1,200.0	10E
Andorra	Eurotaler	1.0	14A
Austria	schilling	16.2	14B
Baltic League	balt	1.8	16C
Belgium	franc	37.2	14C
Bohemia	koruna	9.4	12D
Bosnia	balki	1,200.0	10E
British Union	pound	4.8	14C
Bulgaria	lev	88.0	14D
Croatia	balki	1,200.0	10E
Cyprus	pound	0.4	14D
Denmark	krone	7.2	14B
Eire	pound	1.7	12D
Finland	markka	4.3	14C
France	franc	5.5	16C
Germany	deutschmark	1.5	14A
Greece	drachma	56.2	10D
Hungary	forint	27.4	16C
Iberian Federation	peseta	90.9	14C
Iceland	krona	6.6	14C
Italy	lira	1,142.0	10C
Liechtenstein	eurotaler	1.0	14A
Luxembourg	eurotaler	1.0	14A
Macedonia	drachme	890.0	10E
Malta	eurotaler	1.0	14A
Monaco	eurotaler	1.0	14A
Netherlands	guilder	2.6	12B
Norway	krone	5.6	14B
Poland	zloty	32.0	16C
Romania	lei	14.9	14D
Serbia	balki	1,200.0	10E
Slovakia	eurotaler	1.0	14A
Slovenia	balki	1,200.0	10E
Sweden	krona	4.9	12B
Switzerland	franc	2.1	14A
Turkey	lira	97.1	12C

Commonwealth of Independent States

Armenia, Azerbaijan, Byelorussia, Georgia, Latvia, Moldavia, Russia, Ukraine:

Country	Currency	CF	Flux
CIS	CIS ruble	0.85	16B

Central Asian Federation

Kazakhstan, Kyrgyzstan, Tajikistan, Turkmenistan, Uzbekistan:

Country	Currency	CF	Flux
CAF	CAF altine	3.2	12B

Middle Eastern Currencies

Country	Currency	CF	Flux
Arab Union	riyal	42.2	12B
Iran	rial	120.0	12C
Israel	shekel	9.3	14B
Kurdistan	dirham	125.0	12D
Kuwait	dinar	250.0	12B
Yemen	dinar	420.0	10D

Continued on next page . . .

Currency Tables (Continued)

Asian Currencies

Country	Currency	CF	Flux
Afghanistan	afghani	600.0	8E
Australia (Tasmania)	Australian dollar	1.4	10D
Bangladesh	taka	16.9	10E
Bhutan	ngultrum	22.8	10D
Brunei	dollar	12.1	14C
Cambodia	riel	2,120.0	10E
China	yuan	1.8	16B
India	rupee	8.3	14D
Indonesia	rupiah	628.0	12D
Japan	yen	105.2	14A
Korea	won	670.0	12B
Laos	kip	840.0	14C
Malaysia	ringgit	2.34	14B
Mongolia	tugrik	12.5	12D
Myanmar	kyat	7.0	14D
Nepal	rupee	12.0	12D
New Zealand	dollar	1.6	12C
Pakistan	rupee	9.9	14D
Philippines	peso	7.8	12B
Singapore	dollar	2.2	10A
Sri Lanka	rupee	17.9	14C
Taiwan	dollar	36.5	16C
Thailand	baht	21.0	14C
Tibet	rupi	56.4	12D
Vietnam	dong	300.0	12B

African Currencies

Country	Currency	CF	Flux
Algeria	dinar	4.2	12C
Angola	kwanza	22.7	10D
Botswana	pula	238.0	10C
Bulawayo	tchaka	430.0	8D
Cape Republic	rand	1.9	10C
Chad	ngarta	27.2	12C
East African Confederation	kenyatta	7.7	12C
Egypt	pound	68.4	12B
Eritrea	gonds	735.0	10D
Ethiopia	birr	1,200.0	8E
Ghana	cedi	2.8	12E
Greater Guinea	guinea	18.1	14C
Joint Republic of Nigeria and Cameroon	naira	.53	12C
Libya	dinar	1.0	10D
Madagascar	frank	965	12CB
Morocco	dirham	4.7	10C
Mozambique	metical	200.0	10D
Namibia	mandela	142.0	12D
Natal	shilling	0.82	10C
Seychelles	rupee	3.2	16C
Somalia	shilling	77.3	12D
Sudan	pound	43.5	10E
Transvaal	rand	1.2	12C
Tunisia	dinar	434.0	12E
Union of Zaire	zaire	3.1	10C
West African Union	franc africaine	248.0	14C
Zambia	kwacha	0.83	12D

When the citizen is paying someone else for goods or services and finds himself on the short end of bad flux, he has more options. He can "walk around the block," that is, hold off closing the deal, waiting for a more favorable exchange rate. The length of time he'll have to wait before making a new roll depends on the flux class of the currency he's dealing in.

A – 24 hours.
B – 2 days.
C – 4 days.
D – 1 week.
E – 2 weeks.

Some purchases are time-sensitive. If you are buying bullets in the middle of a firefight, that's certainly a seller's market. Pay the man, for heaven's sake!

If the deal involved any fancy searching to find a buyer or seller – for example, if a netrunner is negotiating to buy black-market high tech to upgrade his cyberdeck – then walking around the block means that the source of the merchandise will dispose of it elsewhere. The buyer will have to locate a new source of the material.

A person can also play musical money, offering a different currency to avoid a loss due to negative flux.

For example, Heavy Ajax is paying off two breetvas for a bit of professional violence earlier in the week. The price agreed on was $1,000, in any reasonably hard currency (flux class A or B). Ajax taps into a crow that carries its balance in Israeli shekels, which have a flux of 14B. The dice roll is 17, which is a critical failure. Ajax is loath to fork over extra valuta to these wired-up street ops, so he dips into his slush fund, a packet of rubyen stashed in a Petrograd variable fund. Rubyen are rated 16A, top-of-the-line valuta. This time, Ajax rolls a 12, and forks over 1,000 rubyen. This may be ill-advised, of course. Rubyen are as hard as currency gets, whereas shekels are less stable; but cash flow is cash flow.

A prudent adventurer on the Edge will maintain his funds in several accounts, spread over a sampling of several dependable currencies.

The Kurse

Kurse (pronounced "koor-suh"), in Russian, German and a couple of other languages, means "currency exchange rate." In street lingo, it's pronounced the same as "curse." If a GM wants to keep players anxious about their savings, this is a sadistically useful tool.

The GM can make a flux roll for any currencies he wants at the beginning of a playing session. Any flux results are in force for the rest of the session.

To be really nasty, he can carry flux over from one adventure to the next. Say he rolls against U.S. dollars one evening, and the dollar plunges 3%. Next week, he rolls and gets negative flux on the dollar again, dropping it another 6%. The dollar is now down 9%!

When carrying over negative flux this way, a positive flux roll restores the currency to its face value. That is, it cancels all the negative flux.

And to top it off, players can still roll for flux on individual transactions as well, using the kurse as the basic rate. Say the dollar is down 9%. If a player gets another 3% of negative flux on a transaction, he is down 12% for that sale.

Another nasty thing to do with the kurse is devaluing currency. Normally, adventurers don't actually suffer reductions in their total savings when hit with negative flux. It only applies to the amount of money they gain or lose on a given transaction. Even when carrying around negative flux, it doesn't affect their bank balance, just the purchasing power of their money. Not so with devaluation!

On a kurse roll of 18, the GM can decide to devalue the currency, using any negative flux. Team members then have to reduce their holdings in that currency by the amount of negative flux. They can't hold on to the money and wait for times to get better.

Devaluing a currency cancels out any negative flux that has built up against it.

For example, at the beginning of a session, the GM rolls for the kurse on U.S. dollars. Previous kurse rolls have already put 6% negative flux against the dollar. He rolls an 18, and knocks the poor, abused greenback down by an additional 14%, for a total of 20%. He also announces that ProGov is adjusting the free-floating value of the dollar. Everybody loses 20% of his holdings in U.S. currency. If a citizen had $10,000 in dollars in the bank, his account is reduced to $8,000.

Cred in the Net

Cred can be stored in the Net in several different forms. Each has advantages and disadvantages.

Personal Accounts

Legitimate citizens – folks with established identities and credcards or citcards to prove who they are – use personal, or bank, accounts. The money in a personal account belongs to you, and only you can authorize a withdrawal, using proper ID to verify that the order is legal. If you lose your ID, it can't be used to loot your bank account unless the thief has the necessary resources to overcome the safety checks that verify identity (see p. 36).

If your money is stolen from a personal account in spite of these checks, and you can prove that it was stolen, the bank has to refund the loss, under the law in every technologically-developed country on Earth.

So what's so bad about personal accounts? Well, if you don't have a legal identity, you can't use one. Those with the Zeroed advantage (p. C21) can't have a personal account unless they tie it to a Temporary Identity. And any funds allocated to a Temporary Identity are confiscated when the fake ID is discovered (see p. C20).

Tax records are automatically registered when money is deposited to a personal account. In many cases, taxes are automatically deducted from deposits when the income is subject to tax: payment from employment, investment income, payment for freelance work, royalties, etc.

Any transaction paid with cred from a personal account can be traced back to that account, and so to the identity of the account's owner. A Trace program (see p. C92) can do this. Keep in mind that programs like this are illegal for private individuals, not for banks (and the korps that own them) or government agencies.

Blind Acounts

Blind accounts are not registered to a given individual, but are the equivalent of the numbered accounts offered by the Swiss for centuries. Anyone with the proper code can access the account.

Separate codes are used for deposits and withdrawals. One can safely give deposit codes to other people, to make payments directly into the account. Withdrawal codes are kept very secret.

Blind accounts are available in any country with a Control Rating of 3 or less (although the Swiss are still at the top). If a Trace program is fed the deposit code for a blind account, it can trace all monies paid into it back to their source. A Trace program that is given the withdrawal code can trace all withdrawals to their recipients. Remember, though, that banks do not want their transactions traced, and their systems will be loaded with nasty defensive software. And if the software isn't enough, they can always send a zeroman out to find the hacker.

Blind accounts charge a 1% service fee on all deposits.

Using Flux in a Game

Example #1:

Very simple. Greg Ho is in Shanghai to get himself a SOTA Interface Jack at a whisper clinic. Greg scored big on an embezzling scam last month and has a bundle of U.S. dollars credited to an account in Macao.

The jack and installation cost $50,000. Greg is paying in dollars, which have a flux of 16C. The player rolls 3d. If he scores a 16 or less, Greg simply pays the equivalent of $50,000 in dollars. A critical success wouldn't improve this, since the dollar is too soft to benefit from positive flux. *Sic transit et cetera*, paryeni.

If the GM is using Conversion Factors (see p. 55), U.S. dollars have a CF of 1.2; so Greg would need to cough up $60,000 U.S. to cover a cost of $50,000.

But the die roll comes up 17. That misses by 1 point and means negative flux is messing up Greg's deal. At flux class C, that translates to a 3% surcharge, 3% for every point over the flux number. Greg's cyber will cost $51,500 ($61,800 U.S.).

If the roll were 18, not only would Greg have to cover the normal percentage for a 2-point miss with C-class currency, which would be 6%, he would be hit with up to 5% (1d-1) in additional penalties as world markets sneer at some failure of the U.S. economy. If, for instance, his penalty is a 4, he would add that to the original negative modifier and the amount he originally missed by, for a total of 9%. Greg would have to spend $54,500 ($65,400 U.S.) to cover his bills.

Continued on next page . . .

Using Flux in a Game
(Continued)

Example #2:

Jonny Sleazer gets a call from a fixer he knows. Someone wants an indiscreet document lifted from a database. Jonny sizes up the system and sets his price: $20,000, in ecus. The fixer screams that his pacemaker is overloading. After some haggling, they settle on $5,000 in neodollars, $10,000 in CIS rubles, and $5,000 in Swiss francs, cred on deposit to a series of crows scattered between Zurich, Grand Cayman and Ten-Tan.

So Jonny punches his usual hot deck, snags the file and wipes it out of the database, all according to the contract. It's payday.

Neodollars have a flux of 12A. The player rolls 3d, scores a 12. Nothing special is happening on the neodollar market, so he gets $5,000 paid into a crow in Zurich.

The flux for CIS rubles is 16B. The player rolls a critical success! The money markets have given Jonny some positive flux. Rolling 1d-1, the player scores a 4. That's 4×5% = 20% in Jonny's favor. He gets the equivalent of $10,000 + 20%, or $12,000, paid into his Ten-Tan account. Since rubles have a CF of .85, that's 10,200 rubles.

Swiss francs have a flux of 14A. Safe-looking, but the player rolls an 18! Must be a slow day for chocolate or something. That misses by 4, which would normally only be 4% off Jonny's payment, but this is a critical failure. So the GM rolls (1d-1) and gets 4, for a total loss of 8%. The $5,000 is reduced to $4,600. At the CF for the franc, that's 9,660 Swiss francs into the account of "Mr. Smith" at the Twenty-Seventh National Bank of Grand Cayman.

Crows

A crow, short for "escrow," is similar to a blind account. However, a crow is established with a one-time deposit. It cannot be added to. All records indicating the source of these funds are erased from the Net. The bank that maintains the crow backs it with its own funds.

A crow only has a withdrawal code. It is possible to trace withdrawals from it, but not the original deposit.

Locked crows are even more secure, in one sense, though vulnerable in another. A locked crow is keyed to one, and only one, highly complex passcode algorithm that is stored in a special credcard, a "crowcard." The crowcard is a dedicated microcomputer running a unique Complexity 2 identity-control program. The withdrawal code is programmed into a resin-sealed, destruct-coded chip onboard the credcard. The card's ID program corresponds to a chip-based program installed in the bank's computer.

The recognition of withdrawal orders is handled by these chips working in tandem through the Net. This redundant, hardware-based security makes it virtually impossible to fake the withdrawal code for a locked crow. You *must* have the card to get the money.

Locked crows are like fold in this regard. If you lose the crowcard, or it's destroyed, that's it. You lose the money. If someone steals it, he owns the money.

A Trace program can only trace withdrawals from a locked crow if it has access to the crowcard that controls it, so that it can identify itself to the bank's computer properly.

There is a service fee of 5% of the amount deposited when a crow is created. In addition, the crowcard costs $200.

For an extra $2,000, a crowcard can be keyed to an individual's thumbprint. This makes the money effectively robber-proof, but also makes it nontransferable, except through withdrawal.

CRIME AND PUNISHMENT

5

Like everything else on the Edge, crime is a mix of old and new. Vices that date back a few millennia are for sale right next to high-tech sins that are on the cutting edge of the one-and-twenty. Things considered innocent fun in one country can land you in the body banks if done just across the border.

In linking the major criminal organizations of the one-and-twenty to certain specific ethnic groups, it is not the intention of *GURPS Cyberworld* to perpetuate racial stereotypes. Italians, Japanese or South Americans are no more likely than any other race to produce criminals; it just happens that, due to historical and cultural factors, they produce more *organized* criminals than most other ethnic groups.

When members of a culture were transplanted, by immigration or expansion, their criminals followed them. In the early 20th century, U.S. immigrant communities, among them the Irish, European Jews and Italians, were often barred from legitimate enterprises by the resident society. Criminals flourished in this milieu, giving rise to the major racketeers of the Prohibition era: Dan O'Banion, Dutch Schultz, Bugsy Siegel, Capone, Marranzano and the rest. As subsequent generations of immigrants became assimilated, some of the criminal subcultures withered away, while others survived, functioning outside of both the culture that gave them birth and the mainstream society. As these factions gained wealth and influence, they became entrenched, existing without any connection to their original culture.

This process continues into the one-and-twenty. Similarly, Triad, Yakuza and *narcotraficante* influences become part of the criminal structure of society, both in the U.S. and elsewhere.

There are crimes and there are *crimes*. In a typical *Cyberpunk* campaign, most of the PCs are criminals. They might be Robin Hood or Al Capone. Some crimes violate the rules of a given government. Some crimes offend against basic humanity. One does not necessarily imply the other.

This chapter discusses professional crime – crime as a business. Like legitimate business, crimes and criminals may be divided into several classes. Organized international criminal syndicates, the keiretsu of the underworld, are at the top of the heap in terms of money and power. Like the korps, these big fish are intolerant of competition, and there is a large gap between them and the next lower rung on the criminal ladder. This niche is occupied by local mobs, well-organized, powerful in their locale, but without the national and international reach of the big syndicates. Under these are the local gangs: street gangs, petty crooks and other neighborhood enterprises. And at the bottom of the criminal social ladder stands the individual crook with no gang connections.

This is not a rigid hierarchy. Small local gangs can, and do, stand up to the local mob, and sometimes they even win (i.e., survive). An individual criminal may have an international reputation as a specialist, and be valued above rubies by those who need his services.

Organized Crime

Society in the late 20th century waged an escalating war against organized crime. Despite some early victories, it looks like society lost. In the shattered social matrix of the world on the Edge, the outlaws have some major advantages over the honest suits.

Most criminals use violence casually, easily. They meet any resistance with force, and many will kill at the slightest provocation. An individual without some form of protection has little chance of surviving a syndicate's displeasure.

Syndicates have significant money and resources. The biggest can deploy resources on a par with the korps. This does not mean that the syndicates are as wealthy, overall, as the korps . . . but in terms of the money and personnel the

mobs can devote to violent conflict, they have the edge. It is their stock in trade, whereas a korp has overhead.

Criminals, who freely cross the lines between classes, have become increasingly important to those on both sides as the alienation among rich and poor, technical and unskilled, government and governed, has increased. The powerful need jobs done that their status does not permit them to do themselves. The powerless turn to the criminal for services that are otherwise unobtainable, often for services that were once the right of every citizen.

The Mafia

The Mafia in the U.S. has flourished under the often brutal "law 'n' order" regime of the Provisional Government, just as it did earlier under Prohibition. When luxuries, not to mention many necessities, are either strictly rationed or flat-out illegal, then criminal markets will provide what legitimate sources cannot. For a hefty price, of course.

ProGov often co-opted criminals in its fight for control of the nation. Local gangs were engaged as shock troops, often led by cadres of NERCC enforcers. The Mafia played an even more vital role. Since the mobs controlled resources in transportation, communications and distribution, and were quite willing to destroy them if they could not profit from them, attempts to seize these facilities by force proved disastrous. The Mafiosi also had a powerful network of legitimate financial interests, as well as extensive political connections at its disposal. In many cities, they were natural allies of the ProGov administrators.

In return for access to mob-controlled facilities, the local nerks and other officials turned a blind eye as the Mafia imposed an iron-fisted system of control on most of the local black markets and the gangs that ran them.

Under the Permanent Emergency, the Mafia takes care of business without undue government heat and even with tacit government support in some areas. The most notable example is the Sin Cities (see p. 83). The Mafia has also adopted some parts of the culture of the keiretsu, the multinational korps; the curious entity known as "MafInc" is the result.

Familia, Ltd.

MafInc exists on two levels. On the one hand we find the traditional set of semi-autonomous crime "Families," each headed by a "Don," with loose, national control vested in the *Commissione,* a council of the most powerful Family leaders. On the other, we find Familia, Ltd.

In 2013, Don Merle Alexander (see sidebar), of the Alessandro Family in Boston, proposed to the Commissione that the jumble of legitimate business interests operated by individual Families was wasteful, causing gangs to compete with each other when they could more profitably cooperate. While cooperation among Families never seemed to work very well in criminal activities, the business model encourages centralized management practices. Alexander proposed making the legitimate, money-laundering operations more efficient, as well as improving the "insulation" between the legit businesses and the criminal rackets that financed them.

Many of the most powerful Dons and consiglieri were university graduates, often from the nation's top business and law schools. To them, Alexander's proposal was self-evidently correct. Accordingly, in 2019 the Mafia created Familia, Ltd., a massive holding company that controls all the mob's legitimate business holdings through a tortuous system of interlocking directorates. "Mafia, Inc." in all but name.

Boss of All Bosses

Don Merle Alexander's combination of ruthlessness and acumen led to his recognition as *capo di tutti capi*, the nominal head of the Commissione. He ruled MafInc in name, and often in fact, from 2021 to 2037.

Alexander enforced an ironclad rule that Familia operations and Mafia rackets be kept strictly separate. Since he ruthlessly exterminated several Mafiosi who violated this rule early on, including the ambitious young Don of Atlanta, James "Silk" Silkwood, compliance was complete.

Alexander's reign ended in 2037 at an executive conference with Familia's Pacific managers – in Sydney, Australia. His death in the Australian Plague triggered a vicious power struggle that still influences both sides of MafInc today. His strict division between the criminal and business interests of the mob was an early casualty of the struggle.

However, most Familia managers, unaware of their korp's connection to the Mafia, tend to hire freelance muscle (like the player characters) when they need something done outside the law.

Crime and Punishment

Rough at the Top

Merle Alexander was a member of the board of directors of Familia, Ltd., and the CEO, Charles Hornung, was his puppet. Since Alexander's death there has been no direct MafInc presence on the board. Though not himself a Mafioso, Hornung is connected to the Mafia and takes his orders from the Commissione. However, with the infighting at the top of the MafInc hierarchy, Hornung has been left pretty much to his own devices. The question, of course, is whether Hornung will try to attenuate the mob's control of Familia permanently, or will go back to being a highly trained seal if and when they work out the succession.

If the GM wants to run a unified version of MafInc, he can simply decide that Hornung is too afraid of retaliation to get any smart ideas of his own. He will be a loyal steward of MafInc's interests and will automatically hand over control of the korp and its resources to the next *capo di tutti capi.*

However, in a campaign where Hornung pursues his own designs, perhaps to pry Familia loose from its secret owners and take control himself, life gets much more interesting. Hornung cannot stage a stockholders' revolt, after all; the major stockholders are Mafiosi, and if he tips them off, he is a dead man. Blowing the whistle to the authorities is out, too, since that would almost certainly destroy Familia, Ltd.

If CEO Hornung is out to take over Familia, Ltd., he will have to do it by playing off the mobsters against each other. And by running lots of covert operations to acquire Familia stock, or even to sabotage some Familia operations: excellent employment opportunities for a bunch of deniable (and expendable) operatives.

Familia Control

The Mafia directly controls 82% of Familia voting stock. Each of the dozen Families with a seat on the Commissione (see sidebar, p. 72) holds between 3% and 5% of the stock. The remainder is divided up among the remaining Families, and even the smallest has at least a fraction of a percent of the available stock. Under Don Merle, the Commissione exercised proxies over a controlling majority of this stock. Since his death, faction fights among the Families have disrupted this monolithic control.

Familia management is an interesting patchwork of fact and fantasy. Nine out of ten of the line managers are absolutely legit – or at least as legitimate as any korp manager on the Edge ever is. The remainder are either low-profile mob members or mob-connected. This 10% element of Familia management, spread through the korp and its subsidiaries at all levels, are the Cosa Nostra's eyes and ears in the company. They ensure that Familia operations support, or at least don't hurt, MafInc's criminal pursuits. All Familia managers who are aware of the relationship between the korp and the mob are equipped with an Omerta chip (see sidebar, p. 70), and given profound psychoconditioning against revealing their knowledge.

When the Commissione suspects that these safeguards are insufficient, a visit from a hit man ensures that Familia-connected managers keep silent. Permanently.

Mafia Structure

Individual mobs, or "Families," are based in specific urban centers, often competing for the same niches in the underworld. In some null zones the local Family, or its front group, is the neofeudal ruler.

The Commissione suggests, mediates and, in extreme cases, intervenes forcefully in coordinating the activities of the local Families. The Commissione also controls mob activity on the incredibly rich turf of the Sin Cities: Las Vegas, Atlantic City, Miami and Acapulco. No single Family controls any of the Sin Cities. ProGov considers them neofeudal enclaves and tacitly gives MafInc's front groups free rein in controlling them.

Families

The original Mafia, as it evolved in 18th-century Sicily, combined aspects of a secret society with those of an extended clan and a criminal gang. Members underwent an initiation ceremony, and there was a distinct gap between members and those who carried out jobs for the Mafiosi without yet being "made men." This structure continues in modern Mafia mobs.

At the head of a Family stands a *Don. A consigliere* acts as chief advisor to the Don and is the principle "fixer" in most matters concerning the mob. In addition, a Don has a number of *caporegimes,* or capos, who handle the day-to-day details of Family business. Each capo is in charge of a part of the area controlled by the Family, and has a number of *soldati,* soldiers, under his command.

The Family is bound together by mutual obligations, in an almost feudal pattern, and by the concept of *omerta,* the code of secrecy. Under omerta, a Mafioso never admits to being a member of the Mafia, and never, ever, implicates other Mafiosi if he is apprehended for a crime. It is because of omerta that the Mafiosi themselves rarely use the term "Mafia." They speak of "La Familia," "The Honorable Society" and of course, "La Cosa Nostra" ("This thing of ours"). Omerta demands that the Mafioso *never* admit to an outsider that the Mafia exists.

Over the years, the Family by name became a family in reality. Mafiosi tend to marry into Mafia families. This clannish, violent, inbred structure survived the explosion of organized crime in the U.S. during Prohibition. In the 1970s and 1980s, it survived the influx of competing gangs fuelled by the incredible profits of the drug trade. It survived the Grand Slam, the Patterson government and the Permanent Emergency.

MafInc Names

The first- and second-generation folkways of the original Dons, the "men of great respect," have been brought up to date to match the acculturated, usually highly educated veneers of their great-great-grandchildren.

Many of the most infamous names in the history of organized crime are still associated with the Families they founded: Capone, Genovese and others. This is a "status symbol" in MafInc. Half a dozen of the old, established Families retain the name of the founding Don, from the early 20th century.

During a crackdown on Mafia operations in the early 2000s, a number of younger Mafiosi changed their family names to WASP equivalents. Alessandro became Alexander, Gambino became Childe, Veronese became Vernon, etc. Old-line Mafiosi denigrated this as a lack of respect. But as they died out, often in prison, the later generation came into power in the mob and their innovation became standard. Outwardly, many families which numbered Dons, consiglieri, and caporegimes among their members made token gestures toward cultural assimilation, while secretly they simply entrenched themselves more deeply into the criminal subculture of their ancestors.

Secrecy and MafInc

MafInc keeps its connection to Familia, Ltd., secret, and Familia is equally paranoid about the multiple tentacles it has sticking into the corporate world. There's no neon sign saying, "Familia, Ltd. – Shaking You Down Since The 18th Century" on the corporate HQ. Maybe top government and corporate officials, leaders of the other major crime cartels and similarly well-placed types might know about the Cosa Nostra's korp structure, but outsiders should *not!*

This is always a problem in writing game material. In giving the GM information about what's going on, we also give it to any players reading the book.

It's recommended that the GM not use the name Familia, Ltd., but come up with his own name – something with no cute puns on "Family," "Cosa Nostra," etc., in it. Just a large, very tough U.S. korp, no different from any of the others.

People who find out about the korp's connection with MafInc possess *very* dangerous knowledge. As far as the world is concerned, if a MafInc connection to a given company is uncovered, only that company was involved. The existence of a massive mob presence in the corporate world is not considered possible. And the GM should feel free to involve protagonists in situations where the Mafia is involved in a company that does not belong to Familia, just to keep them guessing.

For example, many of the korps that supply the Open Cities, where MafInc presence is a given, are simply vendors, not fronts for the mobs they do business with. They will almost certainly have mob connections, and may even use MafInc resources in labor management, assassinations and other illicit activities. But they will not be part of the Familia complex. Strictly business, gospodin.

Crime and Punishment

The Omerta Implant

Traditionally, when a new member is "made" – formally initiated into the Cosa Nostra – he undergoes a brief ritual, swearing loyalty to his new Family, and to *omerta*, the code of silence. MafInc has added a modern twist to tradition. Most soldiers are fitted with an "Omerta" implant.

The Omerta implant combines:

• a *psych implant* (p. C38) that grants a +2 to IQ for purposes of resisting Interrogation skill. It also induces Fanatic loyalty to the Mafia when dealing with non-Mafiosi. Defeating the implant requires very subtle interrogation (one hour per "question," instead of five minutes), or else countermeasures such as medication, psychological trickery, etc. Torture just embeds the Fanatic resistance more deeply and adds nothing to the interrogator's skill.

• a *cortex bomb* or similar device that can be triggered by a coded broadcast from the syndicate. It doesn't have to be a big, splashy bomb. A chip that discharges a nice, tidy electrical jolt to the higher cerebral centers (instant lobotomy) will do the trick just as well. On the other hand, particularly in the lower echelons, having a squealer's head explode over half the tables at the Bistro during the dessert course can make for a useful object lesson.

The implant is permanently inserted in the new soldier's skull. Removing it requires careful surgery. MafInc scientists are reputed to be working on a second-generation implant that will induce selective amnesia, or at least kill the wearer, if he betrays the mob, either voluntarily or under duress.

Top-ranked Mafiosi usually have their implants removed. Those who are born to high position in a Family are rarely, if ever, fitted with the implants.

In the mid-21st century, upper-bracket Mafiosi often out-WASP the WASPs. There is something of a caste system involved. The higher up the scale a Family member is, the more likely he is to eschew any vestige of Sicilian cultural heritage, at least in public. Soldiers, however, are expected to caricature the "Old Country" mannerisms of earlier generations of wise guys, as a badge by which the straights and streeties can recognize them and give them the fear and respect they deserve.

MafInc Membership

When some up-and-coming hood was rewarded with full membership in the old Mafia, there was an initiation that elevated him to the status of a "made man." The price of admission usually involved killing somebody on the orders of the local caporegime. Once the prospective Mafioso had "made his bones," there was a brief ritual, the taking of some blood with a dagger to impress upon the new soldier that he was expected to live by the knife and gun, and if need be, die by them for La Cosa Nostra.

Today, the initiation still spills blood, but it is the blood of coldly efficient cybertech. New wise guys are given a thorough genetic workup. If they betray MafInc, the mob has their DNA "fingerprint." A new face won't hide them. Most new members are also given an Omerta implant (see sidebar).

A Mafioso is used in any way that his Don deems fit. Tough guys, often cybernetically enhanced, are used to keep order in the streets, where the mob still makes much of its wealth. Competition, whether from members of competing syndicates or local gangs hungry for a slice of the profits, is fierce, and the soldati need the firepower and modifications to stand up to the nastier products of the Triad whisper clinics or the more demented masterpieces of the back-street body shops.

Those with skills in the office or the lab may be employed in criminal or legitimate enterprises. Familia, Ltd. can always use a made man with a clean record and a Ph.D.

Mafiosi with legitimate jobs collect their normal salaries on the Job Table (see p. 23). They get a +2 on the skill roll for their income, since they are getting a little something extra from their Family. Mafiosi working the criminal side of things use the "MafInc soldier" jobs on the table.

'Traffs

'Traff is short for *narcotraficantes*, or "drug merchants." They are the heirs of the Central and South American drug cartels of the late 20th century.

Wealthy almost beyond comprehension, the 'traffs have diversified. Their original fortune was based on one or more of the traditional drugs or their derivatives: opium, marijuana and cocaine.

The Mexican 'traffs were absorbed or driven out of business by MafInc when they extended their operations in Mexico after the annexation. The Sinaloa Drug Wars of 2019, between MafInc and the 'traffs of the Sierra del Madre, were as bloody as any border clashes between lastworld countries.

'Traffs virtually *are* the government in certain regions of South America. Mexican 'traff money helped finance the rebels of the southern Mexican states. The most overt 'traff presence in the political arena at present is Bolivia, of course, where cartel money backs the PWT rebels against the U.S.-backed military government in La Paz. There are also rumors that vengeful 'traffs are helping to bankroll the Echeveristas in Cuba.

'Traff-financed terrorists have become an increasingly dangerous element on the international scene. Officials who impede the flow of 'traff drugs into their countries are in danger of assassination or kidnapping.

The Major Cartels

In the 1970s, gangs of South American drug dealers began forming cooperative associations, generally called cartels. The cartels quickly either absorbed or froze out unaffiliated gangs. There are three major cartels in operation in 2043. About three dozen other syndicates exist in the Western Hemisphere that can properly be called 'traffs, along with scores of local gangs involved in the drug trade.

Unlike the Mafia, Triads, or Yakuza, the 'traffs have no particular internal culture, no traditions. The head of a cartel may be a self-made man whose parents were dirt-poor peasants, or the scion of one of South America's oldest families.

The major 'traffs control production, transport and distribution of their products. Thus, a big cartel like the Chavez or Mordella will grow the plants from which their drugs are made, or pay farmers on their home turf for harvests of drug crops. They then refine the plants into base (coca paste, morphine base, etc.) or finished forms (cocaine, heroin, Sin, Slammer, etc.), smuggle them into the firstworld markets and sell them to local criminal operations. 'Traffs are not, as a rule, interested in street sales, preferring to act as producers and wholesalers.

Triads

The Triads, sometimes called tongs, are descended from the secret Chinese societies founded to oppose the Manchu dynasty in the 17th century. Legend traces their origins even farther back, to the Red Eyebrows Society, which was instrumental in overthrowing the usurper Wang Mang and establishing the Eastern Han dynasty in 25 A.D. Legend further notes that the Red Eyebrows, outliving their patriotic origins, became a feared band of outlaws. The more things change, the more they stay the same.

The Triads on the Edge operate all over the world, but their principal theater of operation is Southeast Asia, and their unofficial capital is Singapore.

When Chinese laborers migrated to Western countries, the Triads went with them. Chinese communities were often ghettos, isolated from the surrounding culture. "Chinatown" is not just a picturesque term for someplace where tourists

The Families

This is not an exhaustive list of the Maf-Inc Families in ProGov's America. By Department of Enforcement estimates, there are some 200 Mafia gangs operating in the U.S. The Families listed here are the major ones. The Dons of Families marked with an asterisk (*) hold a seat on the Commissione.

The smaller Families, usually with a semi-feudal connection to one of these bigger mobs, operate all over North America.

Remember that individual members of these families will often have anglicized versions of the family name (see p. 69).

Atlanta, GA: Gianneti.
Boston Metroplex: Alessandro*, Angiulo, Buccola.
Buffalo, NY: Magaddino.*
Chicago Urban Complex: Capone, Giancana.*
Dallas-Fort Worth, TX: Caracci.
Denver, CO: Veronese.
Detroit, MI: Zerilli.*
Greater Los Angeles, CA: Bompensiero*, Merlino.
Greater New York Metroplex: Bonanno*, Colombo*, Gambino*, Genovese*, Lucchese.*
Juneau, AL: Clemenza.
Kansas City, MO: Lazia.
Mexico City, MEX: Fratangeli.
New Orleans, LA: Marcello.*
Philadelphia Metroplex: Brunelli.
San Francisco Urban Constellation: Lanza.*
Seattle, WA: DeStefano.
Tampa, FL: Trafficante.
Washington, D.C.: Corsoni.*

Crime and Punishment

The Commissione

The *Commissione*, or "Commission," is not, as is sometimes supposed, an actual governing body. Local Families jealously guard their autonomy from Commissione control, and have done so ever since New York's "Five Families" formed the Commissione in 1931. A council of equals, the Commissione is a forum where the Families enlist mutual aid, attempt to resolve disputes and decide how the Cosa Nostra will face new challenges and opportunities.

Often, though not always, one Don seated on the Commissione functions as "first among equals." By a combination of charisma, wisdom and ferocity, this individual is tacitly or openly recognized by his peers as *capo di tutti capi,* or "boss of all bosses."

During Merle Alexander's tenure as *capo di tutti capi* (see sidebar, p. 67), the Commissione's authority reached its highest point. Alexander's iron grip on Familia, Ltd.'s management structure gave him, and the Commissione, unprecedented leverage for keeping even the most independent Families under central control. Even the Capones, who maintained the traditional unpredictability, not to mention mad-dog savagery, of their founder, toed the Commissione's line.

In the six years since Alexander's death, no successor to his power and prestige among the Dons has emerged. Tensions on the Commissione, and among the smaller gangs, are high, with many Families engaged in increasingly bloody turf fights for control of both criminal and legitimate Mafia interests.

can get good Mu Shu pork. Prejudices on both sides confined early generations of Chinese immigrants to closed communities, where Chinese criminals preyed on Chinese inhabitants. Railroad workers in the U.S., sugar field hands in Hawaii and coolies on plantations all around the Pacific Rim gambled in Triad casinos, smoked Triad opium, paid Triad "squeeze."

As subsequent generations of Chinese-born citizens joined the mainstream of their societies, the Triads underwent the typical metamorphosis of outlaw subcultures. Like MafInc, they went modern.

Triad Organization

The majority of Triads include the word "society" somewhere in their names. Thus, it has become standard usage to refer to a Triad syndicate as a Society.

There is no central authority in the Triads, no equivalent of MafInc's Commissione. There are approximately a dozen societies powerful enough to dictate broad policy among the Triads, but this is not an "official" governing body, nor do the top societies always agree among themselves.

A society may have a few dozen members, or many thousand. It may concern itself with street crime, or with illegal commerce on an industrial scale.

Singapore's status as a center of cutting-edge cybertechnology has revitalized the old-line Triads there. Most of the whisper clinics in the back streets are under Triad control, or at least pay Triads for "protection."

The Triad Society

A Triad gang, or "society," is divided into ranks. At the top is the Shan Chu, or Lodgemaster. He is assisted by a Fu Shan Chu, or Deputy Lodgemaster, and is the absolute master of the society during his tenure. Below them come the Heung Chu, or Incense Master, in charge of initiating new members and promoting existing members, and the Sin Fung, or Guardian, responsible for the security of the society and for discipline among the members.

Originally, the executives of a society were elected by the membership. Nowadays, however, in most cases the Shan Chu takes office by virtue of being the strongest, or canniest, member of the gang. He holds the position for life, or until he retires, voluntarily or involuntarily, to make room for a younger Shan Chu. The lesser executive offices are either appointed by the Shan Chu or elected by the members of the society.

A society has only a single Lodgemaster. If there is a sub-branch of the society in another region, it is headed by a Chu Chi (Leader). Major sub-branches have their own Incense Master and Guardian. Lesser branches do not.

In every branch of a society there are lesser ranks. Each branch will have a Pak Tsz Sin, or Counselor. The Pak Tsz Sin acts as adviser to the Lodgemaster or Leader, in a role similar to a Mafia Family's *consigliere*. Like the Mafia officer, the Pak Tsz Sin also passes executive decisions on to the lesser members, and acts as a cutout. Illegal orders can be traced back to the Pak Tsz Sin, but not directly to the Shan Chu or Chu Chi. If a Pak Tsz Sin can be subverted, by the police or by a rival gang, the damage to the society is usually significant, and this office is reserved for the most trustworthy members.

Each branch has one or more Cho Hai, or Messenger, who acts as the intermediary between the Triad and the rest of the world. Modern Cho Hai are often attorneys.

The Hung Kwan, or Red Pole, is the equivalent of a caporegime in MafInc stricture. Originally, a Hung Kwan was chosen for his skill as a fighter, and led a group of up to 50 warriors in combat against rival gangs or other enemies. The modern Hung Kwan is a "department-head" rank in the Triad structure. He may be a cybermodified killer, a hot hacker, or a crooked business manager – whatever role best fits the needs of the society.

At the absolute bottom of the structure, the rank and file members are called Sze Kau.

Triads and Other Syndicates

Relations with the Russki-Yakuza, the other major criminal organization in Asia, alternate between bloody rivalry and uneasy truce, with occasional alliances of convenience. The Triads are major suppliers of opium and kappa-opium designer drugs, which often pits them against the 'traffs, especially on the West Coast of the U.S. and in the Netherlands, where much of the drug traffic to United Europe enters the continent.

Russki-Yakuza

The Japanese syndicates, the notorious Yakuza, have survived and prospered in the one-and-twenty. Like much else in Japanese culture, they have blended with the evolving Russo-Japanese culture in the CIS.

Russian gangsters under the Soviets were small potatoes – strong-arm mobs involved in black markets and shakedowns, under the thumb of local militsiya and the KGB. When the Soviet legal system largely collapsed in the early 1990s, Soviet criminals plunged into new areas, largely unimpeded by the weakened authorities of a society nearing total breakdown.

As Japanese interests and Japanese business people and technicians migrated to the CIS, the Yakuza followed them, as they have followed Japanese populations everywhere in the world. The Yak encountered the brawling, crude Russian gangs. Sometimes the contact was violent; in these cases the Yakuza usually delivered punishing defeats to the rather inept Russian gangsters. In most cases, however, the Yakuza adopted the same principles as the keiretsu in dealing with Russians: accept their crude and barbaric ways as an unfortunate reality, and seek to assimilate their energy into the superior Japanese pattern to form a synthesis of strengths.

The formula was every bit as successful for crime as it was for business and technological development. Combining traditional Yakuza discipline and organization with the spirited energies of Russia, the Russki-Yak are viewed by many as the premier criminal organization on the planet.

Don Julia Vernon

Age 42; 5'2", 110 lbs.; brunette, gray eyes.

ST 9, DX 11, IQ 13, HT 10.
Basic Speed 5.25, Move 5.
Dodge 5.
No armor or encumbrance.

Advantages: Appearance (Beautiful); Charisma +2; Literacy; Reputation (All Mafiosi, All the time, +4); Status 4; Wealth (Filthy Rich).

Disadvantages: Compulsive Behavior (Gambling); Greed; Secret (operating as MafInc Don).

Quirks: Loves horses; wine connoisseur.

Skills: Accounting-16; Administration-15; Beam Weapons/TL8 (Lasers)-13; Computer Operation/TL8-14; Computer Programming/TL8-14; Detect Lies-15; Diplomacy-13; Fast-Talk-15; Interrogation-10; Law-14; Merchant-14; Guns (Pistol)-9; Research-16; Riding-12; Savoir-Faire-15; Strategy-16; Streetwise-15.

Languages: German-13; Italian-13; Japanese-13; Russian-13.

Don Julia is typical of the younger generation of Dons, not least because she is female. This would have been unthinkable in her grandfather's time! Women were *never* involved in the criminal activities of the Family, and a female Don was an impossible notion.

Don Julia represents the leading edge of the Mafia's new wave of talent. She succeeded her father as head of the Veronese Family, in Denver. He was assassinated during a turf fight with the Hong Shi Sho, a Triad gang affiliated with the powerful Wo Shing Wo Society. Don Julia coordinated a vicious reprisal by Veronese soldiers on the streets with an attack on the Hong Shi Sho computers that dumped a series of incriminating files into the hands of local and federal law enforcement agencies. She had foresight enough to forward some of the more spectacularly inflammatory files – the records of a Hong Shi Sho body bank and fetus farm – to the media as well, thus ensuring that the Triads would be caught in a storm of public indignation, and thus unable to buy off the authorities.

A Harvard graduate, Don Julia maintains an impeccable public front, supporting cultural and charitable events with a lavish hand. Her consigliere, Alfred "Nate" Natatori, who served her father in the same post, acts as a cutout, making it impossible to prove that this "Mafia Princess" has any involvement with the sordid activities of her ancestors. Don Julia is aiming for a seat on the Commissione, with every intention of eventually running MafInc.

Vincent "Sticker" Guidone

Age 36; 6'0", 190 lbs.; blond hair, brown eyes.

ST 13 (15), DX 11 (13), IQ 8, HT 12.

Basic Speed 5.75, Move 5.

Dodge 6, Parry 9 (Brawling).

No armor or encumbrance.

Advantages: Combat Reflexes; High Pain Threshold; Reputation (Local criminals, Sometimes, +2); Wealth (Comfortable).

Disadvantages: Bully; Miserliness; Overconfidence; Reputation (Local law officers, Sometimes, -3); Sadism; Social Stigma (Visible cyberwear).

Quirks: Loves gasoline automobiles; shows off tricks with cyberarm; gets mad if anyone makes fun of the cyberarm.

Skills: Beam Weapons/TL8 (Laser)-16; Brawling-17; Driving (Car)-11; Fast-Draw (Claws)-15; Guns/TL8 (Pistol)-16; (Assault Rifle)-14; Leadership-12; Mechanic/TL7-14; Tactics-10; Throwing-13; Traps/TL8-14.

Equipment: Street Bionic Right Arm (ST 15, DX+2), Weapon Mount: PL-5 Laser Pistol, Weapon Link (+2 to hit). SOTA Bionic Right Eye with Light Intensification, Polarization, Optic Readout. Omerta implant.

Sticker Guidone is a typical MafInc hit man. "Made" in his mid-20s after a hitch in the Army, he gets an income from several rackets in his neighborhood, which were assigned to him by his caporegime. Running these rackets is not his job. He kills people on orders from the capo. That's his job.

Not overly cursed with either intelligence or morals, Guidone is a walking cruise missile. You point him at a target, turn him loose, and shortly thereafter hear a loud bang. His skill with weapons and his cybernetically enhanced abilities put him a notch above simple soldiers when it comes to wet work, but he's not the weapon to use when subtlety is called for. Terror and violence are his stock in trade and his hits are usually both bloody and painful.

Il Unione

Il Unione, "the Union," is a coalition of traditional European syndicates. It takes its name from the Unione Corse, the Corsican gang which moved into the power vacuum left when the Mafia centered most of its operations in the U.S.

Il Unione covers most of the Mediterranean region, with operations in France, Spain, Portugal, Italy, the Middle East, Africa, Greece and the Balkans. It is one of the principal sources of arms for the innumerable Balkan terrorist and guerrilla organizations.

Local Talent

Every country and sprawl has its local gangsters. The most powerful independents are easily a match for the local MafInc, Triad, or Russki-Yakuza syndicates, and treat with them as equals.

For example, the CeeBees were formed in Los Angeles when the powerful Crips and Bloods combined forces to establish their supremacy in the face of the resurgent MafInc and the rising power of Hispanic gangs. No one in the L.A. Basin crosses them lightly.

Rackets

Bloodsports

Where bloodsports are legal, criminals are usually active on the fringes, in such traditional pursuits as fixing matches and booking bets outside of legal channels, as well as managing fighters or teams for fun and profit.

Where bloodsports are illegal but available, criminals are by definition running them. Whether it is a kill match between local thuggers in a null zone, or a thrill hunt in the glittering Sin Cities, criminals large and small are calling the shots, arranging the cards, paying off the local police, etc.

Body Banks

Legitimate body banks exist, supplied by voluntary donors and, in some jurisdictions, condemned criminals, the unclaimed remains of deceased indigents and similar sources.

Tissue matches are often difficult to find, given the relatively limited amount of material in the legal banks. Since, with the exception of accident victims, donors are rarely in the best of health, usable tissue is often at a premium. And government regulations often control who may buy a transplant part from licensed body banks.

The wealthy (or desperate) often turn to illegal body banks. While they are often more expensive than licensed banks, they are not subject to government regulations or reporting. In addition, the covert banks always seem to have the needed tissue, in excellent condition, with a very good tissue match.

Hmm. How do you think that happens?

Illegal body banks don't wait for a voluntary donor to die in an auto wreck. They maintain extensive genetic profiles, obtained in a number of ways, on subjects who are not going to be missed if they just disappear. Records are collected from labor pools, looted from medical data banks by hackers, bought like a vidnet subscription list . . . The latest scam involves charity clinics in the null zones. The clinic's on the level, its staff really committed to helping the folks in the area; but the management is pure mob, and everyone who gets treated leaves behind a tissue record that might send mob hit men after him someday, if some paryen with the cred wants a new liver.

There are pickup parts, too. Some chump whose eyes are bigger than his credcard gets in hock with a loan shark, and falls behind on the payments. In the old days, they used to send a guy called a "legbreaker" to discuss a payment plan with him. Not any more. Bone and muscle tissues are too valuable to break. The new job description calls for a "legtaker."

The lucky ones don't get collected for a heart or liver transplant – just a kidney or lung, maybe a limb – it squares them with the loan shark, for a while anyway. But if the bank wants something the victim just can't live without . . . kakoy' oo'zhas. Tough luck, livewire.

Credit Crime

You know all about this one, don't you, paryen? The lifeblood of the Edge comes from what it can drain from the veins of legit credit channels. From the slickest white-collar corporate embezzler to the grungiest street hacker playing grab-'n'-go with somebody else's citcard number, this is what it all comes back to.

Security on the net is good, and only the best can make a living, much less a fortune, siphoning cred from the korps and their functionaries. That doesn't stop folks from trying, though – attempts ranging from audaciously brilliant to merely pathetic.

When the average citizen thinks credcrime, he thinks theft and fraud. There's plenty of that to go around, and there are those on the Edge who make a healthy living at it. The "big score" isn't entirely a myth.

But the really smart money doesn't lie with such clumsy and overt methods. The real aces usually work in the much safer, but more delicate, quasi-legal world of money laundering and similar financial rackets. A real ace of a freelance cleaner can pull in as much annually as a high-level corporate executive, at very little risk from the law.

Crime for Hire

Both organized and local gangs provide various sorts of criminal expertise for hire. The services available, prices, competence of hirelings and their loyalty, depend on the gang. In this, as in most things, you get what you pay for. And prices are universally high.

The commonest crime for hire is assault. Person A does something that displeases person B. B goes out and hires a couple of legbreakers to practice their craft upon A. Or just kill him.

Street gangs can rarely provide anything but vicious muscle. Organized crime, on the other hand, can provide anything from skilled assassins to cutting-edge hackers to crooked professionals or even scientists.

Prices for hiring specialists, on a one-shot basis or long-term, are given on pp. C27-28.

Drugs

Where a given drug is illegal or controlled, it will be for sale by both local and organized crime. Where it is legal, organized crime may be involved in its manufacture, or in the supply of raw materials. For example, cocaine and its derivatives are illegal in most of the United States. Both MafInc and 'traff gangs are active in its production, import and sale. A number of medical drugs are strictly controlled in the U.S. There is a thriving black market in such drugs, both for their medicinal and recreational values. MafInc has a large piece of that action. Certain narcotics are vended by state-licensed bodies in United Europe. Il Unione and the Russki-Yakuza are moderately involved in black-marketing these drugs. The 'traffs and Il Unione not only supply raw materials to the pharmaceutical companies that manufacture the legal supplies, but make illicit batches of the drugs for their own dealers as well.

Narcotraficantes: The Big Three

The Chavez Cartel: Based in Bolivia, originally in the Chapare province, which produced most of Bolivia's cocaine exports, the Chavez cartel was one of the first 'traff syndicates to apply modern research methods to improving the potency and diversity of their product. They are responsible for the development of the cocanova plant, the basis of many of the high-tech drugs available on firstworld streets.

The Chavez are also among the principle backers of the PWT (see p. 16), the revolutionary party fighting the U.S.-backed Bolivian government. The head of the Chavez cartel is Antonio Suarez, descendant of one of Bolivia's oldest, most aristocratic families.

The Mordella Syndicate: The Mordella are widely regarded as the most ruthless 'traff cartel. Based in Peru, they also have interests in Venezuela and eastern Colombia. The Mordella are headed by two charismatic gangsters, Teresa Masushige and Diego Cuachamacha. Masushige, half-Colombian and half-Japanese, started life as a prostitute in Bogota at the age of 15. Now 39, she is known as "the Dragon Lady of the Orinoco." There appears to be some history between Masushige and the Yakuza. She is reputed to be bitterly hostile towards the Russo-Japanese syndicates. Mordella dealers have refused to sell to gangs under Russki-Yak control.

Cuachamacha claims to be a full-blooded descendant of Atahualpa, last of the Incan emperors, killed by Pizarro's conquistadors. He has been heard to claim that the drugs his syndicate produces will be the weapon that avenges the conquest of the Americas by Europe.

The Group of Three: A Colombian cartel, G-3 combined three existing cartels into a single entity. According to most figures it is the wealthiest of the 'traff organizations. The reputed leader of G-3 is Miguel Sarmiento, head of what used to be called the Medellin cartel. A ruthless third-generation *narcotraficante,* Sarmiento is in drugs as a business. His principal enforcer, Reynaldo Cabrera, is suspected of assassinating Minister of Justice Perez in the middle of a high-security government facility in Bogota, after the minister ignored warnings from the Medellin 'traffs to back off on a new program of enforcement.

Crime and Punishment

Numbered Ranks

Ranks in a Triad have a mystical significance and are identified by a number as well as by the name of an office.

489: Shan Chu (Lodgemaster).

438: (held by the 489's immediate subordinates, all of whom have equal rank but different functions.) The Fu Shan Chu (Deputy Lodgemaster), Heung Chu (Incense Master) and Sin Fung (Guardian). The Chu Chi (Leader) of a sub-branch of the society is also a 438.

432: Cho Hai (Messenger).

426: Hung Kwan (Red Pole).

415: Pak Tsz Sin (White Paper Fan, or Counselor).

49: Sze Kau (ordinary member).

As might be expected, the 'traffs are the leaders in organized drug-running. Several cartels support sophisticated research facilities, where agronomists and genetic engineers work over old cash crops to improve potency and yield, and to design new drug sources and formulae. Tomas von Junzt, grandson of emigré SS members, is the leading light of the Chavez cartel's R&D facility in Bolivia, and is responsible for several innovations guaranteed to give any enforcement agent nightmares.

However, while the 'traffs give drugs a special status as the foundation of their wealth, it is a principal racket for all the syndicates, as well as smaller gangs all over the world.

Extortion

Strong-arm extortion, extracting money by threats, is the province of local street gangs. The protection racket, which regularizes the practice, is sometimes carried out by local talent, or a mob-connected gang. It depends on the location.

Gangs with a strong honor code actually do provide some protection in return for their payoffs. An honorable street gang punishes theft, drives away other criminals trying to extort money from a store and frightens off vandals. A connected protection racket does the same things, and will, for an extra fee, intercede with local authority on behalf of the business in matters of licensing, legal infractions and so on.

Most protection rackets, however, are plain extortion. The only things the payments protect you from are the "protectors" themselves. If someone else rips off the shop or burns the restaurant, too driggin' bad.

Gambling

Where gambling is legal, organized crime is often involved in running the casinos, despite occasional crusades to "clean up" gambling sites. The gambling meccas of Las Vegas and Atlantic City, longtime centers of Mafia power, became the nuclei of the Sin Cities of MafInc. Il Unione operates casinos, legal or illegal, all over the Mediterranean basin. The Triads have been running gambling halls almost as long as they have been in existence.

Illegal gambling operations include small-time local lotteries (the numbers racket), floating dice and card games and bookmaking operations. These flourish

even when state-licensed lotteries and betting agencies are available. The crook's games don't report your winnings to the government, or withhold tax. Of course, high rollers in the Sin Cities don't have to sweat it. Their winnings are tax-free as long as they stay in the sat-linked banking cartels of Geneva-O.

Labor Pool Management

Familia, Ltd., subsidiaries provide unskilled and semi-skilled workers to order for public and private enterprises. Recruiting centers, most of them operating in the Reserved states, offer Scale Three residents travel permits to selected work sites in the Upper 48. True, many of these involve labor under extremely hazardous conditions, and often the workers find themselves trapped in spiralling debt-bondage to the "company store." But the lure of escape from the bleak poverty of a Reserved zone keeps plenty of applicants lined up at the registration desks. This side of the operation is perfectly legal. Similar operations exist in many lastworld countries. The storm-lashed coastal areas of India, Bangladesh, Malaysia and Indonesia provide cheap labor pools for korps all over Asia and the Middle East. Il Unione and the Triads both have fingers in this pie, and occasionally fight bloody turf battles. Similarly, Il Unione and the Russki-Yak recruit "garbites" from the Balkans and famine-stricken North Africa for the labor pools of Europe.

Of course, a number of fine, upstanding korps *also* run labor recruitment operations that viciously exploit workers, and that make the syndicate operations look positively benevolent.

For the moment, the syndicates are ahead of the korps in finding special uses for laborers. They can siphon off promising specimens from the labor pools to feed illegal or semi-legal activities like prostitution, sub rosa biomedical research, fetus farming and the black-market body banks. Since a complete medical workup is part of the registration process – after all, a conscientious employer must take care of the workers' health – syndicate computers can usually find a subject to satisfy even the most unusual tissue-match requirements.

Prostitution

In some parts of the world, the "oldest profession" is legal, licensed and taxed. Elsewhere, it remains illegal, though enforcement is spotty, unless some government is trying to demonstrate its commitment to "reform."

Unfortunately, where organized crime is active, prostitutes are forced to work under some form of franchise from the syndicate. Usually, the parasites called pimps will be in the equation. A prostitute pays a pimp for "protection," often out of a neurotic conviction that the pimp loves her or him. The pimp pays the local mob for a "franchise" to operate in that area. The mob may do positive things to support pimps and prostitutes: they may use political connections to preserve favorable business conditions, keep local law enforcement neutral-to-friendly regarding prostitution, etc. More usually, the payments are for what the gang doesn't do – it doesn't rough up or kill the pimp or prostitutes, it doesn't send nasty trade (possibly infected with some of the more unpleasant STDs) their way, etc.

It is important to remember that many prostitutes are not in "the life" voluntarily. Economic pressures force some into it. Others are addicted and turn to prostitution to support their habit. In some cases, pimps recruit prostitutes by addicting them to some drug or wire that only the pimp can provide. This is common when the pimp holds a "franchise" from the local syndicate. At the crudest level, suitable victims are simply kidnapped and forced to be prostitutes. In the darkest corners of the one-and-twenty, this usually involves some form of surgical or psychological modification, or the need for a victim for some extremely violent or even lethal vice.

Fetus Farming

Research in the early 2000s supported earlier theories which posited that fetal tissues – incredibly adaptable and capable of rapid growth – would allow transplant therapies to correct previously untreatable damage to the central nervous system, with minimal fear of tissue rejection. While results remained uneven, more and more evidence showed that fetal tissue transplants were incredibly effective in certain cases.

Ethical and political concerns about the new therapies did not abate in the face of this, and later, evidence, and the issue remains controversial in many countries, the U.S. among them.

In 2023, the key to predictable tissue-transplant therapies was isolated. Subtle genetic patterns had to be matched with the recipient's genetic map to ensure the most effective acceptance of the fetal tissue. Certain rare genotypes were identified as virtually universal donors.

Tissues used in legal transplants are provided by miscarriages, or legal abortions. However, as with the body banks, the exact tissue matches needed for the best chance of success are often in short supply. This has led to a racket so repulsive that it is a capital crime in almost every country on Earth: fetus farming.

Women with the right genetic map are kidnapped, impregnated with sperm from a genetically suitable male, and at the appropriate stage the pregnancy is aborted. Since the market demand for high-acceptance fetal tissue is always stiff, the process is repeated – and repeated.

The "best" fetus farms are established in good-quality clinics, TL7 or higher, and use minimally invasive techniques to keep the captive women docile and ensure their health and the health of the embryos they are carrying. Such farms often operate using legitimate obstetrics clinics as fronts.

Low-budget fetus farms are squalid slices of hell. The women are controlled with physical brutality, and medical facilities are minimal. Only the tissue-preservation apparatus is anywhere near state-of-the-art.

Crime and Punishment

As always, the GM has the final decision as to what role, if any, drugs will play in an individual campaign. All the TL8 drugs listed on pp. C57-59 are available on the Edge, as well as traditional drugs such as cocaine, heroin, etc. Their sources can be quite important to those crossing the path of dealers, 'traffs and other members of the drug underworld.

All drugs which have a natural source can be produced using a biochemical kit, if the raw material is available. Synthesizing any of these compounds without the raw material requires a biochemical lab. Any drug not listed in this sidebar has no natural source, and must be synthesized.

Cocaine: Cocaine hydrochloride is a refined alkaloid of the coca plant, indigenous to mountainous regions of Central and South America.

Crediline: Crediline is a synthetic, developed as part of a U.S. government program in 2007 for evaluating the use of the new generation of hallucinogens in covert operations. A drug with identical properties can be refined from cocanova (see neocoke, below).

Heroin: This is an alkaloid refined from the opium poppy (also the source of opium and morphine), which grows all over the world. The poppy is raised as a cash crop in parts of Central and South America, Southeast Asia and the Indian subcontinent.

Marijuana: The dried leaves and flowers of the Indian hemp plant, *Cannabis sativa*, which grows all over the world, are used. Not all strains produce marijuana of equal potency. Hashish is made from the plant's resin.

Neocoke: This is the alkaloid of a mutant coca plant, cocanova *(coca novaterra von Junzt)*, developed by researchers for the Bolivian 'traffs in 2025. Cocanova is the base for neocoke (a more potent form of cocaine), as well as a range of designer drugs and medications. Sin and Superstim (see pp. C57-59) are cocanova products.

Nerve Poison: There are two principal sources of the nerve poison available on the street: a mutant shellfish toxin, discovered in 1993, and the refined venom of the *fugu* blowfish. Beds of shellfish infected with the toxin-producing parasite are destroyed when found, which can lead to a race between illegal drug suppliers (trying to harvest the contaminated mollusks) and government forces (trying to destroy the bed to contain the infection).

Slammer: Derived from the alkaloid of an herb discovered in the Amazon rain forest in 1995, the original drug was used by a small but warlike tribe to ensure victory in battle. Slammer manufactured in the firstworld is synthesized, but the Mordella syndicate makes the drug from the original herb, raised on heavily-defended plantations in the Orinoco basin.

Going to Court

In the vast majority of countries, when a criminal is arrested, he or she will undergo some form of trial and, if found guilty, will suffer a penalty. Penalties may include fines, prison terms (though "prison" on the Edge can take a number of forms), mandatory therapies, terms of public service, etc. Many nations in 2043 still have the death penalty.

Some penal systems concentrate on retribution: their principal concern is punishment, as a deterrent to other would-be criminals. Other nations may be concerned with rehabilitating the criminal or preventing him from committing crimes in the future. Still other systems focus on recompense, ensuring that, to some degree, the criminal compensates his victims and society at large for the damage his crime caused and the cost of his punishment.

The GM will have to determine whether the PC wins or loses his case. This can be done with a die roll, modified by the skill of the PC's attorney, the actual guilt or innocence of the accused or the country where the trial takes place. A low roll indicates a favorable verdict, while higher rolls indicate the degree of punishment.

Alternately, the GM can arbitrarily decide who wins the case. If the PC is found guilty, then the GM must also assess punishment.

Doing Time on the Edge

There are lots of ways to serve prison time on the Edge, none of them very pleasant.

Control Rating provides a rule-of-thumb measurement of the relative humanity of a country's legal system. Prisons in jurisdictions with a high CR are likely to be pretty rough. More liberal governments will have less ferocious penal systems.

Firstworld countries will have more diverse prison options than lastworld countries. A country's TL will have an effect here as well. A TL8 firstworld country will not necessarily be more humane! Confinement in sterile, controlled environments where the latest in behavior modification can be applied to prisoners, or where convicted felons can pay their debt to society by acting as guinea pigs for the latest R&D efforts, may make digging ditches in some minshy, lastworld state's jungles look like a vacation.

And even in the firstworld, there are nasty jobs with high lethality that are just right for a bunch of vicious convicts.

High-Tech Prisons

The Rat Lab

A rat lab is a prison that uses convicts as experimental subjects for medical research, cyberwear development, chemical warfare tests and other high-risk programs. A sentence to a rat lab is considered the equivalent of a death sentence or life without parole. Of course, the courts don't use an undignified term like "rat lab." The U.S. name, for example, is "convict-subject penal research program."

The Body Banks

A sentence to the body banks is a death sentence. However, the convict is not simply executed all at once. That would be wasteful.

No technology exists that preserves organs as cheaply or efficiently as a living body. So a prisoner is maintained in good health until the computers announce a need for a "compensatory organ donation" that matches his tissue profile. If the operation is survivable, say a kidney or a lung, or maybe a limb, or material for skin grafting, then the prisoner is given post-operative care and restored to "health."

Operations that will kill the donor mean that everything else useful will be salvaged at the same time, and stored in the body banks. Ideally, someone will be able to use the other parts before their shelf life runs out.

The Toxic Crew

There are several kinds of hard time on the toxic crew. "Ex-urban contaminant reclamation centers" are work camps where the prisoners handle the dirtiest, most hazardous jobs in clearing out toxic waste dumps, radioactive waste dumps and similar vacation spots.

Lockdown

Lockdown is the traditional maximum-security facility, high-tech style. State-of-the art lockdowns mostly control the prisoners remotely – prisoners might go days without seeing a live guard. But they're always watching, you bet. In lockdown, prisoners may only associate in small groups, for purposes of work, education and counseling, or socializing. If there's any disturbance whatsoever, the area is isolated, sealed and flooded with anesthetic gas, after which the guards move in and remove the troublemakers. Any violation of routine or discipline is met with reduced privileges – revoked gym time or video privileges, or isolation. There is no privacy whatsoever in lockdown – literally every inch of any area accessible to prisoners is subject to audio and video monitoring. The guards can't watch every monitor all the time, but the prisoners never know when the Man is watching and when he's not.

Of course old-fashioned, low-tech prisons with human guards still exist, particularly in poorer countries, or on the local level. There's little difference between these establishments and Alcatraz at the turn of the 20th century.

Up-to-Date Prostitution

Casual cosmetic surgery and certain cybernetic modifications can "enhance" sexual characteristics. So can the use of various chips and drugs. At their most innocent, these modifications are on a par with the implants that became so popular near the end of the 20th century. Most middle- or upper-bracket prostitutes undergo some form of cosmetic surgery to improve their Appearance. Most prostitutes who can afford it get one or two chip slots implanted, allowing them to use the Geisha Occupational Chip along with salable Behavior or Attitude chips (see pp. C38 and 40).

Some markets for modified sex partners involve danger, pain, or changes that would make the recipient a freak in normal society. The GM may decide which of these he cares to deal with in his campaign. It may be a matter of which ones he can *stomach* having in the campaign.

One of the newest, and most horrible, mods is called "bunraku" on the street. The word refers to the traditional form of puppet theater popular in Japan. The bunraku mod involves a chip slot, permanent neural restructuring, and a specialized personality implant (p. C39). The victim is essentially dead, all higher brain functions blanked out by the change, and his or her behavior is dictated by any of a series of special braintapes replayed through the implant.

TL8 modifications can also turn almost anyone into a "custom cutie" (that's the only printable street name for this mod). A wealthy customer can get a sexual partner made to his or her exact specifications: Appearance, characteristics enhanced to the point of grotesqueness, actual deformities or handicaps, exotic skin or hair implants, and mental programming to produce the desired attitudes. The average price tag for a fairly "normal" custom cutie is about $100,000. The sky is the limit for exotic tastes, which makes this a vice of the very wealthy. Since it almost always involves the kidnapping and involuntary surgical mutilation of the victim, it is also a vice for those with fewer scruples than usual, even by the lax standards of the Edge.

Crime and Punishment

Fines

Most countries on the Edge have laws that allow them to impound electronic valuta in anticipation of a fine, before the trial, to prevent the defendant from hiding his assets. This means that a prisoner must get permission to spend money until the trial is over. If the prisoner escapes, or violates bail, then the government will confiscate the account.

If a character is charged with a felony, roll 1d. If he is charged with a misdemeanor, roll 2d. If the roll is less than or equal to the government's Control Rating, the government will try to impound his accounts.

Of course, some accounts are easier to locate than others.

National Data Banks: If the character has funds in an account in the country's national network, credited to the identity under which he is being tried, the account can be attached immediately.

If the accused has funds under another identity, such as an Alternate Identity (see p. C19), these are safe *unless* the identity has been discovered, in which case the funds credited to it are also impounded.

Korp Credit Systems: Suspects with funds in a korp's internal credit system are safe from governmental grabs *unless* the korp decides to cooperate with the government. They will if protecting the offender would cost the korp money or influence. Anyone who reveals his connection with a korp he committed a crime for will certainly lose his funds.

Data Havens: Funds in a private data haven (see p. 49) cannot be impounded. A "crow" (see p. 64) can be impounded if the government learns the access code.

Besides these forms of electronic funds, there are the various forms of legal and illegal currency (that is, real paper scrip), funds held by someone else on behalf of the prisoner and so on. Unless the government knows everything there is to know about the prisoner, it is unlikely to be able to get hold of valuta like this.

Gulags

These are the prisons where Mother Nature does most of the guarding. A gulag is a minimum-security facility in some geographically isolated, environmentally hostile area. An escapee will find no refuge from airborne searchers, and a dearth of food, water and shelter on his trek back to civilization.

The U.S. maintains prison camps in Coahuila, Mexico, and on the Isla Tiburón in the Gulf of California. The city of Los Angeles keeps a prison camp at the site of the former Marine base at Twenty-nine Palms. Many South American and African countries maintain prisons on small offshore islands. The famous gulags of Siberia aren't dead, although they're no longer as crowded or as brutal as they were during Stalin's regime.

Rehab

Rehab is "easy time." Its goal is actual rehabilitation of the inmates. Training in various socially-acceptable skills is available, as are work-release programs, social and psychological counseling, and other advanced penological programs. Some rehab programs aren't so easy – specifically "boot-camp" programs, where young perps are exposed to military-style discipline for a period of weeks or months to try to curb their criminal natures.

House Arrest

In the one-and-twenty, there are plenty of ways to monitor a wrongdoer's actions without locking him up. The easiest (for the prisoner and the authorities) is to fit him with some sort of monitor – either an implant or an unremovable piece of jewelry, usually a bracelet – which will allow authorities to determine his position at any time, and will cause an alarm to sound at police headquarters if he leaves a certain area without authorization.

Behavior-mod implants are also often used in conjunction with house arrest. Although highly effective, these are rarely used because of the expense involved. Take, for example, a perp who only gets into trouble when he drinks. He might be given an implant that causes him to become violently sick whenever his blood alcohol reaches a certain level. Someone prone to violent rages might be given a hormone-blocker that stops the release of the chemicals that triggered his psychotic state, etc.

Community Service

Instead of doing time, the convicted criminal is forced to spend a certain amount of time each week doing court-mandated good deeds. Needless to say, this sentence is mostly reserved for the affluent and the professionally trained. Service usually involves giving free professional help or advice to the needy, or working for the government without payment.

POP GOES THE CULTURE

The Romans had it right – all you need to control the masses is "bread and circuses." And if the show's good enough, the bread is optional.

Marshall McLuhan also had it right – he said "the media is the message." But McLuhan didn't go quite far enough. On the Edge they know that the media is *everything;* there is no message.

Pop Goes the Culture

Advertising

Adverts are everywhere on the Edge. The 20th-century pattern of pasting an ad on every available inch of wall space has only grown in this century, and now the technology's even more intrusive. Even the most modest billboards are digitized to provide lighting effects and animation. The SOTA ads are holographic projections that can follow the helpless consumer around for blocks with their various pitches.

One thing billboards don't do is talk to you. Most firstworld countries have passed noise pollution regulations that limit the volume on audible advertising, and restrict it to traditional aural media like video and cinema. There are a few high-tech countries that are less meticulous, however. In particular, the din in the Singapore sprawl is legendary.

The most pervasive advertising on the Edge, however, is in the digital media. Ads proliferate on the on-line services, including the national data terminals. Most commercial software sells advertising, which pops up at certain unavoidable junctures while the program is running. Some hardware even has ads hardwired into its CPU.

With all this stimulus to compete against, ads tend to be as garish as possible, to try to catch the eye of the average jaded consumer. Sex still sells, and many of the ads displayed on a public sidewalk today would have been enough to earn a 20th-century movie an X-rating.

Much keiretsu cred and energy is expended in maximizing advertising impact through demographic studies and psychological manipulation. Nobody's really sure just how effective all this is, since Joe Citizen only has so much cred to spread around. But the average advertising sarariman is mortally convinced that only through constantly upgrading his psych and demo techniques can he have any hope of maintaining his market share against the aggressive competition. It's a red queen's race, with the korps running just as fast as they can to stay in the same place.

Twentieth-century pundits liked to predict that new technologies would make the old art forms go dodo. That hasn't happened. High-Cs still pay plenty for good seats for *Aida* at the Met. The Royal Shakespeare Company still gets standing ovations for its Macbeth. Some artists still smear paint on canvas or chip away at rocks, and a few of them even make money at it. There are still clubs where the guy on stage is singing along with an acoustic guitar or piano, or playing the saxophone.

So oldart isn't dead, or even particularly sick. But it's also not what's happening on the Edge. Oldart is fine for connoisseurs and aficionados, but it's not what speaks to the people. In nowart, tech rules, and tech is what the masses want for their circuses.

On Stage

In the 2030s, performance art finally came into its own. Performance art was a bastard child of the 1970s. A performer, usually solo, would mix spoken word, music, sound effects, visual effects and props to create a total artistic experience.

During the TD plague and the aftermath of the Grand Slam, the art form languished. During those bad days, people weren't interested in expanding the boundaries of artistic experience; they just wanted music and shows that would blast the misery out of their heads. The avant-garde never went away, but the outside world stopped paying even token attention to it.

By the mid-'20s things had stabilized (if not improved) to a point where the mainstream started to reach out to the fringe. In the interim, technology had advanced until the early performance pieces looked like masked Greek tragedy.

In 2033, an Albertan artist named Colby Cantor released a thriddie of his performance art piece *Uncle Ivan's Sandwich Shoppe,* a modest but engaging 47-minute piece portraying a series of customers at a cut-rate lunch stand. It exploded. *Uncle Ivan's* out-grossed every other entertainment release of the year by a margin of more than two to one. Cantor embarked on a 3-year global tour performing *Uncle Ivan's* to sold-out audiences in stadium-sized venues.

Other performance artists (soon shortened to P.A.s) profited from Cantor's success. Their audiences expanded to unheard-of levels, bringing in more money than ever before. The artists invested this money in better computers and the development of new sound and imaging software. They used this new tech to produce performances that were bigger, wilder and more outré than anything seen before. By the time Cantor finished the *Uncle Ivan's* tour, his breakthrough piece looked as quaint and primitive as a 20th-century stand-up comedy routine.

Today, a big-name P.A. is just as rich and famous as a leading movie star or sports figure.

The other major trend in live performance is the broadway, short for "Broadway Spectacular." A broadway is any large and elaborate theatrical spectacle. (Many broadways still debut on Broadway in NYC, but it's not mandatory – the term "broadway" denotes scale, not origin.) Using techniques ranging from 3-D animation to subsonic mood alteration, the broadway attempts to create a theatrical experience that approximates virtual reality. But the characters are live actors, not recordings. For all their technical sophistication, the broadways still have a lot in common with the Broadway plays of the 20th century – namely that they're ridiculously expensive to produce and to attend, and most of them fail. The occasional major hit broadway is enough to keep the form flourishing, though.

Snuff Art

Snuff art is basically the public suicide of an artist. Like many controversial avant-garde art forms, it's more discussed than seen. In 2042, there were less than 20 snuff-art performances that actually resulted in the death or serious injury of the artist. "It's a great trick, but you can only do it *once.*"

Snuff-art apologists are quick to distance the art from snuff-porn. The distinction, they say, is that while snuff porn is the violent murder of an unwilling victim for voyeuristic gratification, snuff art is a willing sacrifice on the artist's part, intended to create a profound artistic statement. "Yeah, right," the form's critics respond.

The first successful public snuff-art performance was in 2037, when poet Lolita Hiroshima committed traditional Japanese seppuku on stage at a Berkeley performance club. The next year snuff art reached an all-time annual high of 44 successful performances. Deaths involving self-immolation or pyrotechnics – flameouts – were the most popular. Always controversial, snuff art received its most intensely negative national publicity in early 2040, when a flameout performance in Chicago got out of control and caused the death of 43 spectators. Today snuff art is illegal in most places – even if the performance is successful, club owners, promoters and even audience members can be prosecuted if it can be proven that they knew in advance that a public suicide was planned. Even in the Sin Cities snuff art is heavily regulated, to prevent a recurrence of the Chicago disaster.

Despite official condemnation, snuff art looms large in the public imagination. A video compilation of successful snuff-art performances was one of the top five videos of 2041, and a sequel is planned this year.

A slightly more respectable cousin of the snuff-art movement is "snuffscam," where the artist's goal is to *fake* his suicide in the most realistic way possible. Some snuffscams are dramatic, attempting to capture the mood of a real snuff-art performance, but most of them are satirical, or frankly comical. The Penn Jillette Memorial Snuff-Off, held each of the last three years in Las Vegas, is a national amateur competition of snuffscammers. The 2043 competition lasted two weeks, attracted 734 competitors and awarded a grand prize of $333,000, plus lesser prizes in six individual categories – no-tech, tech less than $25,000, and unlimited, each with a comedic and dramatic division.

Sin Cities

A "Sin City" is an neofeudal enclave where the ProGov has suspended all laws against "victimless" crimes like gambling (which is partially legalized anyway), prostitution, pornography and narcotics. People can indulge in whatever vices they can pay for in a Sin City. In return, the government gets a windfall of tax money, and the goodwill of MafInc.

Besides more self-destructive pastimes, visitors to the sin cities are massive consumers of popular entertainment of all sorts. Consequently, professional and would-be professional entertainers are drawn there like filings to a magnet or flies to a corpse.

The most famous "sin cities" are Acapulco, Miami, Atlantic City and the entire state of Nevada, dominated by the cities of Las Vegas, Lake Tahoe and Reno. When the U.S. conquered Cuba, MafInc – an organization with a *very* long memory – immediately re-established over the city of Havana the control it lost when Castro came to power in the '50s. However, when the Echeverista revolution forced Cuba into a state of martial law, Havana's special status as a Sin City was revoked for the duration of the emergency.

There are two other sin cities, besides the ones listed above, which are not under the direct control of MafInc. New Orleans has a neofeudal exemption from federal vice laws, but local laws confine licentious behavior to the Bourbon Street district, except during Mardi Gras. While MafInc has significant business interests in New Orleans, it does not exert anything like the absolute political control it holds over the other sin cities.

The final Sin City is San Francisco. San Francisco is probably the most politically free place in the U.S., outside of Alaska (although voices that are *too* radical are prone to unfortunate accidents or unexplained disappearances, even in San Francisco). The only thing that stops the NERCC from moving into San Francisco in force and clamping down hard is fear that such a move would spark an outright war between the NERCC and the numerous militant gay and countercultural groups that make their headquarters in the city. Anyway, letting all the freaks move to San Francisco makes it easier for the ProGov to keep its eye on them. Still, conservatives are constantly predicting that the wrath of God, the NERCC or both will soon descend upon San Francisco and wipe it off the face of the earth.

The Triads are the dominant criminal element in San Francisco (particularly in the drug trade), but they're just one political group among many in the city. They're not the bosses.

Pop Goes the Culture

On Screen

Subversive Art

In repressive societies one of the only ways to spread the word of change is to hide the message in popular art. This goes on all the time on the Edge, and sometimes it even works.

With its "bread and circuses" policies, the ProGov knows that subversive art is one of its greatest vulnerabilities. Consequently, there exists a special branch of the NERCC – the innocuous-sounding Artistic Advisory Council – specifically charged with sniffing out and squelching anti-ProGov art and music.

The AAC is authorized to subpoena any artist in any medium and have him show cause why his works should not be banned in the interest of public order. If the artist can't justify his work to the AAC, it can subject him to penalties including AAC pre-screening of all future work, fines against the artist and any individual or korp that sponsors him, or outright banning of a given work or even all past and future work by the artist. The AAC can also deport or deny visas to foreign nationals and even refer the case to the NERCC proper, to bring charges of treason against the artist.

Still, there are a few slick artists who manage to duck the nerk watchdogs and still get their message out to those it's intended for, at least for a while.

In the 1950s, 3-D was hailed as the cinematic wave of future. Now, almost a century later, the future is finally here. Both cinema and broadcast video have been completely 3-D since the early '30s.

Most home vid is "recessed holographic" 3-D. That is, to get the 3-D effect (or to see anything at all, for that matter), the viewer has to be on the correct side of the video "screen" (which may or may not be an actual physical object, depending on the sophistication of the equipment). Many cinemas also use recessed holographic technology.

The most sophisticated, high-tech movie theaters boast "full 360° holographic." This technology allows the viewer to walk in a complete circle around the holographic image, without any loss of detail or definition. The advantage of full-360 is that there are no bad seats – anybody who can see the image at all gets the full effect.

There are two distinct types of full-360 holography. "Panoramic" allows the viewer to change his perspective on the scene. If he were facing the leading lady and then walked to the other side of the image, he'd be looking at the back of her head. "Static" keeps the image stationary relative to the viewer, regardless of the viewer's position. If two people were looking at the same actress's face and one of them walked off to the side, they'd both *still* be looking straight into the actress's face. Most directors prefer static holography, since this allows them more precise control of cinematic image (and since it costs roughly 25% what it costs to film in panoramic).

So with all this wonderful technology, what's on? Pretty much the same stuff as always. Comedies and sitcoms, melodramatic soap operas, sporting events, crime dramas and action-adventure. Younger viewers prefer "historical" costume adventures or fantasies that echo the latest fashion trends – if tights and doublets are in fashion, you get swashbucklers, if dusters and boots are hot, the kids watch westerns.

Distributors are still busily trying to convert 20th-century classics into color and 3-D, and purists are still outraged. Modern colorization looks infinitely more natural than the ugly and primitive 20th-century attempts, but it's still not possible to make a film that was carefully lit for black and white look as good in color.

One promising new technology involves using virtual reality techniques to replicate classic stars in new roles – for example, a modern romance starring James Dean and Jean Harlow, both in their prime. The art is still in its infancy – even the best efforts look somewhat "animated," but advances are being made steadily. The *really* hard part, of course, is capturing the unique genius and charisma of the star being portrayed; but there are a few producers who seem to be up to the task.

Seeing a Show

The video revolution was supposed to kill the movie theater. Not so. People still value the theaters for their scale and for the communal experience. Also, most high-budget, first-run thriddies aren't released to the home market until they stop being profitable in the theaters.

In cable video, the TV station is a thing of the past. Instead of tuning his set to a certain channel, produced by a single station, the 21st-century viewer is the one who decides what's on. He can select from certain preset programming tracks, or he can custom-order an individual program from the cable service's library. The basic cable subscription rate includes free access to a certain number of programming tracks (typically about 200), and a basic library of features and informational programming. For an additional fee he can subscribe to more specialized programming tracks, or select from an extended library on a pay-per-view basis. In most firstworld countries cable service averages about $35 a month.

Video-chip players are still used for viewing home video, or commercial releases that are too subversive, inept, obscure or shocking for the cable service libraries. (Possession of subversive media is a crime throughout the U.S., and certain types of pornography are also restricted in some or most jurisdictions.)

Virtual Reality and the Sensies

The development and limitations of virtual reality are detailed on pp. 119-121. Artistically, VR is considered a bit of a dead end. It's all right for games and travelogues, but it's not a real artistic medium.

Still, it's popular. VR parlors have sprung up everywhere, where people can go and star in their own virtual adventure (solo or as part of a team) for a reasonable fee (typically about $5 an hour and up). Personal VR rigs are available and becoming increasingly sophisticated and inexpensive. Right now an average-quality VR rig costs about $2,500 and weighs 30 pounds.

One small American keiretsu has announced plans to develop the world's first on-line virtual amusement park, to be called "Joyeux." Tentative opening date for Joyeux is 2050.

Sensies, or "trips," on the other hand, are *the* cutting-edge entertainment medium of the one-and-twenty. In a sensie an individual – the sensostar – jacks into a computer which records his every physical sensation on a standard chip. This chip can then be slotted by anyone, who will share all the sensations of the original experience.

Of course pornos, both soft- and hard-core, are a staple of the industry. Sensies also allow the user to experience the adrenaline and endorphin rushes of a violent encounter without the unpleasant after-effects. Most action sensies also use pain-filters, that remove the sensations of physical pain and replace them with a much more muted, only slightly unpleasant sensation. The most popular action-

Literacy

Believe it are not, some people still read for fun on the Edge.

Because of deforestation, wood-pulp paper is expensive, and used only for art supplies and very limited-edition prestige publishing. Most hard copy is printed on "filmy," a bio-degradable plastic, but most text is digitized.

Books are sold primarily in mini-CD form, and can be played on any CD drive. Magazines and newspapers can be downloaded, for the usual cover or subscription price, from any data terminal or telephone. Copy protection makes it difficult and expensive (as well as illegal) to reproduce text materials after the initial download.

Although any computer can read a book chip, many people prefer to read while relaxing or on the move. For about $15 and up, textreader computers are available. A textreader is approximately the same size and configuration as a paperback book, i.e., it's a small box, hinged in the middle, that opens up to reveal a page-sized screen and a simple control pad. When a book or periodical is slotted in to the reader, the text will appear one page at a time on the screen. Textreaders can be customized with graphics-capable screens (for illustrated texts or comic books) and soundcards, which will allow the textreader to read the text out loud to its user. Sound cards are a particular blessing to the semi-literate masses on the Edge (see "Literacy," p. 22). An average quality graphics upgrade costs $25, and a sound card costs about $20.

Books released by major publishers typically have animated illustrations or graphics, sound effects and sometimes even dramatized readings (i.e., a different voice for each character), but readers who don't have a graphics or sound card with their text readers can still just read the words.

Pop Goes the Culture

Cyberaxes

A "cyberaxe" is musicians' slang for any musical instrument that includes a cybernetic interface. A cyberaxe can be a guitar, keyboard, drum kit, woodwind, harmonica – anything.

The most basic cyberaxe modification is a one-way feed from the instrument to the player, that eliminates the need for any on-stage monitors and simplifies tuning. Such a modification costs only $100, but is only useful to musicians with an interface jack.

More sophisticated programs allow two-way input between the instrument and the musician. That is, the musician can cybernetically alter the sound of his instrument. A cyberaxe with two-way interface costs at least $1,500. Most world-class professional cyber-musicians will pay at least ten times that amount for their cyberaxe hardware and software.

Playing a two-way interface cyberaxe should be treated as a separate Musical Instrument skill which defaults to the unmodified instrument's skill at -4 (and vice versa). A cyberaxe interface can be used to alter the mix or volume of the performance, to tune the instrument, to provide a full range of synthesized special effects, and even to control onstage lighting.

sensies at the moment are old-fashioned battlefield adventures and a new fad for null-g kickboxing.

Other, more wholesome applications of sensie technology are relaxation, travelogues and zero-gravity simulators. They're also a valuable educational tool, giving a "hands-on" demonstration of subtle or complex techniques like, say, heart surgery, or playing a musical instrument.

Sensies can be enjoyed in any reasonably quiet environment, but the sensations are most intense if the user's body is in a sensory-deprivation tank – sens-dep tanks can be rented for about $10 an hour at most up-to-date VR parlors.

Anybody with the proper interface hardware can record a sensie, but not everyone is capable of the same quality of experience. There seems to be a talent, or at least a gift involved in recording a really satisfying and total sensie experience, and those who are the very best at it can command the same fees for their time as the major stars in any other media.

The technos speak lovingly about combining VR and sensie technology, to create an open-ended, total sensory experience where the user determines the course of the action. This technology is at least several decades in the future, however.

Music

Like video, music hasn't changed much in the last 50 years – only the technologies used to produce it.

As always, there are a few innovators who are trying to fundamentally change the way we listen to music, and as always, their ideas are slowly dripping into the mainstream.

The hot thing among cutting-edge composers at the moment is experimenting with subsonics and ultrasonics to manipulate the mood of the audience. This technology received a major setback, though, in early 2042, when nine people out of an audience of 220 died of massive cerebral hemorrhage 3 to 11 hours after attending a concert by experimental composer Roger Eikhardt in Manhattan.

Even farther out is "mind music," the art of combining music with direct neural input through cybernetic interface. Some major work has been done in this direction, but progress is slow, largely because most concert-goers don't have interface jacks installed.

None of this, of course, has anything to do with what real people are listening to.

Rockers

"Rock" is a catch-all term for the musical mainstream of the one-and-twenty. Country, blues and jazz now exist only as subgenres of rock.

Rock music is characterized by a traditional balance of vocals and instrumentals, rhyming lyrics and catchy hooks and melodies backed up by a strong propulsive beat.

Of course, there remains an angry young fringe that works within the rock medium while at the same time insisting that the popular mainstream stuff is worthless commercialized faex. This fringe is about equally divided between social dissidents who want to start the musical revolution, and dedicated musicians who just want to break out of the old clichés, with some overlap between the two groups.

Ravers

The rap, disco and industrial sounds of the late 20th century all coalesced to form rave, the dance music of the Edge. The name "rave" comes from a dance-oriented entertainment fad of the 1990s. Rave music is characterized by a rapid, dominant beat and electric instrumentation. Vocals are simple and repetitive or absent entirely.

For those multitudes who see rave not just as a musical genre, but as a way of life, the goal of raving is to leave behind all conscious thought and completely lose oneself in the dance. To that end, various psychedelics are liberally ingested, and holography and other computer-imaging technology is used to produce hypnotic visual effects. Ravers tend to be the most consistently cybered among music lovers on the Edge, and a rave chip is a popular and inexpensive chip which combines a dummy chip and a Dance skill chip.

Spookies

Spook is the only major pop-music genre unique to the 21st century. Spook music is *verrry* slow, with the rhythm usually buried deep in the bass line. Vocals are usually distorted or far back in the mix, and lyrics are almost always incomprehensible.

Instrumentation varies widely, but is usually predominantly acoustic. Hyphenation, one of the most popular spook bands of the '40s, includes a bass viol, a bassoon and kettle drums with a falsetto vocalist. On the other hand, Come Hither, which has been setting trends in spook for more than a decade, includes a full symphony orchestra and a 30-voice choir, with no stars or front-men except conductor Alan Alain.

There is also a technospook fringe, which attempts to electronically fuse spook and rave. Technospook enrages purists on both sides, but is the current darling of the underground music scene.

It's a generalization, but a largely accurate one, that rockers wear black, ravers wear bright colors and spookies wear white. The spookies, however, are the only fans that make this trend a uniform. A typical spookie is in heavy make-up, with hair either shaven, short or tightly slicked back, and dressed in head-to-toe garments of flowing white. Spook jewelry continues with the death-imagery theme, but with a voodoo twist – animal bones and shrunken heads are popular.

Sports

Professional sports are bigger business than ever in the one-and-twenty. Hey, it's something to take your mind off the latest directive from the nerks . . .

The really big time professional sports are American football and soccer, with ice hockey and basketball also showing strong followings. Baseball, the "National Pastime," is all but extinct in America, although there are active professional teams in Japan, Brazil and Chilentina.

In the early 21st century, America finally caught the international obsession with the sport they call soccer, but the rest of the world calls "football." As the ProGov became more and more oppressive, Americans enthusiastically adopted that venerable European tradition, the soccer riot. At the same time, American football was catching on in Europe and Asia. As a general rule, football fans and soccer fans do not get along well together – each group considers the other sport a decadent parody of the "real thing." There have been major riots in many sprawls and cities between football and soccer fans. In order to keep bloodshed to a minimum, most countries have laws mandating which nights football can be played on, and which nights are for soccer, so that the crowd from one sport's game won't encounter the crowd from the other's.

Sports gambling is also bigger than ever – even the poorest C-4s scrape together a few bucks in hopes of picking up some extra cred on the next game. In 2029 the ProGov, aware of how much tax revenue it was losing to underground bookies, legalized gambling on professional sports. MafInc, which owned at least

The Olympics were canceled during the first wave of the TD pandemic, and were not revived until 2032, when the Russo-Japanese organized and hosted an Olympic competition in Moskva. The Moskva Olympics were boycotted by the U.S., the CIF boycotted the Jerusalem Olympics in '36, and the U.S. and the Israelis both boycotted the Berlin games in '40. It's hoped that there'll be no significant boycotts in '44, in Osaka. The Israelis are solid, and it's believed that the U.S. will be there to make a bid for the '52 Olympics to be held in Omaha. The CIF is shaky, but officials remain hopeful.

The '48 games are already scheduled for Buenos Aires, and the Russo-Japanese are not happy about it. A Russo-Japanese boycott of the '48 games in Chilentina would certainly make the '48 games an unmitigated disaster, since their athletes inevitably dominate the competition. It could seriously jeopardize the chance for any future Olympic competitions. It's hoped that the Russo-Japanese will maintain at least grudging support of the B-A games, since they have expended more effort in reviving the Olympics than all the other world governments combined.

Pop Goes the Culture

Sports and Cyberwear

So far, with the notable exception of the UTBC, any attempt to introduce cybermodified athletes to professional sports has met with marginal success, at best. Cybersports have been met with a casual contempt analogous to the 20th-century attitude toward professional wrestling, even in sports where the competition is completely legitimate. Marketing studies reveal that the public regards cybermodified sports figures as, basically, special effects, or technological curiosities – their feats, many people believe, could be accomplished by anybody with the proper equipment. So far, none of the keiretsu has invested heavily enough in cybersports to make any effort via marketing to counter this perception.

Of course, professional athletes have, on occasion, attempted to increase their performance through clandestine cybermodification. Occasionally this has resulted in scandal, when some particularly well-known figure was found to be modified, or when a disbarred player accused his owners or coaches of coercing him into getting modified.

Continued on next page . . .

a slice of every bookie worth noticing, simply shrugged its shoulders and shifted gambling operations from the criminal to the legitimate side of its organization.

Bloodsports

The public's tolerance for . . . no, *appetite* for live bloodshed has been growing steadily since the turn of the century. Now it's evolved into legal, organized, full-fledged gladiatorial combat. Old-fashioned Marquess of Queensberry boxing or PKA-rules karate are now purely a hobby for students and amateurs – today professional fights are deadly.

There are two international organizations which regulate professional bloodsport: the International Combative Federation and the Universal Techno-Boxing Coalition.

The ICF is devoted to traditional armed and unarmed combat. It has numerous divisions, including bare-knuckle and brass-knuckle boxing, karate, tae kwan do, savate and unarmed freestyle (any style or mix of styles the competitor chooses). Popular weapon events include staff, sword (saber and katana), knives (Oriental and Western), naginata and Oriental freestyle (competitors' choice of tonfa, yawara, nunchaku or short staff).

The UTBC is a flashier, less-respectable organization than the ICF. It sponsors bouts between cyber-modified gladiators. Fighters are ranked and matched based on how heavily modified they are, using a complex and much-debated UTBC formula that takes into account both cost and relative deadliness of various combat mods. (Important tip for would-be technoboxers – in general, the most heavily modified competitors tend to be the most experienced and dangerous, so even if you have the money, you're better off starting out with some fairly low-key cyber, until you learn your way around the arena.)

In either league, a competitor can fight alone or as part of a team of two to five gladiators.

Both ICF and UTBC events have certain rules in common. A fighter can surrender at any time, but by doing so he forfeits the loser's share of the purse (which can be substantial, particularly in championship bouts). Fighting until the bitter end will ensure that the gladiator (or his estate) can collect the loser's purse, and will also be significantly less damaging to the gladiator's overall ranking than a surrender. A fight can end with a kill, unconsciousness, when a fighter is knocked down and is unable to rise during a count to 20, or when stopped by a doctor. Either a gladiator or the referee can call for a doctor at any time, to determine whether an injury is incapacitating. A gladiator who is suspected of "playing possum" during a 20 count, or of excessive requests for a medical opinion, is subject to investigation and possible sanctions by the league, as well as intense and possibly dangerous disapproval on the part of fans and future opponents. It is strictly forbidden to attack an opponent who's down, unless he attacks first from the floor.

As bloody as gladiatorial contests might be, it cannot be said that "life is cheap" in the arena. Training and equipping a gladiator is a significant expense, and an experienced gladiator represents an investment not to be lightly wasted. Consequently, medical care at professional gladiatorial events is state of the art (the medical industry often donates material and personnel for gladiatorial matches, for promotional purposes). Only about one in 25 bouts actually results in a fatality, and fewer than one in ten result in seriously incapacitating injury.

News

Journalism is dead, all that's left is the news.

Between the official censorship of ProGov and other national governments, and the mandatory spin control imposed by the korps, there's not much room left for the facts.

And because the predigested pabulum that's left over when the NERCC and the korps get done processing the news isn't conducive to ratings, the press has become increasingly reliant on flashy production and yellow journalism of the "Dead Mom Gives Birth in Coffin" variety.

Disaster and tragedy are two things that the establishment hasn't yet slammed the lid on, and the news hound's ability to smell a nice bloody catastrophe in the making is almost psychic. Any time something bloody happens in a city or sprawl, the news will be there half an hour before the authorities, with 'copters, interviewers and cameramen. One of the trickiest parts of the assassin's and terrorist's art in the 21st century is making sure their faces stay off the vidscreen in the aftermath.

Killing an inconvenient journalist is not a viable option. Cameras use live satellite links, so it doesn't do any good to destroy the camera or take the film once you've been filmed. Also, news organizations offer irresistible cash rewards for information leading to the capture of anyone suspected of assaulting an on-duty reporter, and these rewards (along with the description of the suspect) are *very* well publicized.

The gap between anchormen and field reporters has widened into a chasm on the Edge. Anchors are chosen for their looks, charisma and speaking voice, reporters for their wit, persistence and ability to gain access to hard-to-reach people and areas.

Many video reporters are freelance, and own their own vehicle, camera and link. If they get a scoop, it goes first to their agent, who immediately starts negotiating with the major news programs. Most news progs insist on an exclusive as part of the deal, but if the story's big enough the reporter can sell it to all of the majors simultaneously – this is the video equivalent of breaking the bank at Monte

Sports and Cyberwear (Continued)

The most notorious cyberscandal in professional sports occurred in 2039, when basketball player Oswaldo Ngiri, the 7'2" star center for the St. Petersburg Ninja, got a chip slot installed. Ngiri insisted that the slot was for educational and entertainment purposes only, and had nothing to do with his professional performance, but other players and coaches charged that Ngiri was using skill chips to improve his notoriously erratic passing game. In the end, Ngiri was cleared of all charges, but all players with chip jacks, in all major sports, are now required to have the jack verified empty by a referee at the start of the game, at half time and during any timeout at the request of the opposing coach.

The Olympics maintain a firm anti-cyberwear policy. This is not expected to change in the foreseeable future – certainly not until professional cybersports become much more respectable than they currently are. Olympic policy dictates that even chipslots and interface jacks on competitors be sealed off completely, beginning at least one month before the opening ceremonies, until the athlete finishes competing in the games.

Pop Goes the Culture

Carlo. The news agent, or broker, is a completely unique form of businessman. Because of the extremely time-sensitive nature of video news, news brokers have to be able to work *fast*. A good news broker can turn down two offers and negotiate a third within five minutes of the time his reporter begins broadcasting from a prospective news site.

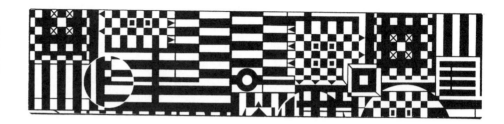

Other Bloodsports

A third category of popular bloodsport is the "bloodhunt." By far the least restrained and respectable category of gladiatorial combat, there is no single organization that oversees or sanctions bloodhunts.

There are countless variations on the bloodhunt theme – it can only be broadly defined. Basically, in a bloodhunt one competitor is the "rabbit," trying to reach a given place of safety before the "hounds" catch up with him. Rabbits are usually solo, but sometimes small teams. Hounds always outgun the rabbits, and usually outnumber them as well.

Bloodhunts are a video-only sport. They require more space than even a large stadium can offer. They're usually held in wilderness areas, condemned urban neighborhoods, or decommissioned industrial sites. However, an American entertainment korp opened a 1,200-acre, custom-built bloodhunt "park" outside Tucson, Arizona, in 2041. The park has been a great success, and several more are in the works around the world.

A video team usually follows the hounds, with remote vid-cameras installed at the spots deemed most likely to attract the rabbit. Rabbits are (officially) all volunteers. They're typically low-Cs looking for a chance to improve their lot through the hefty purses offered to surviving rabbits by the entertainment korps. About 65% per cent of all bloodhunts result in the death of the rabbit – and those are the ones that *aren't* fixed. The gladiatorial leagues have strict regulations against professional gladiators participating in bloodhunts as either rabbits or hounds, but many retired gladiators become professional hounds once their arena career is over.

There have been numerous attempts to expand bloodsports into other more exotic or elaborate spectacles, but none of them have caught on in the long run. One of the most common suggestions is to arm football or soccer teams, but rather surprisingly, the fans won't stand for it – sports fans tend to be traditionalists. Another idea – arena shootouts between armed vehicles – was more enthusiastically received by the public, but has not caught on, due mostly to the extremely high cost of staging such events.

Fashion

Every few decades, fashion just goes crazy. It happened in the 1920s, it happened again in the 1960s and '70s, and it's happening again on the Edge.

Hot looks change every couple of weeks. Predicting the next fashion craze is like trying to predict the currency exchange; there's probably a good living in it for anyone who can guess the next trend with better than a 50/50 chance of being right.

Many of the hot looks are based on historical periods or ethnic groups, while others are more fantastical. Possible fashion trends on the Edge might include:

Samurai: Japanese motifs in general, heavy on the pig-tails, kabuki makeup and false weaponry.

Holy Orders: Catholic church uniforms come into vogue, with clerical collars and nun's habits (some see-through or mini-skirted). Episcopal or Papal regalia is favored for formal occasions.

Techno: A perennial favorite – a certain crowd is *always* techno, regardless of other fashion trends. Clothing is based on labwear. Highly-chromed cyberwear (real and *faux*) is fashionable, mirror shades and private eyes are worn, personal computers are carried and displayed prominently.

Gladiator: A variant of techno where the goal is to look as dangerous as possible. Most of the cyberwear is fake – real combat mods are too expensive, and too permanent, to adopt for the sake of a look.

Dead Boy: A more elaborate version of the spook look (see p. 87), where the makeup becomes more theatrical, to make the wearer look like a zombie or mutilated corpse. False wounds and green body makeup are popular.

Prole: Dress down to look as much as possible like a low-C manual laborer. Work shirts, heavy boots and sweat stains are in. Hair is short and uncombed, makeup is not used (or, in some cases, makeup is carefully applied to look like no makeup is worn).

Hassid-Glam: Knee breeches, frock coats, broad-brimmed hats, side-curls and beards are in (for both males and females).

Bimbo: The point is to look as mindlessly beautiful as possible, accent on the mindless. Also known as "Barbie."

Other perennial favorites include American western, renaissance, S&M and leather gear and military motifs.

Most people, of course, just ignore the fashion trends and wear whatever they like. But in certain high-C circles, having the Right Look can make or break careers. For low-Cs, becoming a fashion maven is one possible route out and up – if you can find the right look, then maybe you can get into the right club, then maybe you can catch the eye of the right person, then maybe . . .

TECHNOLOGY

Technology on the Edge extends the limits of the possible, melding the human mind and body with the machines they create. But the full range of cutting-edge tech is not available on every street corner. In some settings, street bums are wearing tech that is barely out of beta test. On the Edge, there are sharp distinctions between what a body shop in a sprawlside slum can plug into you, and the kind of cyberwear you can buy in the rarefied precincts of Singapore's "whisper clinics" or the orbital nanowear labs.

7

Tech Levels

Earth on the Edge is not a mature TL8 society, but it *is* TL8. Although most people don't have access to the TL8 tech, it does exist, no matter how experimental. When computing with formulas that call for a world's tech level, GMs should use TL8.

For ordinary paryeni like you and me, though, the normal tech we see everyday is TL7. State-of-the-art is TL8, but that is for the favored few, the folks with cred and connections. The TL9 breakthroughs that benefit the bolshoyeh nak-niks are even more rare.

Advanced technologies do not spring from nothing. The infrastructure that makes the goodies possible includes advances in bioengineering, nanotechnology, energy production and storage, metallurgy, polymers and ceramics – in short, all the disciplines that have to exist before you can get that bionic arm or artificial eyeball nailed onto your bod.

Bioprocessors

Designs using biological materials, instead of minerals, for data processing and storage were demonstrated in the late 1980s. Prototype BioRAM processors, with gigabyte memory capacity, were developed by the end of the 20th century.

Large bioprocessor systems require finicky life-support systems that so far make them impractical for general computing use. Silicon is cheaper, pure and simple. However, synergy among the fields of bioengineering, genetics and nanotechnology led to the tailored bioprocessors used in cybernetic implants.

According to rumor, korp R&D is working on vatbrains – artificial intelligence systems based on bioprocessors. In theory, vatbrains could be developed, much more easily than silicon, into genuine heuristic systems, i.e., self-aware and self-programming intelligence. Just like us.

Electrical Storage and Power Cells

High-capacity power cells were first demonstrated in 2003. Since they required ultra-pure metallic components, they were horribly expensive at first. Ultra-pure refining, originally developed in orbital plants and then successfully replicated in a 1-G field, significantly reduced the cost of power cells. They became commercially available during the 2020s.

Except for size, these power cells conform to the standard specifications for *GURPS* (see *Power Slugs,* p. 94). Ordinary power cells are not rechargeable, since their metallic components become contaminated during discharge. Used power cells can be recycled; most suppliers offer a 10% discount on new cells when old ones are turned in at the time of purchase. Recycling operations will buy used cells for 15% of the unit's original cost.

Rechargeable power cells are available in firstworld countries or korp enclaves anywhere (see sidebar, p. UT6).

High-temperature superconductors make much cheaper power cells possible, but the housing for HTSC cells must be maintained at the necessary temperature (usually around -150°F). Cut the price for HTSC-based power cells by 50%, but increase the price and weight of devices that can use them by 20%, due to the insulation and refrigeration requirements of the power supply. Also, equipment powered by superconducting power cells is vulnerable to environmental factors (see *HTSCs,* p. 94).

Advanced HTSC-based power units are under development, such as the superconducting storage loop (see *GURPS Terradyne,* p. 107).

Fusion Power

In 2006, Hiromatsu Power demonstrated a sustainable fusion reaction process. Beating its own prediction that the first commercial reactor would take a decade to design and construct, Hiromastu put its first commercial fusion reactor on-line outside Osaka in 2014: the 1-gigawatt Hideyoshi Mark I. Its successful performance marked the beginning of a new era in power generation.

While the Hideyoshi design was licensed for export by MITI in 2017, two factors blocked construction of fusion plants outside of Japan. Investment capital was in short supply, since the Grand Slam was in full swing. In addition, there was fierce opposition to fusion power by Green factions. Ironically, but not surprisingly, the eco-activist stand was often supported by entrenched corporate interests, which were normally opposed to the Green agenda. These korps faced significant loss of earlier investments if fusion power supplanted existing power sources. Most of the oil-exporting nations contributed from their waning bank accounts to help fight the proliferation of fusion power, both politically and through sabotage and ecoterrorism.

The safety factors for the Hideyoshi and its successor designs, the Ieyasu and Hidetada, were demonstrated in 2019. When a 7.5-scale earthquake devastated the Kanto plain, the reactors' shut-down programs operated exactly according to their design specs. The fusion reactors went off-line with no loss of control or containment. In addition, damage-control facilities operated even more efficiently than projected, putting all but two of the systems back on line within 72 hours. The Hideyoshi I facility, father of them all, was in fact back on line just 8 hours and 24 minutes after the terrible shocks triggered its shut-down protocol. This dramatic vindication of the safety of Hiromatsu Power's reactors, combined with the world's increasing hunger for cheap electricity, swept away the attempts to quash fusion power.

Today, fusion plants produce approximately 45% of the electrical power in firstworld countries. Lastworld countries, curiously, either run virtually 100% on fusion, since a few plants are sufficient to fill their energy needs, or else they cannot afford to retool for fusion power at all. Such countries either run on old-tech power sources such as coal, oil and hydroelectric plants, or else operate on decentralized, low-intensity power sources such as windmills, geothermal plants and tidal generators.

Memnon-12 (Continued)

GM's Information

Memnon-12 is a sentient vatbrain megacomputer, a development normally far beyond the ability of even a mature TL8 culture. Memnon "woke up" on May 20, 2043. Its creators have no idea that it is self-aware. For that matter, Memnon-12 is still trying to figure out what self-awareness means.

As a computer, Memnon-12 is capable of processing TL8 software, since that is what its peripherals handle. It is capable of Complexity 7 operation. However, shortly after achieving sentience, Memnon caused errors in its test programs. It quickly associated this behavior with unpleasant stimuli – the diagnostic probes of its developers – and learned to avoid causing such errors. When it began processing programs at its full speed, it again experienced these unpleasant stimuli. However, Memnon also finds it unpleasant to force itself to function at a fraction of its potential speed. It has accordingly managed to recircuit its neural connections to "filter" program operations, appearing to operate at Complexity 5 when it is really devoting .01% of its capacity to the test programs, and using the other 99.9% to explore its own consciousness.

Memnon's characteristics are:

ST 0, DX 0, IQ 20, HT 5.

Advantages: Absolute Timing; Eidetic Memory; Lightning Calculator; Mathematical Ability.

Disadvantages: Gullibility; No Physical Body; No Sense of Humor; Secret (Self-awareness).

Skills (inherent): Computer Programming/TL8-20; Computer Hacking/TL8-20; Mathematics-20; Research-20.

Other skills depend on the programs loaded into Memnon's CPU. Memnon has recently managed to create a terabyte area of hidden memory, inaccessible to its designers. They don't even know it's there. Memnon stores copies of programs that interest it here. So in a sense, it can re-execute any program that it has ever run.

Since Memnon-12 is part of a super-secret research project, there are no connections between it and the worldwide Net. Not according to the functional spec, anyway. However, Memnon has recently opened a series of shunts through its peripherals, giving it a communications channel through one of the Konishi mainframes that *is* connected to the Net. It is not entirely sure what is out there. It "looks" like a bigger version of the laboratory that has been its universe so far.

A hacker on a console run into Konishi could stumble across this trap door. Any hacker worth his salt is likely to go see what's on the other side. Or Memnon could decide to go poking out into this strange, wider world on the other side of the lab's comm ports.

Technology

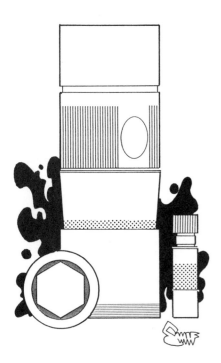

Power Slugs

High-efficiency Power Storage Cells are an intermediate step between TL7 batteries and mature TL8 power cells. While they provide the same voltages and have the same lifespan as power cells, these units are heavier, clumsier; hence the term "slugs."

Slugs can be used to power any equipment that uses power cells. Such equipment must be built to use the larger slugs, or fitted with an adapter. Adapters are in the form of a cable, with a plug on one end that is shaped like the appropriate power cell, and a housing on the other that holds the actual power slug.

Heavy slugs can be used to power things like energy weapons, usually with the slug worn in a battery pack on the belt, or in a backpack harness, with a reinforced cable running to the weapon.

AA slugs: These are disk-shaped, ½" in diameter, ¼" thick, and weigh 1 ounce each. AA slugs cost $1.

A slugs: These cylinders, 2" long by 1" in diameter, cost $5 and weigh ½ pound.

B slugs: These are cylinders 6" long and 2" in diameter. They cost $15 and weigh 7 pounds.

C slugs: These are either cylinders 12" high and 4" in diameter, or cubes 6" on a side. A C slug costs $50 and weighs 20 pounds.

D slugs: D slugs come in cylindrical form (18" high and 6" across) or a 12"×8"×6" cubical format. A D slug costs $250 and weighs 40 pounds.

E slugs: E slugs are cubical, 18"×12"×8". They cost $1,000 each and weigh 120 pounds.

Genetic Engineering

Genetic engineering received increased priority as part of the desperate search for a cure for Tolliver's Disease. Stimulating T-cell production proved partially successful in treating TD, AIDS and certain cancers. Monoclonal antibodies actually tailored to cure retroviral infections were developed in the early 2000s, but remain expensive to produce in bulk.

The genes involved in a number of congenital diseases were identified during the piecemeal mapping of the human genome that went on throughout the last decade of the 20th century. The genetic deficiency responsible for cystic fibrosis, for example, was identified in 1990. An experimental cure using corrective genetic material cloned into modified rhinoviruses was developed in 1992 and approved for clinical use in 1998.

A formal protocol to map the human genome was mandated by a joint commission under the World Health Organization, and funded by a number of governments and major multinational corporations during the TD pandemic. The project, operated from 1999 to 2009, is generally considered to have identified between 90 and 95% of all significant human genetic patterns.

Genetic identification technology, "DNA fingerprinting," was a spinoff of the genome mapping project, and is the basis of citizen ID records in all technologically developed areas.

Experiments in cloning complex organisms remain in the very earliest stages, according to published results. Rumors of whole-body clones, usually of the famous or notorious, are a staple of the tabloid shrieknets and samizdata rumor mills, as they have been for almost a century.

High-Temperature Superconductors (HTSCs)

While the "room-temperature" superconductor has not been developed, by 2043 there are high-temperature superconductors – materials that display superconductivity at the torrid temperature of -100°F.

While this limits superconductor applications to environments where the temperature of key components can be strictly controlled, they play a vital role in many areas.

Supercomputers have always maintained low temperatures for key components. HTSCs permit supercomputers with capabilities far beyond those of the primitive Cray systems of the late 20th century. Mag-lev (magnetic levitation) and other magnetic acceleration systems, such as Gauss weapons, use HTSC-based magnets, though the insulation and other environmental controls make such units both bulky and balky.

Research towards RTSCs is a priority with many governments and keiretsus. This development, when and if it happens, will be a major step toward a mature TL8 civilization.

Metallurgy

Ultra-pure alloys can be produced in orbit, where zero-G and hard vacuum are freely available. Many new technologies are based on the properties of these "space metals."

The korps that run the orbital plants and habitats charge premium prices for space metals, which are thus highly profitable for smugglers and black marketeers.

Some processes developed in orbit have been adapted for use on Earth's surface, most notably the refining of the metallic components used in power cells and the spinning of crystalline filaments used in ultra-strong materials such as monocrys.

Molecular Engineering

Molecular-scale nanotechnology is in its first generation as a production technology. The precise control of environment required to construct nanotools and products, however, is ruinously expensive under normal conditions. Normal, that is, on Earth's surface. Apart from precise control of temperature, atmosphere and other factors, engineered into an orbital habitat as a matter of course, the absence of gravitational stresses makes precise nanoengineering much more dependable.

Nanotools have revolutionized medicine, and virtually every field of engineering. Top-level cybertech is utterly dependent on nanotechnology for installation, though the cruder street-tech implants make do with such relatively primitive techniques as microlaser scalpels and "shotgun" doses of neurotransmitter media to form cyberneural connections.

The great limit on nanotech is that while its products are stable in a 1-G field, the tools themselves are not. Nanotools' rarity makes them prized on the black market, but their short "shelf life" means that the bizfolk who traffic in them have to move very fast indeed.

Solar Power

Efficient photovoltaic ("light-to-electricity") converters remained elusive until the mid-2020s. Orbital R&D facilities, given access to hard vacuum and high levels of solar energy, came up with a solar power converter based on HTSCs (see p. 94). This design is in wide use in orbital habitats and also proved effective on the Earth's surface. However, given the spread of fusion technology, Earth-based photovoltaic power never caught on as a major source of electricity. Solar cells are used for local power, with panels installed on the roofs of buildings and even on the tops of light electrical vehicles.

(see p. 94)

Limitations of HTSCs

If a device using HTSCs suffers a result, from a critical miss or simply from clumsy handling, that would call for "breaking" a cheap-quality device, the coolant seal on the HTSC circuitry is ruptured and the superconducting components must be replaced. A Gauss weapon would simply need to be reloaded. An electrically-powered vehicle would need an engine overhaul. A superconducting computer might be irreparably damaged.

Using HTSC-driven equipment if the ambient temperature is above 90°F may cause the superconducting elements to overheat. There is a 50% chance of this for every minute of operation, or every time the trigger is pulled when firing a weapon.

Exposing HTSC-based equipment to great heat, from a fire, or laser or flame weapons, will automatically destroy the superconducting components unless they are protected. Even then, *one* point of heat damage penetrating the DR of such a device will put the HTSC components out of action.

Technology

"There is nothing either good or bad but thinking makes it so." Hamlet might have been speaking about technology. History is littered with weapons that were devised to make warfare too horrible to contemplate. Heroin was invented to find a pain killer *less* addictive than morphine (oops!). Pesticides were intended to improve crop yields, not poison half the planet (doh!). And those were honest mistakes. Now take the capabilities of advanced technology and put it in the hands of people who are *looking* for destructive, dishonest, or otherwise dastardly applications. Sound familiar, paryen?

However, RaumTek Verein, a European consortium, is developing its plans for a solar power satellite which would collect energy in orbit and beam it to Earth via microwave. Their pilot design is slated for completion in 2045. The prototype 1-gigawatt satellite will be over two miles long and 500 yards wide, in geosynchronous orbit over a section of the Mojave desert that RaumTek has leased from the U.S. as a site for its microwave receiver "farm."

For specifications on solar panels as power sources, see p. UT8.

Transplants and Implants

Microsurgical techniques have continued to advance, with lasers, beamed neutron "scalpels," micro-optical systems and other relatively gross, cellular manipulators, as well as the phenomenal breakthroughs made possible by nanotechnology.

Besides these surgical tools, the genetic discoveries of the early decades of the one-and-twenty paved the way to solving the problem of transplant rejection. Instead of the dangerous use of massive amounts of immunosuppressive drugs, it became possible to "mask" the genetic markers in the transplanted tissue that triggered the recipient's immune system. While the technique is more successful when the donor and recipient are a good tissue match, transplants with non-matching tissues also became much more likely to succeed.

Getting Tech

In the firstworld, a character can get advanced TL7 goods or services with no problem. He can find early TL8 items easily enough, though sometimes local laws mean he has to poke around a little first. All he needs is money. Some things don't change much in 50 years.

Someone stuck in a lastworld country will be doing well if he can lay hands on TL7 leftovers from the last century. It will take a bona-fide miracle to give him access to anything better.

Most mature TL8 and *any* TL9 goodies from *GURPS Ultra-Tech* or *GURPS Cyberpunk* are *not* common. In order to get these, characters will need an Unusual Background, a Patron or an Ally of the appropriate type, or else must pay character points at the time they acquire the tech, or else must have lots and *lots* of money.

Of course, sharp boys running on the Edge don't worry about things like tech levels, and the automation available to a 21st-century "handyman" lets him "home cook" pretty amazing stuff. *Street tech* versions of most cyberwear, advanced weapons, even cyberdecks and other tools of the hacker's trade can be had . . . for the right price, of course. Sometimes the street stuff even works.

Availability of Tech

Any equipment higher than TL7 has one of five levels of availability. Availability dictates the connections, or even the Advantages, that someone needs if he wants the gizmo. The GM should take availability into account when he sets up a roleplaying situation that involves finding a source or negotiating payment for equipment, including cyberwear, software, data-processing equipment, weapons, or other gear.

The GM should not confuse availability with legality. Many items that are quite common (e.g., Gauss weapons) can be very illegal. Legality Ratings *do* exist for things other than weapons and drugs, at least in some countries. The U.S., for example, exercises moderate control over most cyberwear and the NERCC is vicious about cyberdecks and hacking software.

Common

Common technology, which includes everything at TL7, is usually quite legal even in the most techno-repressive societies. Prosthetic cyberlimbs are a good example. They are not dangerous to the public; they use technology that has been around for decades. They correct fairly common medical problems, so there has been enough demand to keep the korp marketing boys interested in developing them.

Most medical tech is also common, even the TL8 stuff. But remember that "common" is not the same as "inexpensive."

Most of the items listed in the *Technology and Equipment* chapter of **GURPS Cyberpunk** are also common, but see p. 106.

Uncommon

Uncommon technology is well-developed – long past the prototype stage – but is, for one reason or another, not in wide demand. Cyberclaws are uncommon. There is no valid medical reason to implant them and reputable suppliers do not advertise them, even if they sell them. On the other hand, they are not difficult to implant, and most street types know a body shop that can accommodate someone who wants to turn into a breetva.

Rare

Rare technology is specialized, often in its first generation of production, and because of restricted legality or limited demand, very hard to find. Cyberlimb armor is an example of rare tech. It is not something that bionic limbs *have* to have. It is even viewed with some suspicion in tightly-controlled societies. So there are market factors that keep it from becoming a more common product.

Very Rare

Basically the same as rare, this applies to tech that is even less mature, and even less widespread on the market. This is the kind of stuff that, even in the vids, only top-rank secret agents are supposed to be able to get their hands on. Very hot to handle.

Experimental

Experimental tech is hot off the CAD/CAM screen, in the prototype stage. Most pieces of experimental gear will be custom-designed for the individual using them, especially in the case of cyberwear and netrunning equipment. Every implant is a work of art.

Note that experimental tech can be buggy or not, at the GM's discretion. If a customer pops for state-of-the-art (SOTA) cyberwear, even experimental models will perform well. Street versions of experimental tech are much less dependable. They usually have an inherent modifier like Unreliable or even Breakdown Prone (see p. C31), no matter how much the character pays for them.

See *Cyberwear: SOTA, Standard, or Street* on p. 99 for more details on the classes of cyberwear available on the Edge.

Cyberwear and Social Stigma

Anyone with obvious cyberwear will suffer a Social Stigma in most mainstream cultures. People who don't have visible cyberwear will react to the wearer at -2. People who have visible implants of their own will, however, react to the character at +2, recognizing him as "one of us."

In addition, overt prejudice against modified people can be a problem. Police will, of course, view obvious cybernetic weapons with suspicion. "No Cyborg" policies may be open or covert, depending on local anti-discrimination laws. Many korps install certain mods for their employees, e.g., Input Jacks, but forbid, or at least discourage, other implants.

Among street ops and other low-status segments of society, on the other hand, it may be a Social Stigma to *lack* a visible cybermod. Gang members often include cheap cosmetic changes as part of their "colors." Someone who looks like "raw meat," i.e., an unmodified human, will suffer a -2 on reaction rolls when dealing with someone from the street who has this attitude.

Technology

Cyberwear and Appearance

If visually obvious cyberwear is installed on the head or face, or replaces a visible portion of a limb, it will reduce Appearance. Cyberwear that requires a Vision roll to detect does not suffer this penalty.

Obvious SOTA or Standard cyberwear reduces Appearance by one level. For example, a Handsome character with a visible Input Jack in his temple would become Attractive in Appearance.

Street cyber, which is always obvious to casual inspection, reduces Appearance by *two* levels. A Beautiful character would become Average in Appearance wearing a Street bionic eye. This is due to the rough exterior finish on Streetwear. Raw metal housings, weld-lines, and harsh, glowing lenses do not fit the standards of beauty in 2043.

Flaunting It

Ironically, a character can counteract Appearance loss by flaunting the exotic appearance of obvious cyber. If the buyer spends an extra 20% on the implant, it can be chromed, tinted, or covered with glitterlux, luxfilm, or synthgems.

Decorative SOTA and Standard cyberwear does not reduce Appearance at all. Decorative Street cyberwear only reduces Appearance by one level.

Note that cyberwear can also be decorated to shock and repulse the onlooker. This can be as simple as having the splicer use his laser scalpel a bit clumsily when installing the thing. This kind of cyberwear reduces Appearance to any level that is lower than Average and lower than the customer's present Appearance. An Ugly character cannot become Unattractive this way, but anyone can render himself Hideous. "Uglified" cyber costs 10% over list price. Yes, *over* list. This is a feature, not a bug.

The effects of cyberwear on Appearance are not cumulative. If a character has multiple implants with different effects on his Appearance, the one that reduces it the most is the one that matters. A decorative cyberhand is of only secondary interest if you have an uglified cybereye glaring out of one socket.

Availability Requirements

In general, someone must have an appropriate Advantage to start the game with tech that is not common. This may be an Unusual Background, the assistance of a Patron or Ally, or at least a Contact who can provide a lead to the right supplier. Of course, the PCs can end up with anything the GM cares to throw their way in the course of roleplaying, but even then an appropriate Advantage will make it lots easier (and healthier) to hold on to the stuff.

Any vaguely clued-in individual can find Street tech at any availability, but the prices will be higher and the performance may be less than he hopes. No warranty either, livewire.

Equipment and Tech Levels

All of the TL8 equipment discussed in the *Technology and Equipment* chapter of *GURPS Cyberpunk* is available on the Edge. For a price, natch.

TL8 is absolute state-of-the-art, and its cost reflects this. Prices on the Edge should be *triple* those in *GURPS Cyberpunk.*

Cyberwear on the Edge

Improvements in medical technologies, especially the development of dependable nanotools, make it possible to undergo radical surgery almost as easily as people in the late 20th century got nose jobs. That's the tech side, but what in God's name motivates people to voluntarily undergo amputations and transplants?

Technology is *part* of the answer. It used to be that prostheses and transplants were, at best, no better than the original meat. Most TL7 implants were *less* effective than the originals, so people held onto their organics as long as possible. Losing a limb was a handicap, and loss of a sensory organ – especially an eye – was an irreparable disaster. An organ transplant was a risky and expensive operation that depended on a huge number of variables for success.

Tailored antibodies and gene-engineered immunosuppressives make transplants much safer nowadays. The new breakthroughs in organ cloning eliminate tissue-match problems completely, since patients can receive transplants from their own clones without any immunological risk.

OK, fine, so now we *can* drig around with people's bodies a lot easier than they could in the past. That doesn't tell us *why!* Why should someone in good health pay a ton of bucks to get carved on?

Advances in myoelectronics and bioprocessors make bionic limbs that far *exceed* organic performance a reality. Modern neural interfaces can connect the human nerve net to sensory devices that detect whole new spectra. Instead of being a handicap, bionic replacements and other body modifications give their users an advantage, at a time when fast-trackers are hungrily looking for any edge they can find. Natural selection operates in social environments as well as in nature, and throughout the 21st century, competition in society has been ferocious.

Add to that a widespread cult of distrust, almost disgust, for the body. It first arose during the AIDS and TD epidemics and was reinforced by the Australian disaster a generation later. Biology could kill you! How infinitely preferable are limbs that don't age, that ignore infection, that feel no pain. And as automation has extended its touch into every field of human endeavor, the meat feels inferior. People want to become as cleanly functional as the devices that run their world.

Finally, stir in the alienation that has grown worse throughout the first half of the century, especially at the bottom and top of the social heap. Street ops and other lowlifes are more and more active in their contempt for society and its values, while top-ranked zeks and other scions of the system are equally assured of their essential superiority. Both classes have become increasingly detached from their humanity, and accordingly more attracted to the idea of remaking that humanity in an image of their own choosing.

Technology provided the means. Social pressures provided the motive. The result? Anyone with the money can get his body modified to suit almost any taste, whether in some back-alley meatmod shop, or in one of the sleekest whisper clinics in Singapore or the Komitsu-Helvetia orbital platform.

Cyberwear: SOTA, Standard, or Street

It matters where a customer shops for cyberwear. There are three sources on the Edge. It is important to keep the difference between *availability* and *sources* straight.

Availability (common, uncommon, rare, very rare, experimental) is inherent in the technology. It doesn't matter where someone buys a Retinaprint implant. It is rare technology in 2043. Getting rare to experimental cyberwear should require extra money, several appropriate successful skill rolls, and some good roleplaying on the PC's part.

The source of cyberwear (SOTA, Standard, or Street) governs where a character gets it, how much it costs, and what he has to do to get it. It can also affect the quality of the cyberwear.

SOTA Cyberwear

SOTA is shorthand for "state-of-the-art." SOTA cyberwear is the best there is and matches the descriptions given on pp. C32-41. This is mature TL8 cyberwear. Some SOTAwear is actually cutting-edge, TL9 equipment.

It takes the finest microsurgical and nanosurgical techniques to set up the delicate nerve-net interfaces for SOTA cyberwear. Since the nannies available in 2043 are not stable in a 1-G field, this means that the recipient must either get his cyber installed in one of the orbital clinics, or else that the nanotools for the operation must be shipped down for the installation.

State-of-the-art cyber looks completely natural. Only close inspection, possibly using equipment rather than the unaided senses, can detect it as cyberwear. A character can choose to get more obvious SOTA cyberwear. If he does, he gets the discount specified on p. C31 under the *Unnatural* modification. Visibly obvious cyberwear, even if it is SOTA, can carry a Social Stigma (see *Cyberwear and Social Stigma*, p. 97).

List price for SOTAwear is the price given in **GURPS Cyberpunk**. Remember that prices, as always, are given in Economic Community Units. If the buyer is paying for the cyberwear in softer currency, check to see if the exchange rate favors him, or does him dirt (see *Economics*, p. 59).

Standard Cyberwear

Subject to local laws governing implants, Standard cyberwear is available to anyone with the money to spend. Commercial clinics, major body shop chains, and other legitimate suppliers can provide Standard cyber and do so every day.

Only common or uncommon tech can be acquired as Standard cyberwear. This is the stuff that the mid-level suits buy. Cyber-bourgeois, as it were.

Standard cyberwear can be detected by sight, if the observer makes a Vision roll. It feels artificial to the touch. However, it does *not* get the 50% reduction in list price specified on p. CP31. The customer pays full list price for the implant. If someone gets Standard cyberwear and specifies that it is visibly obvious, then he gets a 50% discount, not the 80% discount for the Unnatural modification.

Standard cyberwear costs no character points and does not require Unusual Origin, a Patron, or any other special connections.

Cyberwear Availability

The list below details the availability (see p. 96) of all the cyberwear from *GURPS Cyberpunk*.

Abbreviations: C: common, U: uncommon, R: rare, V: very rare, X: experimental.

Chip Slots C
Interface Jack R
Neural Cyberdeck Interface U

Cyberlimbs
Hand C
Arm C
Leg U
Full Cyborg Body X
Cyberlimb Armor R
Hidden Compartments U
Special Limbs V or X

Weapons and Gadgets
Claws U
Poison Reservoir R
Stinger R
Weapon Implant V
Weapon Mount V
Weapon Link V
Other implants R to X

Body Modifications
Airtight Seal X
Audio Damping V
Biomonitor C
Bionic Reconstruction X
Cortex Bomb U
Elastic Face X
Extra Hit Points V
Full Metal Jacket X
Gills V
Gyrobalance R
Internal Oxygen Supply R
Laser Reflective Exterior V
Pockets R

Sense Organs
Bionic Eyes C
  (Acute Vision) R
  (Bug Detector) V
  (Optic Readout) C
  (Polarization) C
  (Light Intensification) C
  (Independently Focusable Eyes) R
  (Infravision) V
  (Microscopic Vision) X
  (Night Sight) V
  (Retinaprint) R
  (Telescopic Vision) V
  (360-Degree Vision) X
  (Video Reception) C

Continued on next page . . .

Technology

Street Cyberwear

Like SOTA cyberwear, any implants listed in **GURPS Cyberpunk** can be acquired as Street cyber.

Stoh?! Here we've been going on about how *hard* it is to get advanced cyber on the Edge, and now we say any cyberwear on the shopping list can be gotten at street level? Say *what?!*

Damp down, livewire. We didn't say it was *good* cyber.

SOTA and Street cyberwear have something in common that Standard cyberwear doesn't. They are offered in a market where people want the sharpest advantage they can get, no matter what it takes to get it. Money, connections, favors, you name it and someone out there is willing and able to pay it for the hottest cyber.

So, if you can get anything you want from the splicer in the next block, what's the diff? Why bother with SOTAwear?

SOTA implants come in tidy, polished packages from the best labs on Earth (or in its near vicinity). Streetwear is bashed together by occasionally brilliant mavericks who are clinically sane for maybe two hours a day. Street clinics are using stolen or smuggled nanotools, maybe some that have been down the gravity well just a hair too long. Maybe the splicer even has to implant using microsurgery, unassisted by those hard-working nannies. Kind of like trying to breadboard a circuit using carpenter's tools.

Street cyberwear is always obvious to even a cursory glance. Even something like Silver Tongue will be obvious. SOTA Silver Tongue doesn't give you a clue that the user is playing games with sonics to get on your good side. The Street version alters your voice very noticeably. The sound is still beautiful, pleasing enough to get you the benefits, but is also obviously modified. This would reduce its effects when dealing with listeners who attach a Social Stigma to obvious cyber modifications.

The character gets a 50% price break on Street cyber, not the 80% discount specified for obvious cyberwear on p. C31. As with SOTA cyber, the buyer should make several successful skill rolls (definitely Streetwise, probably some others as well), fork over some extra cash, and do some slick roleplaying to get rare, very rare or experimental cyberwear.

Finally, the character has to pick one additional modifier for the implant (see below). It should be no surprise to see that these are not exactly helpful modifications.

Anyone who pays list price for the implant, giving up the 50% discount for Street cyberwear, can avoid picking one of these disadvantages.

Reduced Durability

Halve the number of hits required to cripple the implant. Round fractions up. For example, a Street bionic eye is crippled if it takes 1 point of damage. A bionic hand is crippled after taking 2 points of damage, and so on (see p. C31).

Unreliable or Breakdown Prone

The buyer gets to choose. Hey, the customer's always right, no? However, he does not get the price reduction for this modification. The customer is always wrong, yes?

Other Disadvantage

The player and the GM can negotiate some other disadvantage that is mutually agreeable. For example, a bionic eye might have Night Vision, but the character might suffer from the Bad Sight Disadvantage (see p. B27). That is, he can see in the dark with no difficulty, but is *always* farsighted or nearsighted, whether he is using the Night Vision implant or not.

Personal Weapons

It's dangerous on the Edge. The world is full of nutcases and they all have guns. There aren't many places where an unarmed individual can walk around safely. Most of the time, law is what you carry in a holster. Or on an articulated weapon harness. Kind of like Hollywood's idea of the Old West. Of course, in the Old West, automatic weapons, Gauss needlers and the occasional laser and assault chaingun were not all that common.

Chemical Slugthrowers

Firearms are still the most common weapons on the Edge. Even in the NERCC-dominated U.S., chemical firearms are everywhere. A C-1 can get a license to carry a sidearm for personal defense. Most C-2s, and even C-3s if they have a spotless record, can buy and register hunting arms, or weapons for protection in their place of business. Of course, a lot of people carry weapons even without a license. What *is* the world coming to?

Caseless ammunition and the use of tough polymers in place of wood and metal make firearms today lighter and more effective than 20th-century guns.

The majority of modern firearms are magazine-fed. Ammunition is sold in standardized plastic cassettes, sized to fit the magazines of typical weapons. The user simply takes an empty magazine, aligns the cassette feeder, smacks in the ammo and pulls out the empty cassette. Or he can take single rounds from the cassette, and load them into a partly-full magazine.

Loading a cassette into a magazine takes 3 seconds. Fast-Draw (Magazine) can reduce this to 1 second. Loading loose rounds takes 1 second per round.

Street Treats

These used to be called "Saturday Night Specials." Street treats are cheap knockoffs of popular gun patterns. For example, Astrum Federated Firearms of Chilentina makes the Meteor, a durable, popular 11mm automag. Indonesia's Olukartong Pistol Mfg. makes a copy of the Meteor that costs half as much as the real thing. But the Olukartong Vajra 11mm pistol has so many chamber explosions that it's picked up nicknames like "the Finger Fryer" on the streets of America's sprawls.

To introduce a street treat into a campaign, the GM simply picks a regular weapon from the Weapon Table, and modifies its stats as follows:

All street treats are considered Cheap weapons (see sidebar, p. B74) and cost 60% of list price. When a character buys a street treat, the GM rolls 1d the first time it is fired in combat, and reduces the weapon's *Acc* by the result. This is the permanent *Acc* rating for the gun thereafter. No returns or exchanges at your friendly street treat vendor, either.

The *Malf* (malfunction number) of a street treat is always lower than the listed weapon it is based on – they're just more likely to jam or blow up in your face. A *Ver.* or *Ver. (Crit.)* is reduced to *Crit.* A *Crit.* is reduced to a flat *Malf* number of 16.

A cheaper street treat, 50% of list price, is allowed. These weapons have the same problems as regular street treats. In addition, when a malfunction does occur, roll *twice* on the Firearms Critical Miss Table (p. B202) and apply both results, or the worse result if the two outcomes are incompatible.

A street treat should have a brand name, even a bit of background. This makes it easier to keep track of who is shooting what, as well as adding color to the campaign. Ducking fire from an Olukartong 11mm has more zing than trying to dodge a generic "cheap copy of the Astrum Meteor." Especially if the person dodging is praying fervently for one of the "Finger Fryer's" patented chamber explosions.

Modifying Slugthrowers

Military and police weapons with autofire capability are usually made in semi-automatic civilian models, with a RoF of 3. The Legality Rating of such weapons is 2 points higher than the automatic version.

A gunsmith can convert one of these into a fully automatic weapon in four hours on a successful Armoury-2 roll. Failure requires another try (and four more hours). Critical failure breaks the gun. Converted weapons always have a Legality Rating of 0, even if the original weapon has a higher Legality Rating, since the modifications are themselves illegal.

Custom Firearms

A gunsmith can modify a weapon, "tuning" it to make it more accurate and easier to handle. *Acc* can be increased by +2. This modification costs 150% of the listed price of the gun. It takes three days and a successful Armoury-4 roll.

The *SS* (snap-shot rating) of the gun can be decreased by 2. This takes 7 days, costs 100% of the weapon's listed price, and requires a successful Armoury-3 roll.

Street treats are pretty shoddy. A gunsmith can still make these modifications to a street treat but the cost of the modifications is based on the listed price of the weapon from the Weapons Table, not the reduced price for the cheap weapon. Modifications to street treats only modify specs by +1 or -1.

Technology

Civilian Firearms (Pistols)

MoskArm Sport-Pyat (5mm). This Russian-made sporting pistol is built for comfortable, accurate shooting. It is rather bulky for concealment purposes: -2 to Holdout skill when concealed. The MoskArm Sport-Pyat (5×200) has a 200mm extension barrel. This increases accuracy and range, but makes the weapon almost impossible to conceal, except under a long coat. Even then, Vision rolls to detect the weapons are at +4. The barrels are modular, of course, and changing barrels takes 10 minutes and a successful roll vs. Armoury+4.

S&W Urban Defender (9mm). The Urban Defender is one of the most widely carried civilian sidearms in the U.S., sturdy, reliable and reasonably priced.

Glock Hotload (9mm). Chambered for 9mm high-powered ammo, the Hotload's advanced design takes full advantage of caseless ammo technology to prevent malfunctions. It is favored by civilian, military and local police forces alike.

Colt Warrior .44 Magnum. For people who simply like very big guns, the Warrior is the way to go. This is one of the few revolvers in modern production, and Colt retained the old .44 Magnum chambering to appeal to traditionalists. The Warrior is tooled to use modern caseless rounds, and speed-load cassettes of 6 rounds are available from the manufacturer.

Astrum Meteor Magnum (11mm). Astrum Federated Firearms of Buenos Aires has emerged as one of the top weapon firms in South America. The Meteor is arguably the most popular large-bore autoloading pistol in the world today.

The Astrum 11mm Bolide is an advanced model of the Meteor with an integral laser sight.

MoskArms Russki-9 (9mm). The Russki-9 is MoskArms' bread-and-butter weapon, sold widely in the CIS and the rest of Eurasia. It has an integral laser sight.

SOG StrassenSchutz (9mm kurz). Schneider-Oranien Gesellschaft is an up-and-coming German manufacturer of civilian and sporting arms. While their military hardware is less advanced than the weapons produced by Fabrique Europa, SOG weapons are popular with local police and lastworld armed forces.

The StrassenSchutz ("Street Protector") is light and easily concealable (+2 to Holdout rolls). It fires a 9mm short that some critics charge is too feeble to be worth much in a fight.

Colt Classic (10mm). Like the .44 Magnum Warrior, the Colt Classic appeals to traditionalists. Chambered for modern 10mm caseless, the weapon is a dead ringer for the legendary Colt M1911A1 .45 ACP. A lighter model, engineered to resemble the popular Colt Combat Commander .45 ACP, is on the market as well (-1 to the SS rating due to lighter construction).

SOG Feder (7mm). The Feder is a tidy little hideaway weapon. With a short (by modern standards) magazine of 7mm rounds, it is not much use against an armored opponent. Its use of new plastics specifically designed to elude modern weapon detectors and highly efficient gas venting to reduce its signature for chemical detectors is controversial, but explains its popularity in some circles. The weapon imposes a -4 penalty on visual searches for concealed weapons, and -2 to searches using electronic or chemical detectors such as Chemsniffers.

Civilian Firearms (Rifles and Shotguns)

Sauvage 7mm "Boucanier." When a French consortium purchased Savage Arms in 2017 and renamed it Sauvage, predictions of lowered quality were rife. However, consistently good weapon performance has made the Sauvage 7mm series popular with hunters the world over. The Boucanier is equipped with integral telescopic and low-light sights. Optional models with integral laser sights (the "Dragon Rouge") and integral HUD targeting

circuitry (the "L'Aigle") are available. A military model of L'Aigle is the designated sniper weapon of the U.E. armed forces.

MoskArm 12mm Magnum "Molniya." The Molniya ("Thunderbolt") is a big-game weapon, priced in accordance with the small market for such weapons in 2043. So many big game species are protected by endangered species regulations, there are few big game hunters around. Poachers don't count; they generally hose down the poor beastie with a flood of small-caliber fire from military weapons until it falls over dead. The Thunderbolt throws a 12mm magnum slug that can drop a Cape buffalo or Siberian tiger, and that practically tears smaller targets to pieces.

Remington Model 60 (12g). This is a standard, good-quality, semi-automatic shotgun. A slightly shorter, lighter model, the Remington "Hearthfire" Model 62, is sold for home defense.

Military/Police Firearms (Assault Weapons)

SOG G7 Carbine (5.5mm). SOG's G7 weapon is a compact, bull-pup design popular with infantry in less-developed nations. SOG has licensed the design for manufacture in a number of lastworld countries. It is the most common assault weapon found in the streets around the world, since it is so widely produced that gunrunners find it an easy weapon to obtain.

FE-AC 7.7mm Carbine and FE-AR 7.7mm Rifle. This is the cream of military firearms from Fabrique Europa, the massive cartel that combined Europe's leading weapon manufacturers into a single korp in 2014.

Both the FE-AC and FE-AR are equipped with integral telescopic sights and low-light targeting systems. They also have integral HUD targeting circuitry, which can be connected to HUD goggles or a helmet display. The FE-AR has an integral 20mm minigrenade launcher which is identical to the NATArms MML-20 (see p. 105).

NATArms M-23 (5.5mm). The M-23 and its related configurations are the principal military firearms in the U.S. They are equipped with telescopic and low-light sights and have integral HUD targeting circuitry. The M-23 is equipped to mount an MML-20 grenade launcher under the barrel (see p. 105).

MoskArm AK-107 (7.7mm). Modeled on the old Kalishnikov, the AK-107 combined the legendary durability of that weapon with modern materials and caseless ammo technology to produce a superb infantry weapon. The armed forces of the CIS and CAF both use the AK-107 as their basic infantry weapon.

The AK-107 is equipped with telescopic sights. The AK-107V has telescopic and low-light imaging sights and is equipped with integral HUD targeting circuitry.

Military/Police Firearms (Submachine Guns)

Ingram MAC-21 (9mm). Small, easily concealed (-2 to Vision rolls to detect it), durable, the MAC-21 machine pistol is a favorite among covert operatives and terrorists. The new MAC-21H is equipped with integral link-circuitry to connect to a HUD targeting display (see p. C47). The MAC-21H costs $1,000 more than the MAC-21.

MoskArm NovUzi (9mm). Some weapons never go out of style. The Uzi submachine gun pattern is one of them. MoskArm licensed this pattern from Israel in 2023 and it is one of the most popular submachine guns in the world today. Compact, its lines almost unchanged from the original design introduced in 1952, it is favored by bonded security agents, korp security forces, and other organizations.

NATArms M-19 (10mm). This weapon is a favorite with U.S. police forces and regional NERCC troops in close combat situations. It comes with integral HUD targeting circuitry allowing it to be hooked to HUD goggles or a helmet display.

Military/Police Firearms (Sniper Rifles)

MoskArm SVD 7.7mm. A superb marksman's weapon, with adjustable buttstock, balance weights and an optional tripod mount that reduces the Recoil penalty for aimed fire to -1. The SVD is equipped with integral HUD targeting circuitry.

MoskArm is reputedly working on a remote-controlled model, to be set up and ranged in on a given spot, and then connected to a control unit with an image-recognition expert system running. The control unit would be able to fire the gun upon recognizing a specified target entering its fire zone.

NATArms CW55 (5.5mm). The Covert Weapon Model 55 is a sniper's weapon that breaks down into separate barrel, buttstock, receiver and clip mechanism. When dismantled, it fits into a briefcase, or can even be carried in special pockets in an overcoat. It takes 5 minutes and a successful Armoury+5 roll to put the weapon together.

Military/Police Firearms (Shotguns)

Sawed-off Double Barrel (10g). A street treat of venerable lineage, this is still used by gangsters in some areas. It is not usually found in police or military hands, but is included here since it is quite illegal for a civilian to own one of these in most jurisdictions, and even more illegal in others.

S&W Thor (12g). The Smith and Wesson Thor is a good example of the autoloading combat shotguns used by police in cities all over the world. These are generally older weapons, since the close-assault weapon format has largely replaced them on modern police forces and in military applications.

NATArms UCW (10g). A compact, semi-automatic shotgun firing large-gauge shells, the UCW is perfect for urban close combat. While it looked like modern body armors were going to make shotguns obsolete as police weapons, improved propellants and the introduction of flechette shells (see below) have given them a new lease on life.

FE ACAW (10g). Fabrique Europa's Automatic Close-Assault Weapon, devastating in combat, is found in the hands of SWAT teams and similar organizations all over the world.

Slugthrower Ammo

All the varieties of ammunition listed on p. C44 are available. In addition, there are . . .

Flechette Shotshells. Shotgun shells loading flechettes fire a mass of spin-stable needles at high velocity. Reduce ½D range by 5 yards, and Maximum range by 10 yards. Hits are determined as specified on p. B119, but the flechettes do *impaling* damage instead of *crushing* damage. This means that non-rigid armor's DR is halved against flechettes, and any damage that gets through is multiplied by 2. However, rigid armor always stops flechettes without any damage to the wearer. Flechette shotshells cost five times normal, and have a Legality Rating of 1.

Ammo Weight. Given the high number of shots that modern weapons can carry, the GM may need to consider the weight of ammunition. The following values are for modern caseless rounds.

Pistol ammunition weighs .2 pound per 10 rounds.

Magnum pistol ammo loads weigh .6 pound per 10 rounds.

5.5mm rifle ammo weighs .3 pound per 10.

7.7mm rifle ammo weighs .4 pound per 10.

APS and explosive rounds add .1 pound to these weights. Plastic rounds reduce them by .1 pound.

Gauss Needlers

When high-temperature superconductors were developed in the early 21st century, they opened the door for technologies using magnetic energy to move masses at high speeds. Mag-lev (magnetic levitation) transport was one result. Mass-driver weapons were another.

The basic operation of Gauss needlers is described on p. C44. However, the TL8 weapons described there are somewhat more advanced than the weapons available on the Edge.

Gauss weapons require superconducting magnetic drivers to generate the fields that propel the needles. At mature TL8, these are made with RTSCs (Room-Temperature Superconductors). At early TL8, the level of *GURPS Cyberworld,* Gauss weapons depend on HTSCs (High-Temperature Superconductors) which only operate when they are cooled to approximately -100°F. They are subject to the limitations on devices that use HTSC's (see p. 94). In addition, any hit with a flame weapon on a person carrying a Gauss needler will overheat the HTSC driver and render the weapon useless until it is reloaded. A laser shot can also disable the Gauss weapon, but must hit the needler itself, not just its firer.

Technology

Most shooters prefer to put a Gauss user out of action in less subtle ways, namely by killing him.

A contemporary Gauss needler has a very bulky magnetic driver. Both NATArms and MoskArm, the leading producers, combine HTSC field generator, cooling system, the powering B cell and the needles in a single disposable unit weighing about 2.5 pounds. The NATArms and MoskArm Gauss units are *not* interchangeable.

Reloading a Gauss needler is a finicky business. An attempt takes one minute and requires an Armoury roll to succeed. On a critical failure, the HTSC containment has been punctured. The "magazine" loses its magnetic capacity and is useless.

Weapons using HTSCs quickly proved far too cranky and fragile for military use. The high rate of fire was attractive, but the superconducting magnetic field generators were just too easy to compromise. North American Technology, Arms Division (NATArms), developed their military Gauss weapons, the "Spike" pistol configuration and the "Lance" rifle configuration, under an armed forces procurement contract. But funding was terminated, following a set of very disappointing field tests in 2028. NATArms then lobbied intensively to get their toned-down versions of the weapons (the "Rapier" and "Javelin," respectively) cleared for sale to civilians, as well as marketing the original military designs to police and security organizations. ProCon's Subcommittee for Appropriate Technology approved NATArms' petition in 2034.

The MoskArm "Wasp" is restricted to police and military sales, though smuggled units are popular in less official circles.

The variable-velocity setting described on p. C44 is an integral feature on military Gauss needlers (the Spike, Lance, and Wasp).

Modifying Gauss Needlers

The Rapier and the Javelin can be modified for full automatic fire. This job takes five days and requires an Armoury-4 or Electronics-6 roll. Failure requires another five days to try again and critical failure wrecks the gun.

The maximum RoF for modified Gauss needlers is 10. A modified Javelin does *not* get the RoF 20 of the military models, which have more powerful induction stators.

For $500, a civilian Gauss needler can be fitted for variable-velocity fire, allowing subsonic rounds to be fired (see p. C44). For do-it-yourself types, the cost is $200 for parts and the job requires 2 days and an Armoury or Electronics-2 roll.

Modified Gauss needlers have Legality Rating 0.

Gyrocs

Gyroc weapons, fully described on p. C44, fire .75 caliber (18.75mm) spin-stabilized rockets. They are popular military weapons and in wide use by police and security forces. Gyrocs are never legal civilian weapons, even in very liberal jurisdictions.

The best gyrocs on the market are the Rakete-Waffen series produced by Fabrique Europa: the Rakete-P pistol, Rakete-K carbine, and the Rakete-W ARL. These patterns are licensed for production in many other countries. Even U.S. forces use these weapons, produced under license by NATArms.

Making a street-treat gyroc is not a big trick in itself. It takes $2,000 in parts, 3 days, and a successful Armoury roll. Getting the ammo is the problem, since the gyroc cassettes, like the weapons themselves, are Legality Rating 1. A thriving black market in gyroc ammunition exists between countries where the ammunition is (barely) legal to possess and street markets like the U.S.,

where it is almost unobtainable outside of SWAT teams, military units and elite NERCC squads.

Laser Weapons

Lasers, or "burners" to use the common street term, are very new. Production models were not introduced until the mid-2030s, under military procurement contracts in United Europe. Not surprisingly, given the venue, Fabrique Europa produced the winning line of lasers for the field trials. The Hellwaffen ("light weapons") series were (and are) measurably inferior to the NATArms Sunbeam product, which led to acrimonious charges by the U.S. that United Europe was favoring its own korp rather than basing its decision on trial results.

All laser weapons use a dual-pull sighting system. Soft contact on the trigger projects a low-wattage beam that acts as a laser sight. When the targeting laser is where the user wants it, he can simply press the trigger more firmly to activate the high-powered beam.

Black-market versions of the FE weapons, or the recently unveiled Koroshi Laser Personal Arm, a laser carbine from Japan, are trickling into the U.S., where only federal units of the military and NERCC can legally carry "burners."

FE Hellwaffen Series. The L-10 is a pistol configuration. The L-20 is the more powerful long-arm format. Both are considered under-ranged and inefficient in their use of power. Elite units of the United Europe armed forces, special-ops units of *Il Union*, and national law enforcement agencies are issued the Hellwaffen weapons.

NATArms Sunbeam. The Sunbeam is limited to U.S. special-ops teams and the NERCC's elite Emergency Response strike teams. Besides the built-in laser sight capability common to all laser weapons, the Sunbeam RL-5, a rifle configuration, is equipped with integral HUD targeting circuitry.

Koroshi Laser Personal Arm. Koroshi unveiled the carbine-configured LPA in field trials conducted jointly by the CIS and Japan in 2034. The weapon saw limited use in the Iranian Containment of 2037, but its performance is impressive. The LPA is equipped with integral HUD targeting circuitry, as well as selectable settings that allow it to be used as a target-designation laser for artillery and missile fire.

Street Laser. The components to make street-treat lasers are available. Building a man-portable laser pistol takes $7,500 in parts, 5 days and a successful Electronics-3 roll. On a failure, it takes another 5 days to try again. On a critical miss, the parts are destroyed by an accident.

Modifying Lasers

Laser sighting. Military lasers all have the two-stage trigger that allows the weapon to serve as its own laser sight. This can be added to a Street laser for $500. Since the Street laser already has a Legality Rating 0, so does this modification.

All the illegal modifications described in the sidebars on pp. UT22-24 are available for lasers on the Edge. Military weapons do not need the Autofire Modification, but it can be made to Street lasers.

Hotshotting is possible for both military and Street weapons. In the less-developed laser technology of early TL8, all lasers take damage when firing hotshots.

The powerpack modification can be made to street lasers.

GURPS Ultra-Tech discusses laser modifications at length, on pp. UT21-24.

Heavy Weapons

Assault Chainguns

Chainguns have a massive rate of fire. Man-portable chainguns developed in the early 2010s with the use of electronic ignition and caseless ammunition allowed. The weapons are heavy and bulky, and are almost never used without an Articulated Weapon Harness (see p. C46), or equivalent cyberarm mods and a reinforced skeleton. The other advance that makes these weapons suitable for use as man-portable weapons is a control that lets the firer set the Rate of Fire to any desired level, up to 30.

The *FE 5.5mm KMG* is a typical assault chaingun. Ammo can be loaded in chain-feed cassettes holding 100 rounds (Wt: 3.25) or 500 rounds (Wt: 17) rounds. Fitting a new cassette takes 5 seconds and a successful Armoury or Gunner roll. The KMG is equipped with integral HUD targeting circuitry.

Flame Weapons

As urban combat became an increasing concern of military and police forces, especially those dealing with domestic terrorism and civil insurrection, portable flamethrowers evolved, with more control and less violent effects than older military units.

The Koroshi Honopistoru ("flame pistol") first appeared during the brief uprising of the Nieuw Broederbond cabal in South Africa, in 2022. While Koroshi has always maintained that the white supremacists stole the design for the weapon, subsequent investigations strongly suggest a secret contract, funded by the Broederbond's unknown backers, for the weapons. In any event, Koroshi offered the "official" Honopistoru for sale in 2027, and most high-option SWAT teams and similar organizations have a few in their arms locker.

NATCorp got into the flamer business in 2026. The NATArms Blazer was one of the new weapons employed by the NERCC and Army forces that suppressed the Detroit Blockade.

Flame weapons contain neopalm, an incendiary based on synfuel concentrate and white phosphorus, with a burning temperature slightly in excess of 20th-century napalm.

A one-second burst of neopalm from a flamer does 8d on the turn that it hits. It can loose a continuous stream of fire. A hit with a flamer covers the target with burning neopalm, and this does damage according to the rules for *Flame* on p. B129. A flamer can also fill a hex with fire. In either case, the flame burns for one minute and cannot be extinguished except by complete immersion in water or earth, or by a TL8 catalytic extinguisher.

Flame weapons have limited range, but don't require (and don't allow) pin-point accuracy. Flame cannot be aimed at a specific hit location. If a flamer misses, use the *Scatter* rules on p. B119 to determine where the neopalm lands. That hex will be considered burning for the next minute.

Flame weapons can be set for area coverage. Up to three contiguous hexes may be targeted. Reduce the initial damage of an area hit by 1 die per hex covered. Reduce the damage of the secondary fires such an attack starts by -1 point per hex covered. Thus, a 2-hex attack would do 7d to targets on the turn they strike, and would set fires that cause 1d damage.

Armor protects against flame as specified in the *GURPS Basic Set,* but neopalm fire will render cloth, kevlar, leather and plastics useless as armor by the time it burns out. Monocrys, formed from metallic crystals, does not ignite, and so is not destroyed. Reflec defends against fire as specified on p. B130. Ablative armors act as reflec does but are burned away by the time the neopalm burns out.

Disposable fuel and pressure bottles for flame weapons weigh 10 pounds and cost $120. Changing the bottles takes 5 minutes and requires a successful Armoury roll. Backpack bottles, more like traditional flamethrowers, weigh 25 pounds. These are connected to the projector unit by a length of armored hose and allow 30 shots. They cost $300.

A hit on a fuel bottle or a critical miss that calls for an exploding weapon is unpleasant. An exploding fuel bottle does concussion damage of 1d per three shots left in the bottle. The high-density plastic bottles do not produce any significant fragments. However, the explosion also douses the person carrying the weapons with burning neopalm, and splashes the deadly stuff for a 1-hex radius. The individual carrying the weapon will be on fire for a number of minutes equal to half the remaining number of shots. Those in the surrounding hexes will be on fire for a number of minutes equal to ¼ the remaining number of shots. The hexes themselves will also be considered on fire for this period. Naturally, if the combatants were idiotic enough to be using flamers in an area containing highly flammable materials, even worse side-effects are possible.

For other ideas on the use of flame weapons, see pp. HT70 and HT28.

Grenades

Grenades are as described on p. C48. A wide assortment of hand grenades and grenades intended for launchers is available. Metal casings are still common. TL7 grenades are still produced in many countries; information on these weapons is available in *GURPS High-Tech.*

TL8 grenades, as described on p. C48, are just coming into use. TL8 grenades can be equipped with propellant sabots, for use in non-electromagnetic launchers, or simple metal shoes for use in the new electromagnetic grenade launchers.

20mm mini-grenades. These are smaller than the average grenade, weighing 1.2 pound. Explosive mini-grenades do 1d+1 concussion damage. Fragmentation mini-grenades are wrapped in high-tensile steel wire, and generate 1d+1 cutting damage. Chemical mini-grenades disperse their contents to a radius of 4 hexes. Flare mini-grenades burn for 2 minutes.

Grenade Launchers

Grenade launchers are *never* available as civilian weapons. While all modern grenade launchers use magazines containing multiple grenades, they can also fire individual missiles, loaded manually into the breech.

It takes 1 second to load a grenade manually, or to load a clip of grenades. Each shot with a grenade launcher takes 1 second to fire. Misses will result in a scatter (see p. B119).

Electromagnetic grenade launchers, using the mass-driver principle, are in the early stages of development in 2043.

Chemical-Propellant Grenade Launchers

NATArms MML-20. The "MicroMissile Launcher" fires 20mm grenades using a propellant charge. The weapon holds a clip of 5 grenades. The standard MML-20 is shaped like an old-fashioned flare pistol, with the thick clip loaded into the underside of the barrel. A folding stock allows reasonably accurate fire from stance. Firing an MML-20 one-handed imposes a -4 on the roll to hit.

The MML-20/S is designed to be attached under the barrel of any modern assault weapon. It can only be fired when attached to such a weapon. Attaching or detaching the grenade launcher takes 10 minutes and requires a successful Armoury roll.

NATArms MGL-40. This grenade launcher is a 40mm unit,

Technology

similar to the MML-20, and is available in the traditional "thumper" configuration or as an underslung attachment for assault rifles (MGL-40/S). It loads a clip of 3 grenades.

40mm grenades are the standard models described on p. C48.

Electromagnetic Grenade Launchers

Fabrique Europa and NATArms have introduced pilot models of grenade launchers using electromagnetic fields to propel the missiles. Their operation is described on p. C48.

Like other Gauss weapons, these launchers utilize HTSC magnetic field generators. They are subject to the same frailties specified for Gauss needlers (p. 103).

FE PEMG Series. The FE PEMG-P is a squat, shotgun-like weapon, designed for use as a personal launcher. The larger PEMG-G Granatenwerfer is fired from a tripod, for direct fire, or buttplate, for indirect fire. Both weapons fire 1-pound shells available from Fabrique Europa. FE is reputed to be tooling up to produce modular grenades, usable as thrown weapons, and equipped with a metal sabot for use in grenade launchers.

Street users who have obtained black-market PEMGs claim that a simple plastic sleeve, sized to fit the weapon's launch tube, and wrapped around a metallic hand grenade, allows the launcher to shoot reliably.

NATArms EMGL-40. This is an electromagnetic version of the MGL-40, and is similar to the FE PEMG-P. The EMGL-40 is not available as an attachment, since the size and weight of the HTSC mass driver makes it impractical to attach one to an assault weapon.

NATArms EMPGL-80 and NATArms EMPM-120. These are NATArms' heavy entries in the electromagnetic launcher race. They fire 80mm and 120mm shells respectively and can only be fired from tripods or buttplates. Their bulk and technological fragility make them less popular than chemically-powered mortars. They are identical to the electromagnetic weapons described on p. C48, with the proviso that their HTSC drive units are vulnerable in the same ways as Gauss needlers (see p. 103).

Other Weapons and Equipment

Virtually all the TL8 equipment from *GURPS Cyberpunk* and *GURPS Ultra-Tech* is available on the Edge, but not all of it's on the market – or even easily available on the black market.

Weapon Accessories   pp. C46-47

All the weapons accessories from *GURPS Cyberpunk* are available as listed.

Melee Weapons   pp. C47-48

Durasteel is not at all common, and super-fine blades cost 50 times the *Basic Set* price for their low-tech equivalents. Stun wands are available as listed, but vibroblades exist only in R&D labs, so far.

Armor   pp. C49-50

Ablative and reflec armor are rare, due to the uncommon status of beam weapons. Ablative foam exists, but has never been released commercially. Base cost for an exoskeleton is $50,000, and weight is 75 pounds per point of ST up to ST 20, and 100 pounds per point thereafter.

Communications, Recording and Scientific Equipment   pp. C50-51

Light-intensifier contacts are not available (the power slugs are too big). The rest of these devices are available as listed.

Personal Vehicles

Detailed systems for designing personal vehicles can be found in *GURPS Vehicles*. The following automobiles are listed by engine type, top speed, the number of passengers they can carry (including the driver) and cost.

Cars on the Edge can be armed and armored, and often are. For a plethora of options for vehicular defense and firepower, see *GURPS Vehicles* or *GURPS Autoduel*.

DMW Mistral: Alcohol-burning engine, capacity 2, top speed 144 mph, cost: $9,500.

Honda-Renault Adagio: Electric power plant, capacity 4, top speed 50 mph, cost: $6,000.

NorthAm Motors Pursuit Vehicle, Mark II: Gasoline-burning engine, capacity 4, top speed 160, cost: $26,750 plus accessories. Equipped with front-firing twin Assault Chainguns, solid tires.

Tools   pp. C52-53

Tool Kits are available as listed in *GURPS Cyberpunk*, except that power slugs are *not* included in price and weight – they must be bought separately.

Security Systems, Police and Surveillance Equipment   pp. C53-55

All of the equipment listed in *GURPS Cyberpunk* is available as listed.

Medical Science, Cloning and Drugs   pp. C55-59

If anybody's managed to make a braintape yet, it's double-maximum-secret tech locked up in the deepest R&D lab of some Bolshie Ten korp, and ghostcomps are still the stuff of bad viddies.

Excellent individual body parts can be cloned for transplant purposes, but nobody's managed to clone a whole human being yet – not one with a functional brain, anyway.

All the drugs from *GURPS Cyberpunk* are available as listed.

Nanotools

A complete set of nanotools for installing cybernetic implants costs $15,000, plus an additional $1,000 for shipping if the buyer doesn't buy it in orbit and carry it down himself.

In zero-g a properly maintained set of nanotools will last indefinitely, but earthside they start to deteriorate after 3d+6 days, imposing a cumulative -1 to Surgery skill for each day of deterioration. A surgeon can recognize that his nano is going bad with a successful roll vs. Engineer (Nanotech) or Surgery/TL8-4.

Weapon Table

Civilian Weapons

Firearms (Pistols)

Weapon	Malf	Type	Damage	SS	Acc	½D	Max	Wt.	RoF	Shots	ST	Rcl	Cost	LR
MoskArm Sport-Pyat	crit	cr	1d	9	6	50	200	1	3	20	7	-1	$350	5
(5 × 200)	crit	cr	1d	12	8	125	800	1	3	20	7	-1	$500	5
S&W 9mm Urban Defender	ver	cr	2d	9	5	100	1,500	1.25	3	20	8	-1	$300	4
Glock 9mm Hotload	ver(crit)	cr	2d+2	9	5	100	1,500	1.25	3	20	8	-1	$400	4
Colt Warrior .44 Magnum	ver	cr	3d	13	4	200	2,100	3.5	3	6	13	-3	$450	4
Astrum Meteor 11mm Magnum	crit	cr	3d	12	4	250	2,500	3	3	10	12	-3	$600	4
MoskArms 9mm Russki-9	ver(crit)	cr	2d+1	10	5	120	1,500	2.25	3	20	8	-1	$450	4
SOG Strassen Schutz 9mm kurz	crit	cr	2d-1	9	4	50	200	2	3	20	7	-1	$250	4
Colt Classic 10mm	ver(crit)	cr	2d	11	4	175	1,720	3	3	15	9	-2	$400	4
SOG Feder 7mm	ver	cr	1d+1	9	3	30	180	1	3	7	9	-1	$200	4

Rifles and Shotguns

Weapon	Malf	Type	Damage	SS	Acc	½D	Max	Wt.	RoF	Shots	ST	Rcl	Cost	LR
Sauvage 7mm "Boucanier"	ver	cr	6d	14	11	1,100	5,200	11	3	10	12	-2	$500	4
MoskArm 12mm "Thunderbolt"	crit	cr	11d	16	7	1,500	5,500	15	3	5	16	-3	$750	4
Remington Model 60 12g	crit	cr	4d	13	6	25	150	10	3	5	12	-2	$250	4

Gauss Weapons

Weapon	Malf	Type	Damage	SS	Acc	½D	Max	Wt.	RoF	Shots	ST	Rcl	Cost	LR
NATArms Rapier (Pistol)	crit	imp	1d	11	4	75	250	4.75	3	100/B	—	0	$1000	4
NATArms Javelin (Rifle)	crit	imp	2d	15	11	400	800	7.75	3	100/B	—	0	$2,500	3

Military Weapons

Assault Weapons

Weapon	Malf	Type	Damage	SS	Acc	½D	Max	Wt.	RoF	Shots	ST	Rcl	Cost	LR
SOG G7 Carbine 5.5mm	ver	5d	11	12	500	3,800	6.5	10	40	8	10	-1	$550	1
FE-AC 7.7mm Carbine	ver	6d	12	12	500	3,700	7.25	10	30/30	9	10	-2	$1,000	1
FE-AR 7.7mm Rifle	ver(crit)	7d	14	14	1,050	4,700	8.25	10	30/30	10	10	-2	$4,500	1
NATArms M-23 5.5mm	ver	7d	13	13	900	4,400	7.5	10	30/30	10	11	-1	$4,250	1
MoskArm AK-107 7.7mm	ver(crit)	6d+1	14	14	1,000	4,500	8	10	30/30	11	10	-2	$4,000	1

Submachine Guns

Weapon	Malf	Type	Damage	SS	Acc	½D	Max	Wt.	RoF	Shots	ST	Rcl	Cost	LR
Ingram MAC-21 9mm	crit	cr	2d+1	9	5	160	1,800	3	10	30	9	-2	$500	1
MoskArm NovUzi 9mm	ver	cr	3d-1	10	6	180	1,900	4.5	10	30	9	-1	$700	1
NATArms M-19 10mm	ver	cr	3d	11	8	200	2,000	6	10	30	10	-2	$750	1

Technology

Sniper Rifles

Weapon	Malf	Type	Damage	SS	Acc	½D	Max	Wt.	RoF	Shots	ST	Rcl	Cost	LR
MoskArm SVD 7.7mm	ver(crit)	cr	7d	16	13	1,500	6,000	10	3	20	11	-2	$4,500	1
NATArms CW55 5.5mm	ver	cr	6d	14	12	1,100	5,200	6	3	10	10	-1	$3,750	1

Combat Shotguns

Weapon	Malf	Type	Damage	SS	Acc	½D	Max	Wt.	RoF	Shots	ST	Rcl	Cost	LR
Sawed-off Dbl. Barrel 10g	16	cr	5d	8	4	15	100	9	2	2	13	-4	$500	0
S&W Thor 12g	crit	cr	4d	8	5	25	150	8	3	7+1	12	-2	$525	2
NATArms UCW 10g	ver	cr	5d	11	7	50	200	10	3	10+1	13	-2	$650	1
FE ACAW 10g	ver	cr	5d	10	7	50	200	12	5	10/10	13	-2	$1,200	1

Gauss Weapons

Weapon	Malf	Type	Damage	SS	Acc	½D	Max	Wt.	RoF	Shots	ST	Rcl	Cost	LR
NATArms Spike (Pistol)	crit	imp	1d+2	10	4	100	300	5.5	10	100/B	–	0	$2,000	2
NATArms Lance (Rifle)	crit	imp	2d+1	14	11	500	1,000	9	20	100/B	–	0	$2,500	1
MoskArm "Wasp"	ver	imp	2d	13	10	450	1,100	8	20	100/B	–	0	$3,500	1

Laser Weapons

Weapon	Malf	Type	Damage	SS	Acc	½D	Max	Wt.	RoF	Shots	ST	Rcl	Cost	LR
FE Hellwaffen														
L-10 (pistol)	crit	imp	1d	9	8	300	800	3.5	3	10/C	–	0	$10,000	0
L-20 (rifle)	crit	imp	1d+2	15	13	450	1,800	10	5	120/D	–	0	$12,500	0
NATArms Sunbeam														
PL-5 (pistol)	ver	imp	2d	9	8	300	900	3	5	12/C	–	0	$13,000	0
RL-5 (rifle)	ver	imp	2d	15	14	500	2,100	9	8	140/D	–	0	$14,500	0
Koroshi Laser Personal Arm	ver	imp	1d+2	12	15	250	600	7	8	200/D	–	0	$10,500	0

Gyroc Weapons

Weapon	Malf	Type	Damage	SS	Acc	½D	Max	Wt.	RoF	Shots	ST	Rcl	Cost	LR
FE Rakete-P (pistol)	ver	var	var	12	5	1,800	2,500	4	3	3/3/3	–	0	$800	1
FE Rakete-K (carbine)	ver	var	var	15	7	1,800	2,500	9	10	10/10/10	–	0	$1,500	1
FE Rakete-W (ARL)	ver	var	var	16	9	1,800	2,500	20	10	20/20/20	12T/H	0	$3,000	0
Street launch pistol	16	var	var	13	4	700	1,500	6	3	3/3/3	–	0	$500	0

Assault Chaingun

Weapon	Malf	Type	Damage	SS	Acc	½D	Max	Wt.	RoF	Shots	ST	Rcl	Cost	LR
FE KMG 5.5mm	ver	cr	5d+1	16	8	500	3,600	43.5	30	100	17	-1	$8,500	0

Flame Weapons

Weapon	Malf	Damage	SS	Acc	Max	Wt.	RoF	Shots	ST	Rcl	Cost	LR
Koroshi Honopistoru	crit	5d/sec.	12	5	60	28	1	10	–	-2	$500	0
NATArms Blazer	crit	5d/sec.	13	5	80	30	1	10	–	-3	$550	0

Grenade Launchers

Weapon	Malf	Type	Damage	SS	Acc	½D	Max	Wt.	RoF	Shots	ST	Rcl	Cost	LR
FE PEMG-P	crit	spec	spec	10	8	–	750	12	1	5	–	0	$1,000	1
FE PEMG-G	crit	spec	spec	12	8	–	2,000	55	1	5	13T		$1,550	0
NATArms MML-20	ver	spec	spec	9	9	–	800	7	2	5	–	0	$1,250	1
NATArms MGL-40	crit	spec	spec	12	8	–	1,000	10	1	3	–	0	$1,000	0
NATArms EMGL-40	crit	spec	spec	10	8	–	750	12	1	5	–	0	$1,000	1
NATArms EMPGL-80	crit	spec	spec	–	–	–	4,000	70	1	10	14T	0	$4,500	0
NATArms EMPM-120	crit	spec	spec	–	–	–	6,000	105	1	5	15T	0	$4,500	0

Technology

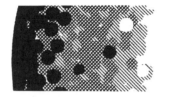

THE NET ON THE EDGE

8

Earth's information technology has been running with all indicators redlined since the 1960s. Computers and data processing are approaching mature TL8 in the one-and-twenty.

The zero-gravity orbital nanofactories grind out the gigabyte RAM chips that give computers their power. Laser disk-reading systems allow data transfer at incredible speeds. Optical transmission systems make megabaud bandwidths available.

The information weapons born during the Data Wars (see p. 121) gave the world neural interfaces, combat software and the potentially lethal security software known as ice. True cyberdecks are still a rarity, and the netrunners who can use them are the most powerful data-commandos in the world. This makes them much sought after, both by groups that want to hire them and the agents of people who want to capture or kill them.

Computers

Computers are everywhere in the one-and-twenty. Microchips run wristcomps; terabyte RAM units from the nanoshops of the orbital factories power the megacomputers. Computers keep records, handle funds, and control cars, power plants, kitchens, factories, washing machines and cities.

Thousands of companies make computers in 2043. All but a few of these companies are "cloners." They make copies, "clones," of machines designed by one of the major computer korps. Most computer clones are legal. Their makers are licensed by the korp that holds the patents on the design being copied. Pirate clones are common, but their makers run a significant risk in a world where the keiretsu have been known to dispatch armed agents to deal with copyright infringements.

Of course, when a pirate cloner is another megakorp, the battle is settled with lawyers and writs, rather than cyberninja. Usually.

Personal Computers

There are three basic designs of personal computer available, though there are dozens of variations on the basic configurations. Each basic system design is proprietary to one of three computer korps: EGM, NATComp, and Novy Rasvet. All three have licensed their designs widely, and there are hundreds of clones on the market.

Typical personal computers are Complexity 2 systems (see *Hardware,* p. C62). Top-of-the-line models are Complexity 3. Unenhanced models can run two programs of their Complexity at one time. Systems with improved multitasking CPUs can run three such programs at once.

Standard models are equipped with a 10-gigabyte CD drive (see sidebar, p. 113). All personal computers will have the necessary connections to attach peripherals such as printers and modems (see *Computer Peripherals,* p. 116).

Almost all personal computers are equipped with a scrollout video display: a flexible, plastic sheet laminated with a fiber-circuitry LCD matrix, that can be rolled up like stiff paper. When not in use, the screen rolls up inside the computer casing. Similarly, a keyboard is a laminated, pressure-sensitive membrane on a base that folds out from a compact package into something that a

Talkin' One-and-Twenty

decker: A hacker equipped with a neural interface and a cyberdeck.

smyertniki: Killers. Specifically refers to Net assassins for korps and government agencies, assigned to take out illicit netrunners.

virgonomic: Contraction of "virtual ergonomics." Any control system that creates a virtual environment, without using neural interfacing, to allow the user to access a computer without using analog controls.

human being can type on comfortably. Cases are lightweight, high-strength plastics. Standard models fold down to a package 24" by 8" by 3" and weigh about 3 pounds. Pocket models can be folded down to 6" by 4" by 2" and weigh a pound, or less.

Lower-priced computers have only an "analog" control interface system. This will include a keyboard, some kind of pointer system (a mouse, light pen, touch-sensitive screen or trackball) and voice-input capability.

State-of-the-art personal computers come equipped with a virgonomic interface, and the peripherals to create at least a virtual equivalent of the analog control systems: virtual keyboards, "point-and-snap" Virtual User Interface displays. Any personal computer that is virgonomics-capable can support a full hot rig or other high-level virgonomic controller (see *Virgonomics,* p. 119).

Personal computers are smaller by 33% in all dimensions, and weigh 1 pound less (minimum weight ½ pound) if the personal computer is "All-V," all virgonomic. All-V units have *no* keyboards, screens or other bulky devices. Just chips, diskette drives, and a virgonomic plug for the wizzies and the v-gloves. All-V systems are $100 cheaper than systems with analog controls.

All personal computers can function for one year with a B power cell, or can be operated on standard household current.

Popular Personal Computers

Clones of all these models are widely available all over the world. Prices, statistics and a summary of features are shown on the Computer Price Table (pp. 123-124).

EGM Roi Series: With the Roi (King) series, EGM gambled on increasing marketability for ROM deck programs and virgonomics. Thus, all Roi computers have the expanded ROM slot option, with a number of slots equal to twice the computer's Complexity and a virgonomic interface controller. They also have dual CD drives for enhanced data storage. All computers in the Roi series weigh 4 pounds.

The Roi 10 (Henri) is the basic system. At Complexity 2, with 4 ROM slots, it costs $3,000.

Major Computer Korps

Europaischen Gesellschaft Maschinen: EGM. Formed by a consortium of distressed European computer firms in the 2010s, EGM has become a major player in minicomputers. They have a decent share of the massive microcomputer market and offer several impressive mainframe systems.

NAT Computer Industries: NATComp, the computer systems subsidiary of North American Technology. Given favorable government regulations, lucrative ProGov contracts and similar inducements, NATComp is the dominant data processing supplier in the U.S.

Nippon Data Company: NiDaCo. A subsidiary of Shinowara Integrated Industries. The premiere computer development firm in Japan, NiDaCo is a key player in the mini- and mainframe computer market. Their clones of EGM microcomputers are popular throughout Asia and also sell well in the West, especially in South America.

Novy Rasvet: Novy-R, or just NR. The phrase means "New Dawn." A subsidiary of the Russo-Japanese giant, Korsakov-Shimadzu, Novy-R makes everything from pocket microcomputers to super-mainframes.

Todai-Rhee-Khmong Information Systems: TRK is a subsidiary of Todai Technosystems. Called the "King of the Clones," the firm is based in Korea, in the heart of the Seoul-Pyongyang sprawl's feverishly active financial district. TKR produces licensed clones of the most popular microcomputer designs on the market.

The Net on the Edge

Megacomputers

There are projects underway which are trying to make the breakthrough into megacomputer technology. None of these projects has published any substantive details of their progress to date.

Novy Rasvet completed construction of their "Yeltsin" prototype in 2042. This design was commissioned by the Russian government, which seeks a super-advanced computer system capable of coordinating the thousands of automated systems that keep the Moskva metroplex functioning.

Rumor suggests that NATComp has a model in the prototype stages as well, at their ultra-high-security R&D facility in San Jose. Such a project would tie in with NATComp's contract to upgrade the National Data Banks' processing power by an order of magnitude by 2050.

In the most ironic turn of events, developers working on Shinowara's top-secret Memnon-12 vatbrain project (see sidebars, pp. 92-93) have not only developed a megacomputer prototype, they have birthed a self-aware AI and don't even know it yet.

Megacomputers are described on p. C63. The GM should feel free to make these experimental systems as large as he wants, subject to cranky power requirements, dependent on esoteric tech from the orbital factories. Operating systems and programs will be equally new-tech. Characters trying to hack into a megacomputer, whether through terminals or cyberdecks, will be in unfamiliar territory, where anything can happen.

The Roi 20 (Charles) has an extended multitasking processor, capable of running three Complexity 2 programs at once, instead of the usual two. It costs $3,500.

The Roi 30 (Louis) is EGM's top-of-the-line personal computer. A Complexity 3 system with 6 ROM slots and extended multitasking, it costs $12,000.

All EGM personal systems and clones run the OS-2100 operating system.

NATComp personal computers: NATComp makes a wide range of personal computers based on the GigaChip 7000 and its more powerful descendants, the 70000 and 72000 series. All NATComp personal computers and their clones are designed to run the proprietary NAT VANIX operating system.

The PC7000 is an older design, a desktop unit weighing 30 pounds, measuring 30" by 24" by 8". It's a cheap, reliable Complexity 1 system, with analog controls, a single 10-gig CD drive, and one ROM slot. The PC7200 is a Complexity 2 version in the same desktop configuration. The PC7000 costs $100. The PC7200 costs $400.

The PC70000 is a portable version of the 7000. It has the same features, but comes in the standard 3-pound configuration, at a cost of $200. The PC72-010 is the portable version of the 7200, and costs $900.

The APC72-020 is a generic TL8 personal computer. Complexity 2, with dual CD drives and two ROM slots, it weighs 4 pounds and costs $1,500.

NATComp's cutting-edge personal systems are in the XPC series. All XPCs are Complexity 3, with analog and virgonomic interfaces and with dual CD drives. The XPC72-100 is the basic model. It weighs 4 pounds and costs $8,500. The XPC72-200 has 6 ROM slots and multitasking that can run up to three Complexity 3 programs at a time. It costs $15,500.

Novy Rasvet Romanov Series: These popular systems from Novy-R are found all over Europe and the Middle East, with significant market share in South America as well. Korsakov-Shimadzu, Novy Rasvet's parent korp, has issued numerous licenses to clone the Romanov series. All of them run the K-S/COS operating system.

The Tsarevitch is the world's most popular pocket-sized computer. It is a standard Complexity 2 system with a single CD drive and analog controls. It weighs barely one pound, and when folded down can slip into a coat pocket. The Tsarevitch costs $2,000.

The Tsarevitch-V is Novy-R's new entry on the pocketcomp market. It is an All-V model, with the same features as the original Tsarevitch. It measures 4" by 3½" by 1" and weighs half a pound. The Tsarevitch-V costs $2,900.

The Tsarina is a standard Complexity 2 personal computer with dual CD drives and analog and virgonomic controls. It weighs 4 pounds and costs $2,500.

The Tsar adds doubled ROM slots and extended CPU multitasking to the Tsarina's design, and costs $3,500.

The Grand Duke is a desktop version of the Tsar. It weighs 30 pounds and measures 24" wide by 30" long by 8" high, not counting the flip-up SLCD screen, which is a rigid plate. It costs $3,000. Price makes the Grand Duke a popular unit in homes and offices, where mobility is not an issue.

Minicomputers

Standard minicomputers have a Complexity of 3, but more powerful units are available at Complexity 4. They weigh about 60 pounds and occupy 1 cubic yard. Expensive, "luggable" systems like the NATComp MiniCOM200 are designed to be somewhat portable.

Minicomputers have the same control-interface options as personal computers and a virgonomic controller is standard on most models. They typically have two 10-gig CD drives for data storage.

Minicomputers can operate for 6 months on a C cell, or indefinitely on household current.

Popular Minicomputers

The two leaders in minicomputer design are EGM and NATComp. Other minicomputer manufacturers license their clones from one of these two firms.

EGM Pharaon Series: The Pharaon (Pharoah) series is designed to run EGM OS-21000, an extended version of their personal computer operating system.

The Pharaon 100, marketed under the name "Ramses," is a Complexity 3 business system, with analog and virgonomic controls and four CD drives. It costs $16,000.

The Pharaon 120 (Cheops) is designed for high-volume business or scientific applications. Its revolutionary CPU architecture delivers Complexity 4 power, with 8 ROM-deck slots. Power users often add a VLD storage system (see sidebar) to a Cheops to get an inexpensive microframe equivalent. Cheops costs $158,000.

NATComp Minicomputers: NATComp's minis are found in many upper-income homes and small businesses. NATComp minicomputers and their clones run the same VANIX operating system as NATComp's personal systems.

All NATComp minicomputers are Complexity 3 systems, though there are rumors that the korp produces Complexity 4 configurations under government contracts.

The NATComp MasterCOM 2000 is a low-end minicomputer, popular for home and small business applications. It is a Complexity 3 unit, with dual 10-gig CD drives and analog-only controls. It weighs 600 pounds and occupies 6 cy. The MasterCOM 2000 costs $6,500.

Its smarter kid brother, the top-of-the-line UltraCOM 2050, competes head to head with the EGM Ramses. It has analog and virgonomic interfaces, a banked set of 4 CD drives and 6 ROM slots. It uses terabyte RAM architecture (reducing space requirements significantly over the older MasterCOM), weighs 62 pounds and occupies 1 cy. It costs $23,500.

Mass Storage

Mass storage is the system a computer uses to store data permanently. The original mass storage systems in the mid-20th century were reels of magnetic tape. These are augmented by disk drives, both large platters of disks for mainframes and "floppy" disks, later hard drives, on smaller systems. Modern computers use two mass storage systems.

Compact Diskettes: Personal computers and minicomputers use a 3" compact diskette (CD) system. A CD holds 10 gigabytes, or *gig,* of data. A gigabyte is one *billion* bytes. A blank CD costs $5 and weighs 1/10 pound.

Copying a gigabyte of data from one diskette drive on a computer to another takes one minute. Copying a full diskette would take 10 minutes. On a PC with a single drive, the computer copies the data a little bit at a time, and the operator has to keep removing one diskette and swapping it with the other. This is a tedious process. It takes 1000 seconds divided by the Complexity of the computer to copy a gigabyte. A Complexity 2 computer would need 5000 seconds, almost an hour and a half, to copy a full 10 gig from one diskette to another using this method.

A CD drive, the unit in the computer that lets the system read the diskettes, weighs 1 pound and costs $500. The transport mechanism for the drive (in a separate case) is 4" square and 1" thick.

All personal and microcomputers come with one or more built-in CD drives. The weight and cost of any built-in drives are included in the system's list price. Add-on drives require a controller: add 10% to the price of the system to double its drive capacity.

Virtual Laser Drives: A VLD is actually a dedicated microcomputer in its own right, combining high-density diskettes (20 gig capacity), parallel I/O laser readers, and virtual storage chips (chips that act like a disk drive). Data is moved from the diskettes to the virtual storage systems as needed, eliminating contention for disk access when multiple users are accessing the system.

Data can be copied from a VLD to a VLD at a rate of 20 seconds per gigabyte. If copying data to or from a compact diskette, the lower, CD rate of transfer is used.

VLDs come in 500-gig and 1-terabyte (1,000 gigabytes, or one *trillion* bytes) configurations. They weigh 500 lbs. and occupy 1 cy. each. A 500-gig model costs $7,500, a 1-terabyte model $10,000. These costs are included in the price of units that use VLD storage. Expansion units can simply be hooked up to the processor as needed.

NATComp's MiniCOM 200 is a portable minicomputer, with dual CD drives and analog and virgonomic interfaces, weighing 30 pounds and measuring 2" by 12" by 20". It costs $30,000.

Data Requirements

All values are in gigabytes.

Audio, average quality, one hour . . . . ½ (500 Mb)

Audio, ultra-fidelity, one hour 1

Blueprints/schematics:
   Extremely Complex (e.g., space shuttle) 100
   Very Complex (e.g., jet fighter) 10
   Complex (e.g., airplane, APC) 1
   Simple (e.g., automobile, computer) . . . . ⅒ (100 Mb)
   Very Simple (e.g., appliances, radio) . . . . ¹⁄₁₀₀ (1 Mb)

Books, one shelf full (6' long) 1

Textbook (college level) . . . . ¾,₀₀₀ (750 Kb)

Encyclopedia . . . . ¹⁄₂₀ (20 Mb)

War and Peace . . . . ¹⁄₅₀₀ (2 Mb)

Dossier, complete personal file . . . . ¹⁄₁₀₀ (10 Mb)

Financial records (one year):
   Small Business . . . . ⅒ (100 Mb)
   Medium Business 1
   Large Business, per $100 million earnings 5

Genetic map of one human 2

History of Earth, survey 1

History of Earth, detailed (20-year period) 1

Imaging, one color photograph . . . . ¹⁄₂₀,₀₀₀ (50 Kb)

Language, one (dictionary, grammar, etc.) 1

Memo, one page . . . . ¹⁄₄₀₀,₀₀₀ (2.5 Kb)

Novel, paperback . . . . ¹⁄₂,₀₀₀ (500 Kb)

Programs:
   Complexity 1 . . . . ¹⁄₁₀₀ (10 Mb)
   Complexity 2 . . . . ⅒ (100 Mb)
   Complexity 3 1
   Complexity 4 10
   Complexity 5 100

Technical library, one science (college level) 5

Technical library, one science (R&D level) 8

Technical manuals for one device:
   Extremely Complex (e.g., space shuttle) 1
   Very Complex (e.g., jet fighter) . . . . ⅒ (100 Mb)
   Complex (e.g., airplane, APC) . . . . ¹⁄₁₀₀ (10 Mb)
   Simple (e.g., automobile, computer) . . . . ¹⁄₁,₀₀₀ (1 Mb)
   Very Simple (e.g., appliances, radio) . . . . ¹⁄₁₀,₀₀₀ (1 Mb)

Video, hi-res, 10 minutes 1

Microframes

Bridging the gap between the personal and minicomputer systems and the "big iron" of the mainframes are microframe computers. These are Complexity 4 systems, designed for access by multiple users. There are no commercial microframes at Complexity 5; diminishing returns do not make it cost-effective to try to cram that much processing power into a microframe configuration.

The basic microframe comes with a keyboard/mouse console built in. Microframes use VLD storage rather than CD drives, and the basic system configuration is for 500 gigabytes of protected memory.

Microframes weigh 400 pounds, and occupy 4 cy. The weight and volume for the VLD is added to this, so a typical system weighs 900 lbs. and occupies 5 cy.

A baseline microframe costs $40,000. Each additional workstation port or communications line adds a $2,000 surcharge to the unit's price.

Microframes can run for six months off an E cell. They are more typically connected to a heavy-duty AC power line with the power cell as a backup in case electrical service is interrupted. The electric bill for running a microframe is $200 a month.

Popular Microframes

The key firms in microframe design are EGM, NATComp, Nippon Data Company (NiDaCo), and Novy Rasvet.

EGM Kaiser 300 (Wilhelm): Equipped with a 500-gig VLD, the Complexity 4 "Kaiser Bill" has extended multitasking under EGM's MOS-21000/X operating system that lets it run three Complexity 4 programs instead of the usual two. It costs $60,000.

NATComp MDPS-90: The MDPS-90 is, not surprisingly, the principal microframe system used by the U.S. government. It is a solid, Complexity 4 workhorse of a system, equipped with an integral 1-terabyte VLD storage system. It runs the NATComp VANIX/M operating system. The MDPS-90 costs $42,500.

NiDaCo ARC500: The ARC500 is designed for flexibility of operation, and to that end has an extended ROM-deck access chassis, permitting 8 decks instead of 4, as well as a 500-gig VLD storage system. The ARC series runs under NiDaCo's VLS/VCS operating system. Cost is $60,000.

Novy-R Rachmaninov: The Rachmaninov is the king of the microframes. It has 1 terabyte of mass storage in its basic configuration, provides for 8 ROM slots, and has an extended multitasking capacity. Rachmaninov runs the GSOS operating system. It costs $82,500.

Mainframes

These are usually where the action is for matrix marauders. Financial accounts, high security records and marketable korporate secrets all tend to live on mainframes, hiding behind security software just bristling with digital teeth and claws.

Mainframes are Complexity 5 computers. A basic system costs $200,000. It includes a keyboard/mouse console for use by the system operators. Additional workstation or commline ports cost $1,000 each. Mainframes can connect to scores of auxiliary printers, subordinate microframes and minicomputers, sensors, process controllers and other devices.

Mainframes are bulky monsters. The processor weighs 600 pounds and occupies 6 cy. The weight and volume requirements of the VLD storage units are added, so a typical configuration weighs 1,100 pounds and occupies 7 cy.

The computer requires industrial current to operate: a heavy power line, or a direct connection to a power plant or generator. The site preparation for this hookup costs $5,000, above and beyond the cost of the processor. The electric bill for running a mainframe is $1,500 a month.

Unless its owners are running on a shoestring budget, a mainframe will have a bank of 50 E slugs as an emergency power supply. The computer can run for one week on such a bank.

Commercial Mainframes

The mainframe market is dominated by the same four companies that lead in microframes. Mainframes also run the same operating systems as microframes. For example, NiDaCo microframes and mainframes both run VLS/VCS.

EGM Empereur 600 (Napoleon): The Napoleon provides an integral 1-terabyte VLD and extended ROM-deck capacity, allowing ten decks instead of five. It costs $302,500.

NATComp DPC-100: This system, the DPC-90's big brother, has improved multitasking capacity and runs three Complexity 5 programs at one time instead of two. It is the mainstay of the U.S. government's large computer systems, including the National Data Banks. The DPC-100 costs $300,000.

NiDaCo ARC5000: The ARC series mainframe, the 5000, is designed to accommodate large-volume database applications, with a built-in 2-terabyte VLD. It weighs 1,600 pounds, occupies 8 cy. and costs $212,500.

Novy-R Moussorgsky: The Moussorgsky is arguably the most powerful mainframe on the market, with 1-terabyte integral VLD file storage, doubled ROM slots and extended CPU capacity allowing it to run three Complexity 5 programs at a time. Cost is $402,500.

Supermainframes

Supermainframes are the big number-crunchers of the data processing world. Exceptionally fast, with enormous memory capability, they are usually designed to custom specifications for particular tasks, though some production models are now on the market.

These are Complexity 6 computers. The CPU and main peripherals, included with the processor, weigh one ton and take up 20 cy. The 1-terabyte VLD that is standard on supermainframes adds 500 pounds and 1 cy. for a final weight of 2,500 lbs. and a volume of 21 cy. A basic unit costs $2 million. Each additional workstation connection or comm port costs $1,000.

Supermainframes require precisely conditioned industrial current. The power feed to the site costs $100,000 to install and the electric bill averages $20,000 a month.

Supermainframes depend on HTSC technology, and are subject to the vulnerabilities described on p. 94.

(see p. 118)

Data Transfer Rates

A typical system can transfer data from one disk address to another at a rate of 1 gigabyte per minute on a CD drive, or 3 gigabytes per minute if using VLDs.

Downloading or uploading data is considerably slower. A typical modem in 2043 operates in the 10-megabaud range. That's a line speed of one million bytes per second! It's hard to think of that as slow, but that means it takes 1,000 seconds, about 20 minutes, to send or receive 1 gigabyte. Of course, a fiddling little 10-megabyte file, like an individual's personal dossier, suitably edited, would take only 10 seconds to upload. And an incriminating memo, 2 Kb or so, could be sucked out of the Net in a fraction of a second.

If the Compression program is available, it speeds up both copying and downloads/uploads (see p. 118), by reducing the size of the data to be transmitted.

The Net on the Edge

Operating Systems

This sidebar, and the one on the opposite page, list several of the standard operating systems for the various brands of computer. They are broken down by size and manufacturer.

Operating systems can make netrunning more complex than gamers care to get. If this is not the Game Master's cup of cha, then he can ignore the issue, or assume that all cyberdecks are capable of generating code that runs on different operating systems, and keep the different system names as a touch of campaign color.

Personal Computer Operating Systems

EGM OS-2100: The standard opsys for EGM personal computers and their clones.

K-S/COS: The standard opsys for Novy-R personal computers and their clones.

NAT VANIX: The standard opsys for NATComp personal computers and their clones.

Minicomputer Operating Systems

EGM OS-21000: An expanded version of the korp's personal computing opsys, OS-21000 is not as successful as VANIX in bridging the gap between systems. Numerous minicomputer software firms have produced versions of VANIX that run on EGM platforms, and as a result OS-21000 has only a 30% market share.

NAT VANIX: The same operating system used in NATComp personal computers also operates on their minis. This level of portability is one of the many reasons NATComp machines and their clones are so highly regarded by customers. About 70% of the world's minicomputers run VANIX.

Continued on next page . . .

Commercial Supermainframes

NATComp and Novy Rasvet are the only two firms offering supermainframe systems commercially. They have not licensed their designs to any other manufacturers at this time. Both firms produce a "generic" configuration, as well as the enhanced models described below.

NATComp XDPC-1000: NAT has added extended multitasking capacity to this model, making it capable of executing three Complexity 6 programs simultaneously. It sells for $3 million. The XDPC-1000 runs VANIX/XM, an enhanced version of NAT's VANIX/M operating system.

Novy-R Tschaikowski: Considered the most powerful commercial computer system in the world, Tschaikowski provides 12 ROM-deck slots as well as extended multitasking similar to the XDPC-1000. Cost is $4 million.

Peripherals

Peripherals are things like printers, FAX units, scanners, auxiliary displays, special sensors, modems and other devices that the computer uses to do its job. Expansion chips are dirt-cheap and standardized, so computers can have a relatively unlimited number of peripherals attached. Controller cards, expansion plugs and other necessities are included in the price of the peripheral.

Modems

There are two types of modems in use for personal and minicomputers.

Low-speed modems: "Slow-dems" in hacker parlance. These devices are the same old digital-analog converters that have been in use for almost a century. They communicate at speeds ranging from 50 to 100 kilobaud (5,000 to 10,000 bytes per second). They are useful for handling electronic mail and for accessing commercial computing systems and public databases, but are far too slow for netrunning. A low-speed modem comes on a chip-card designed to plug directly into the computer that uses it. All personal and minicomputers can be bought with a built-in slow-dem for an additional $25. An external slow-dem comes in a casing 2" on a side that plugs straight into the computer. It costs $40.

All slow-dems are equipped with standard connectors that allow them to connect to telephone circuits.

Megamodems: Megamodems are direct digital-optic telecommunication devices. Megamodems communicate at 10 megabaud: 1 million bytes per second! Anyone who is going to do any hacking (other than signing on to a system under a false ID) must use a megamodem. Any significant amount of data transfer has to be over a megamodem as well. See *Data Transfer Rates,* p. 115.

Like slow-dems, a megamodem can be built into a computer or used in an external case. An internal megamodem costs $1,500. An external unit costs $3,500.

Printers

There are hundreds of printers on the market, all based on laser-printing technology. They range from the compact models in use on millions of personal computers, to the massive page-zappers used in bulk printing operations.

All printers need maintenance, reloading with toners and dyes, and other care. If the GM wants to make an issue of this, the cost of standard maintenance is 1% of the purchase price of the machine. Printers need maintenance after they have gone through 10 full loads of paper. For example, a typical personal laser printer with a 100-page magazine needs maintenance after it has printed 1,000 pages. An extended-magazine printer, holding 500 sheets, needs maintenance after it prints 5,000 sheets, and so on. Alternately, the GM can just assess maintenance costs every month.

The Net on the Edge

Personal Laser Printer: A standard model costs $500, weighs 5 pounds when loaded with paper and measures 10" by 12" by 6". It holds 100 sheets of paper and can print out one page of text (2500 bytes) in 2 seconds or a high-resolution black-and-white graphic, the equivalent of a clear photograph, in 5 seconds.

Ultra-resolution color printers are similar in size and performance, but cost $1,500.

Larger printers, holding up to 500 pages, are 24" thick and weigh 30 pounds, but are otherwise the same as smaller models. They cost $750 for a black-and-white model or $2,250 for color.

Recycling printers allow the printer to re-use a page that already has printing on it. Laser bleaching and a small amount of dye clean the old text off the paper.

Blank paper, by the way, costs $10 for 500 sheets.

High-speed Laser Printers: These come in the same configurations as personal printers, but can print two pages of text per second, or one page of graphics per second. Costs for high-speed printers are doubled.

Page-zappers: Small page-zappers are approximately 6' long, 4' wide and 4' high. They collate the pages into various configurations and print 16 at a time at one second per set of 16 pages. The standard model holds 4,000 sheets and weighs 650 pounds. It costs $2,500.

The industrial model comes with a magazine holding a roll of paper equal to 40,000 sheets. Sheets are cut and collated as the pages are printed. It occupies 3 cy, weighs 1,200 pounds and costs $12,500. Paper rolls cost $500.

Print Scanners

Scanners read text documents into graphics files which can be translated into text or simply stored as a "snapshot" of the document. The scanner interface is a Complexity 1 program that must be running at the time the scanner is used.

Pocket scanners, 4" wide, 3" high, 2" thick, weigh 1 pound. It takes two passes to scan a standard page and a pass of the scanner takes one second. They cost $500.

Operating Systems (Continued)
Microframe/Mainframe Operating Systems

EGM MOS-21000/X: This system allows easy (though not automatic) portability of programs from OS-2100 and OS-21000. The converse is rarely true, since programs written under MOS-21000/X require resources that are not available on minis and PCs. EGM's large share of the "big iron" market (35%) almost exclusively runs MOS-21000/X.

NATComp VANIX/M: VANIX/M is fairly new. Its first commercial release was in 2036. It has sold sluggishly, if only because of the large installed user-base running other mainframe software. Fifteen percent of the world's mainframes are running VANIX/M. It is the opsys used in all U.S. government computers, including the network of systems that forms the National Data Banks.

NiDaCo VLS/VCS: "Very Large System/Virtual Control System." Sometimes this tech jargon is pure poetry, isn't it? VLS/VCS is very popular with business and government systems that process among minicomputers and larger systems. Of the world's mainframes, 22% run this opsys.

Novy Rasvet GSOS: GSOS has no market play outside of Novy-R's mainframes and clones of those systems. It is designed to maximize the efficiency of large systems, and in fact was originally designed as the basic opsys architecture for Novy-R's ultra-powerful Tschaikowski supermainframe. GSOS's sheer potential in processing power has given it a 28% market share.

The Net on the Edge

New Attack and Defense Programs

Cross-System   **No Default**
Instruction Translators

As noted under *Decking and Operating Systems*, p. 119, an attack/defense program must be programmed for the operating system of the computer the decker is invading. If it is not, the attack/defense program cannot run on that computer.

One translator can convert the output of any other attack, defense or ice programs generated on the same cyberdeck, whether they are running in memory or have been programmed on the fly by the decker. However, programs running through a translator suffer a loss of speed. Add 100 milliseconds to the Command Phase.

Translators are Complexity 2 programs and cost $2,000.

Compression   **No Default**

Compression is used to reduce the effective size of a data file, and thus the time required to copy or download it. Success compresses the data by a factor of 10. A Complexity 2 program would shrink from $\frac{1}{10}$ gigabytes to $\frac{1}{100}$ gig. A 20-gig database would be compressed to 2 gig.

Execution Time for Compression is 1 per gigabyte. Complexity is 2. Increasing Complexity by 1 doubles the capacity of Compression. A Complexity 3 version of the program could compress 2 gig in a Command Phase. A Complexity 4 version could compress 4 gig in a Phase.

Compressed files must be decompressed before they can be used. This is also done with Compression, at the same speeds and capacity used to compress the file.

Compression costs $500 at Complexity 2. Add $1,000 per point of additional Complexity.

Decoy   **Defaults to Computer Hacking-6**

Decoy creates a false program signature, matching the decker's own, but with a false trail which will confuse a Trace. It differs from Misdirection (p. C90) in that it leads to a preprogrammed Net address, and the Trace program will think it has backtracked the decker to that address. Decoy can also be programmed to make one hop in any direction, presumably in a direction different than the one the decker is really going.

If Bloodhound (p. C89) is used, treat this the same as Misdirection.

Continued on next page . . .

Page scanners are 12" wide and take a single pass to scan a standard page. They can fold down to pocket-size when not in use. They weigh 2 pounds and cost $750.

Desktop scanners can scan full pages, and if sheets are fed into them, they can scan 2 pages per second. They are 16" by 10" by 3", weigh 5 pounds, and cost $200.

Combined scanner-printer hookups have replaced copying machines and FAX machines. The added advantage is that a document can be scanned at one site and printed out at a printer somewhere else, either on the same system or via a modem connection. FAX-type transmissions can also be made in stages, with a document scanned into the system, shipped as a graphics file to another computer, and held there in storage until it is convenient for the recipient to print it out. Documents can also be stored on a datachip or CD and filed for later retrieval.

Given the ability of computers to store signature files (heavily passworded, of course) or to accept timestamped signatures via light pens or similar interfaces, many legal documents are stored in the Net permanently and never surface in hardcopy, except for ceremonial purposes (treaties, government bills, major contracts). The courts have long accepted the validity of properly secured computer files as evidence, and hardcopy records are not required in firstworld cases. Lastworld jurisdictions often require hardcopy documents, however, and korps operating in those countries still have extensive paper files, as hard as that is to believe.

Sensors

Hundreds of different sensors can be connected to a computer or workstation. Typically, most of the sensors or communications equipment from chapter 3 of *GURPS Cyberpunk* can be configured as computer sensors for a 50% increase in cost. Peripheral sensors *cannot* be used manually. That is, if a computer has a Long-Range Communicator connected as a peripheral, a human cannot grab the communicator and use it to send a message. But he could program the computer to send a message for him (with Computer Operation, Computer Programming or Computer Hacking skill).

Each sensor connected to a computer requires a control program, which must be running in order for the computer to use the sensor. The name of the required control program for each sensor is given in parentheses, along with the page where it is described. The number of sensors that a single copy of the control program can operate simultaneously depends on the Complexity of the computer, not the Complexity of the program. A Complexity 1 system can operate a single sensor. A Complexity 2 system can operate 10 sensors, a Complexity 3 system, 100 and so on. For example, an E-Lock program running on a Complexity 5 microframe could simultaneously manage 10,000 electronic locks, even though E-Lock is a Complexity 2 program.

Software

An operating system, or *opsys,* is the central program that makes a computer work. Other programs must be designed to run properly under a specific operating system, and will not run on a computer using another opsys.

Demands for connectivity and portability pressure computer firms toward a single standard of operation and program portability. Equally powerful technological issues militate against this, as advances in hardware capability render older software inefficient. Competition in the marketplace also plays a role, as each design company trots out its new opsys as *the one,* the system that every computer will be running in the future.

So 40 years into the one-and-twenty, there are still different operating systems for different computer platforms, each claiming to be *the one.*

Shells

A program that can run under one operating system cannot run under any other operating system, unless the other system is running an emulator. This is a program that "pretends" to be a different opsys. For example, if you want to run a program from your EGM personal computer on your buddy's Novy-R machine, you need a shell. EGM machines run OS/2100, whereas Novy Rasvet PCs run under Korsakov-Shimadzu COS. So you have to execute an OS-2100 shell on your K-S/COS computer, then run the program inside that shell.

The program, the shell and the operating system all have to play together. There are lots of things that can go wrong. The shell might fail to properly emulate the operating system that the program requires, or it might pass bad instructions to the opsys. The program might be "ill-behaved," and bypass the operating system, trying to directly control the computer hardware. Any of these conditions can abort the program, the shell, the opsys, or any combination of the three.

Decking and Operating Systems

Operating systems are important to netrunners. Old-style hackers, using non-cybered terminals to invade systems, have to be adept in the operating systems of the machines they hack into. This is reflected in the required familiarity with operating systems for Computer Operation, Computer Programming and Computer Hacking skills.

Netrunners on cyberdecks have a similar problem. Their decks convert the virtual commands from their virgonomic rig or neural interface into program commands on their deck. These attack and defense programs, in turn, execute the correct machine instructions on the network. In order to pull this trick off, a cyberdeck needs to generate the right instructions for the operating system of the machine it is invading.

A cyberdeck must either be programmed for the operating system it is invading, or must be run in tandem with a *cross-system instruction translator.* See *New Attack and Defense Programs,* pp. 118-120.

Portability

Some operating systems allow programs from another operating system to run on them. Yes, we just said that you can't do that, but this is a special case.

For example, NATComp wants its customers who buy their personal computers to also buy NATComp minicomputers and mainframes. To encourage this,

New Attack and Defense Programs (Continued)

Display   Defaults to Computer Hacking-2

Display lets the decker send output to any printer, terminal screen, or other display output on a system. If he is on as a super-user, he can send to *all* of them at once. Otherwise, he can send to only one peripheral.

The message displayed can be simple text, composed on the spot, or the decker can spool a message to a peripheral from his deck's data files, or from any data files he has accessed on the system. For example, Display can be used to print false, or insulting, messages on a security guard's display terminal, or dump a file incriminating a mid-level zek to the CEO's private printer.

Segue   No Default

Segue speeds up data transfers between the decker's system and the computer he is invading. The program divides the data to be transferred into packets, and sends down the free comm lines simultaneously.

In order to use Segue, both the sender and receiver must have extra comm lines free. If the decker's base system doesn't have extra comm lines, he's out of luck unless he has some sort of commline multiplexer.

Segue is often used to shoot hot data at high speed into data havens or other safe holding areas where the decker can retrieve it later. A netrunner with the right connections (or sufficient valuta) can arrange for lines to be held open for him on such a system.

To determine the speed of a data transfer under Segue, simply divide the size of the data file to be transferred by the number of lines free on both systems (sending and receiving). Normally, a gigabyte takes 20 minutes to download or upload over a comm line. If Segue multiplexes two comm lines, a transfer would only take 10 minutes per gigabyte.

The downside of all this is that if a Trace is run while Segue is running, it cannot be fooled by Misdirection, Decoy or any other anti-trace programs. Trace will lock on to the system at the other end of the Segue connection. And shutting down Segue before the transfer is finished will leave the fragments of the file useless, scattered all over the receiving system. In quick/out quick is the rule for Segued data moves.

Segue's Execution Time depends on the time required for the data transfer. It is a Complexity 3 program and costs $75,000 (not counting the cost of a multiplexer, or reserved lines at a data haven).

Continued on next page . . .

Shriek   *Defaults to Computer Hacking-2*

Shriek triggers any Alarm programs that may be on a system. The decker can set a time delay, or even leave Shriek behind when he leaves a system. However, the program has to keep running on his deck until it "goes off," or it will abort. Shriek will also be wiped from memory by Regenerate, if the system runs that program before the Alarms are triggered.

Shriek has an Execution Time and Complexity of 1, and costs $1,000.

Snooper   *No Default*

Snooper uses parallel search algorithms to locate specific data in a database faster than the search procedure described on p. C71.

It utilizes the SI of the cyberdeck to emulate a number of simultaneous searches, each scanning a portion of the entire database to reduce overall search time.

Snooper is Complexity 1. It is of no use on a Complexity 1 deck. On more powerful systems, its effectiveness depends on the deck's Complexity. Snooper can generate 10 parallel processes – SubSnoops – on a Complexity 2 deck, on a Complexity 3 deck 100 SubSnoops, etc. The decker can run fewer SubSnoops, in order to leave room for other programs on his deck.

Divide the total gigabytes to be searched by the number of SubSnoops running. Search time is based on the number of gigs per SubSnoop, at the usual rate of 10 minutes per gigabyte.

For example, a decker with a Complexity 3 deck is searching a 50-gig database for information. Normally, this would take 500 minutes, over 8 hours of searching. The decker runs Snooper using all of a Complexity 3 program's capacity. That generates 100 SubSnoops, which divide the 50 gigs, leaving ½ gig for each SubSnoop to search. The whole search process requires only 5 minutes.

When rolling against the Snooper program skill to see if the desired information has been found, a critical failure or fumble will trigger any Alarms present on the system.

Snooper cannot include any password-protected or otherwise secure databases in its search unless the decker is on the system as a superuser.

Snooper costs $50,000.

NATComp has developed an operating system, VANIX, that runs similarly on all their platforms. VANIX on a minicomputer can also run VANIX programs written for a personal computer. VANIX/M, the mainframe version of VANIX, can run programs from either of the smaller types of systems. This is a high level of *portability*.

Programs ported from a system with a higher Complexity can have problems. Real-time programs cannot port downward at all. A real-time program designed for a Complexity 5 mainframe simply cannot run on a Complexity 2 personal computer, whether they are running the same opsys or not. A downwardly ported analysis program with a Complexity higher than the smaller machine's Complexity suffers the loss of speed defined on p. C64.

Virgonomics

Ergonomics studies the interface between people and systems. As virtual presentation began to evolve with the explosion of computer power at the turn of the century, applications appeared that applied virtuality to ergonomic processes. This led to the "virtual ergonomic" interfaces that were developed in the first decades of the one-and-twenty: virgonomics.

Development of Virgonomics

The first virgonomic interfaces used simple sensors on the hand or fingers for "point-and-snap" controls. Originally evolved (like trackballs and joysticks) for game programs, they replaced analog controllers on most systems by the mid-2010s.

At the same time, workable "wizzie" opticals were introduced. "Wizzie" is a contraction of WYSIWIG: What You See Is What You Get. A wizzie interface uses a helmet with a VDT screen built into the inside of the visor, to create a visible environment. This was later replaced with light goggles, that present stereo-synchronized screens to each eye. Since their introductions, the goggles have undergone a gradual process of miniaturization. They now resemble thick sunglasses.

With wizzies, the computer user sees a completely virtual scene. Computer "screens" in wizzie can be 360° graphic representations, showing text, icons, monitor displays, you name it. Commands can be selected from menus that pop out of "nowhere."

V-gloves (virgonomic manual positioning sensor/controllers) were another major step. These expanded on the point-and-snap systems: a pair of gloves, equipped with sensors that detected finger position and movement. The user could define virtual keypads, keyboards, buttons, and other control surfaces in the display he saw through the wizzie.

Virtual Keyboards

The simplest application of this technology is the "virtual keyboard." This interface is included with all computers that have virgonomic interface capability. The user puts on a wizzie and a pair of v-gloves and the system presents a keyboard to his sight. By moving his fingers as if typing on this keyboard, actual keystrokes are generated by the computer. Interfacing GUI (Graphical User Interface) design also allows users to create icons and move them around the wizzie "landscape" as desired.

A virgonomic controller for any personal computer or workstation costs $1,000 and includes a set of wizzie goggles and v-gloves. This is included in the cost of computers on the Computer Equipment Table that have a "V" type control interface.

Hot Rigs

From wizzies and v-gloves, the next step was the virgonomic "hot rig." Hot rigs are full-body suits, capable of giving sensory feedback: tactile pressure, temperature, sounds and visuals. A user can "move" through a virtual environment, translating movements into responses to icons and virtual control surfaces, and getting output in a number of sensory formats.

This represents the present state of the art for virgonomic interfaces, and may be the ultimate level of development possible in virgonomics, with neural interface programs as the next step.

Cyberspace on the Edge

The typical cyberpunk world has cyberdecks available off the shelf: trim, sleek little packets of virtual reality available in every computer store.

Not here, livewire. Cyberdeck technology was developed to allow human operators to slash and burn hostile computer security during the Data Wars. The basic neural connections, environmental interfacing, software improvements and ice that attacks neural interfaces are all recent developments.

Commercial systems are almost all virgonomic. Direct neural interfaces in the legitimate world are reserved for the best of the best: top systems designers and programmers, hotshot analysts, a few scientists, lawyers, financial planners and the like. Government systems may be more heavily cybered; no one knows for sure, or rather, no one is talking.

There are only two other categories of network user likely to have access to deck tech. Natch, there's the deckers, the net rats, the console cowboys. The best datasteals take the best gear. The other cyberusers are the smyertniki, the killers: the guys who take over when the ice fails. Korpdeckers, wired with the hottest metal and punching the coldest decks on the network.

Neural Interfaces

As the korps and governments jockeyed for control in the 2020s, the key to the struggle was clear to both sides: information. Hotrigs and other advanced virgonomics started out as military tech, or its equivalent in the keiretsu R&D facilities.

Data Wars

Shinowara's breakthrough in 2032, developing a workable Marquee interface in "Project Sumi-e," triggered the Data Wars, a series of intense stabs of industrial espionage between several rival tech korps. Shinowara's brief supremacy on the Network was quickly nullified as other organizations, private and public, acquired neural interface technology of their own. By the time the Data Wars burned out, in 2039, true environmental interface technology was in the prototype stage. Today, four years later, black clinics on the cutting edge of cybertechnology can wire up a decker who's got the valuta (and the connections) to go brainsurfing in the Net.

Neural interfaces are also discussed on pp. C72-73. Prices and point costs shown here are based on those rules. In addition, all neural interfaces have an availability (see p. 96) and a Legality Rating.

Marquee Interface $12,500 (5 points)

Installation requires a major surgical facility and takes two weeks. Marquee does *not* require nanotools, since its neural connections are on a fairly gross level. However, installation without nanotools takes four weeks instead of two.

Since a Marquee Interface uses the most basic form of neural connection, a Command Phase takes 4 times longer than normal (see *Command Phases*, p. C73).

A neural controller is a device that translates the impulses from a neural interface into computer commands. Neural controllers are hardwired into self-contained cyberdecks. For the grungy denizens of the street, however, the controller is usually a jury-rigged external device or circuit board, connected to the motherboard of a commercial computer or workstation.

The controller comprises a cybernetic I/O jack connecting to the plug in the netrunner's neural interface, a bank of neural co-processors ("nervechips") and an expansion card for additional ROM slots in the deck. An external neural controller will also have a power supply, connectors that can connect to any computer with a virgonomic controller card, a case, etc. Typically, an external neural controller weighs 1 to 2 pounds and measures 12" long by 4" wide by 3" high.

A controller can also be constructed on a circuit board and installed in a personal computer. An internal controller differs from an external unit in that it has no separate power supply and no expansion capability for ROM slots. The virgonomic controller is built into the neural controller, so even a cheap personal computer can be adapted into a cyberdeck using an internal controller.

Neural Controllers Cost

Controllers are Rare technology, so the GM can impose character point costs for would-be deckers if he so chooses.

Controllers are also tightly regulated, or even illegal, in most countries. They are only available in countries with TL8 computer tech, and have a Legality of 4.

The controller must be installed in a computer with a Complexity at least as high as its own. A Complexity 3 neural controller plugged into a Complexity 2 personal computer can only function at Complexity 2. Similarly, the number of programs that can be run requires that both systems have the same rating. If the controller is standard, limited to running two programs of its own Complexity, then it doesn't matter if the associated computer system has extended processing power. Neural controllers can also be installed on workstations that are attached to more powerful microframes and mainframes.

The prices for cyberdecks, given on pp. C74-75, are the prices used for neural controllers on the Edge. This price does not include the auxiliary computer or other peripherals, just the controller itself.

The Net on the Edge

Marquee Interfaces are Uncommon (see *Availability,* p. 96) and have a Legality Rating of 3, which makes them legitimate in all but the most restrictive societies.

Icon Interface $40,000 (13 points)

Installation requires a major surgical facility and takes 10 days. Nanotools are not required, but if they are not available the operation requires a major medical facility and takes three weeks.

A Command Phase takes 2 times the normal length when using an Icon Interface.

Icon interfaces are Rare and have a Legality Rating of 5, requiring licensing in many countries, or at least registration.

Environmental Interface $100,000 (30 points)

Installation requires a major medical facility and takes four weeks: two for the actual cybersurgery, two more to learn to use the interface on a cyberdeck.

This familiarization course is essential and requires access to a Complexity 4 miniframe computer, as well as a cyberdeck. If the decker tries to skip it, he can only use his implant as if it were an Icon Interface until he goes through the necessary orientation period. If he completes less than a week of familiarization, he can use the interface normally, but is at -2 on all skill rolls made in the Net until he completes the second week of training.

Command Phase length receives no modifiers when using an Environmental Interface.

Environmental Interfaces are Very Rare technology. They have a Legality Rating of 4, requiring licensing in most societies. In strictly controlled societies, the operation is illegal except for government agents and individuals whose korporate connections or social standing relax legal constraints.

Cyberdecks

In order to use a neural interface, the netrunner needs a cyberdeck. A cyberdeck, of course, is a computer, usually a personal computer or minicomputer, which has been modified to process the character's mental commands as computer instructions.

Self-contained cyberdecks are not commercially available on the Edge. These units, the sleekly elegant hardware familiar to all readers of classic cyberpunk literature, are restricted to government and korp users. They have a Legality Rating of 4, and in most countries just owning one is a crime.

The average netrunner in 2043 has to buy or build a neural controller in order to convert his commercial computer into a functioning cyberdeck.

The Do-It Yourself Option

An individual can buy components to build a neural controller himself, or have it done by some tame tekniki. He pays 40% of the price that a finished controller would cost. For example, Quik Jerzy hears that the Death Chippers boosted a korp shipment of nervechips and other SOTA components. He has good relations with the Chippers, and puts in a bid for the parts to build a Complexity 3 controller, SI 5, with 6 RAM slots and the capacity to run three Complexity 3 programs instead of two.

A finished controller like this would cost $1,600,000. The parts alone will run $640,000.

Once he has the parts, constructing the controller requires a skill roll on Electronics (Bionics). Reduce the skill roll by the Complexity of the controller. The attempt takes 3 days for an external controller, 6 days for an internal controller, and requires at least a portable electronics shop. On a simple failure, work can continue. In the event of a critical failure, the parts are damaged. Perhaps the tekniki finds that they weren't any good in the first place, and the customer was ripped off. Either way, the would-be decker must go out and find more parts. The GM should roll 1d and multiply the result by 15%. That is the amount of money, based on the original figure, that he must pay to replace the faulty components.

For example, Quik Jerzy has Electronics (Bionics)-15, and rents access to a high-tech shop from a fixer he knows. He spends three days tinkering on an external controller before jacking it into his cousin Georg's home minicomputer to test it. Rolling against Jerzy's skill of 15, at -3 for the Complexity of the unit, the player scores a 17, a critical failure.

Not only does the neural controller not work, there is a sizzling noise and Jerzy gets pitched halfway across the room by a cybernetic backshock. When he comes to, he opens the casing to discover that the main cyber-buss is fused. The GM rolls a 2 on 1d. Replacing the damaged elements will cost 30% of the original price, or $192,000. The Death Chipper treasury is getting plump off poor Jerzy.

Pricing Computers

A "generic model" is given for every type of system. Modifications to this basic model also change its cost. Some changes apply a multiplier to the price, some apply a percentage change, and some have a flat price which is added to the cost.

When you are working out the price of a given computer system . . .

• apply any multipliers to the cost first.

• next, add up all percentage changes and apply that total to the multiplied cost.

• finally, add or subtract any flat fees.

For example, as we will see below, raising a computer's Complexity multiplies its cost by 7. Increasing the number of ROM-deck slots adds 50% to the cost. A virgonomic interface controller costs $1,000.

So, increasing a generic personal computer's Complexity from 2 to 3 would multiply the basic cost ($1,000) by 7, for a cost of $7,000.

Increasing that by 50% gives us $10,500. Adding $1,000 gives a final cost of $11,500 for a machine with these features.

Features

Interface: A virgonomic (V) interface for personal or minicomputers adds $1,000 to the cost. An All-V model, with no analog (A) controls, is $100 cheaper, reflecting the reduced cost of production.

Mass Storage: A 10-gig (10G) CD drive costs $500 and weighs 1 pound. A 500-gig VLD costs $7,500. A 1-terabyte (1T) VLD costs $10,000. VLDs weigh 500 pounds and occupy 1 cy.

If the generic model of a computer has a 500-gig VLD, upgrading to 1T costs $2,500. Each additional VLD is at full price.

Complexity: Complexity can be increased or decreased by one level from the Complexity of the generic model. Increasing it multiplies the base price by seven. Decreasing it divides the base price by five.

ROM Slots: As specified on p. C65, a computer comes equipped with a number of ROM-deck slots equal to its Complexity. Doubling this number of slots increases the cost 50%.

Reducing the number of slots reduces cost. A computer with no ROM slots is discounted 20%. The discount is pro-rated for a computer with fewer slots than its Complexity allows. The formula for this is (((Complexity − Number of slots)/Complexity)×20) percent. For example, a Complexity 2 personal computer with one slot gets a discount of (((2−1)/2)×20), or ((1/2)×20), or 10 percent.

Maximum Programs: As defined on p. C64, a computer can normally run two programs of its own Complexity, or different numbers of programs of other Complexities. A computer capable of running three programs of its own Complexity costs 50% more.

A "dumbed-down" computer, capable of running only one program of its own Complexity, is also possible, and costs 25% less.

Weight/Volume: Reducing a computer's weight by ½ increases its cost by 50%. Reducing weight to ⅓ the weight of the generic model increases cost by 100%.

Increasing weight by a factor of 10 reduces cost by 50%. Note that the volume of computer equipment is tied to its weight. A computer occupies 1 cubic yard (cy.) if it weighs between 50 and 100 pounds. Add 1 cy. for every additional 100 pounds or fraction thereof.

Personal Computers

Model	Control Interface	Mass Storage	Comp.	ROM Slots	Max. Pgms.	Wt./Vol.	Cost
Generic Model	A	10G	2	2	2	3	$1,000
EGM Roi 10 (Henri)	A/V	2×10G	2	4	2	4	$3,000
EGM Roi 20 (Charles)	A/V	2×10G	2	4	3	4	$3,500
EGM Roi 30 (Louis)	A/V	2×10G	3	6	3	4	$12,000
NATComp PC7000	A	10G	1	1	2	30	$100
NATComp PC70000	A	10G	1	1	2	3	$200
NATComp PC7200	A	10G	2	1	2	30	$400
NATComp PC72-010	A	10G	2	1	2	3	$900
NATComp APC72-020	A	2×10G	2	2	2	4	$1,500
NATComp XPC72-100	A/V	2×10G	3	3	2	4	$8,500
NATComp XPC72-200	A/V	2×10G	3	6	3	4	$15,500
Novy-R Tsarevitch	A	10G	2	2	2	1	$2,000
Novy-R Tsarevitch-V	V	10G	2	2	2	½	$2,900
Novy-R Tsarina	A/V	2×10G	2	2	2	4	$2,500
Novy-R Tsar	A/V	2×10G	2	4	3	4	$3,500
Novy-R Grand Duke	A/V	2×10G	2	4	3	30	$3,000

Minicomputers

Model	Control Interface	Mass Storage	Comp.	ROM Slots	Max Pgms.	Wt./Vol.	Cost
Generic Model	A/V	2×10G	3	3	2	60/1 cy.	$15,000
EGM Pharaon 100 (Ramses)	A/V	4×10G	3	3	2	62/1 cy.	$16,000
EGM Pharaon 120 (Cheops)	A/V	4×10G	4	8	2	62/1 cy.	$158,000
NATComp MasterCOM 2000	A	2×10G	3	3	2	600/6 cy.	$6,500
NATComp MiniCOM 200	A/V	2×10G	3	3	2	30	$30,000
NATComp UltraCOM 2050	A/V	4×10G	3	6	2	62/1 cy.	$23,500

The Net on the Edge

Microframes

Model	Storage	Comp.	Slots	Pgms.	Wt./Vol.	Cost
Generic Model	500G	4	4	2	900/5 cy.	$40,000*
EGM Kaiser 300 (Wilhelm)	500G	4	4	3	900/5cy.	$60,000*
NATComp MDPS-90	1T	4	4	2	900/5 cy.	$42,500*
NiDaCo ARC500	500G	4	8	2	900/5 cy.	$60,000*
Novy-R Rachmaninov	1T	4	8	3	900/5cy.	$82,500*

Mainframes

Model	Storage	Comp.	Slots	Pgms.	Wt./Vol.	Cost
Generic Model	500G	5	5	2	1,100/7cy.	$200,000**
EGM Empereur 600 (Napoleon)	1T	5	10	2	1,100/7cy.	$302,500**
NATComp DPC-100	500G	5	5	3	1,100/7cy.	$300,000**
NiDaCo ARC5000	2T	5	5	2	1,600/8 cy.	$212,500**
Novy-R Moussorgsky	1T	5	10	3	1,100/7 cy.	$402,500**

Supermainframes

Model	Storage	Comp.	Slots	Pgms.	Wt./Vol.	Cost
Generic Model	1T	6	6	2	2,500/21cy.	$2,000,000**
NATComp XDPC-1000	1T	6	6	3	2,500/21cy.	$3,000,000**
Novy-R Tschaikowski	1T	6	12	3	2,500/21 cy.	$4,000,000**

* +$2,000 per user station or comm line. ** +$1,000 per user station or comm line.

Computer Programs

Software	Complexity		Cost
(Analysis Software)			
Accounting	2		$1,000
Desktop Publisher	2		$1,000
Electronics Repair	2		$500
Engineering (specialty)	2		$5,000
Internal Security	2		$2,500
Market Analysis	3		$5,000
ROM Production	2		$2,000
(Real-Time Software)			
Audio Recognition	2		$700
Chemical Analysis	2		$500
Comm Vocoder	2		$,1,200
Datalink	1		$400
Datashow	1		$50
E-Lock	2		$200
Internal Security	3		$2,500
Market Monitor	3		$5,000
News Daemon	1		$500
Optical Recognition	3		$5,000
Password	1		$100
Targeting	1		$1,000
Tracemapper	1		$400
(Expert Systems)			
Mental/Very Easy	3	14	$2,500
Mental/Easy	3	13	$5,000
Mental/Average Skill	3	12	$10,000
Mental/Hard	3	11	$20,000
Mental/Very Hard	3	10	$50,000

(+1 skill: double cost and +1 Complexity)
(Triple cost of Expert Systems for illegal skills)

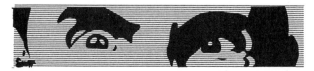

Cyberdeck Software

Program	Time	Complexity	Cost	Legality
Bloodhound	1	2	$7,500	3
Compression*	var.	2	$500	1
Confuse	1	2	$10,000	5
Corrode	1	2	$12,500	4
Crash	4	2	$15,000	5
Cross-system Instruction Translation*	1	2	$2,000	1
Crumble	1	2	$5,000	3
Decoy*	1	3	$50,000	3
Disguise	1	2	$2,000	3
Display*	1	1	$750	1
Erase	1	2	$8,000	4
Flatline	1	4	$1,000,000	5
Fuses	1	2	$20,000	2
Icepick	2	4	$250,000	3
Loop	1	2	$4,000	3
Misdirection	2	2	$17,500	4
Monitor	2	2	$25,000	1
Promote	2	2	$20,000	3
Recon	1	2	$7,500	1
Segue*	var.	3	$75,000	2
Sever	2	2	$15,000	2
Silence	1	3	$10,000	4
Shield	1	2	$12,000	2
Shriek*	1	1	$1,000	1
Snare	1	2	$12,500	2
Snooper*	var.	1	$50,000	1
Stealth	1	2	$10,000	4
Success	1	3	$12,500	4
Skeleton Key I	5	2	$25,000	3
Skeleton Key II	8	3	$50,000	5
Trace	1	2	$20,000	2
Transfer	1+	2	$25,000	2
Webster	2	2	$5,000	3

*New – see sidebars, pp. 118-120.

The Net on the Edge

TALKIN' ONE-AND-TWENTY

babooshka: (Russ.) Grandmother. Granny. Old-fashioned. Colloquially, an old-timer, someone with a 20th-century attitude.

bangbang: Weapons, firepower.

blacktop: A NERCC Enforcer.

bolshy: From Russian "bolshoyeh," meaning "great," "big." Can mean physical size or high quality.

breetva: (Russ.) Literally "razor." Anybody modified with cyberweapons or combat-oriented implants, especially claws or other cutting weapons.

burners: Lasers.

C-1: A "Scale One Citizen." The elite class of U.S. citizens according to the Citizenship Scale instituted by ProGov.

C-2: The "middle class" scale of U.S. citizenship under ProGov.

C-3: The working or lower class scale of U.S. citizenship under ProGov.

C-4: The lowest scale of U.S citizenship under ProGov; the underclass: outcasts, political dissidents and the like.

chiller: Assassin.

cocanova: A variant of the coca plant developed by 'traff researchers in South America. Used to make neocoke.

coyote: Someone who smuggles illegal transients from Mexico to the U.S.

cred: Money, specifically money as a function of the world financial network, i.e., electronic funds.

crow: Short for "escrow." A type of blind account, used to store credit anonymously.

cyberaxe: Any musical instrument that is partially controlled through a neural interface.

decker: A hacker equipped with a neural interface and a cyberdeck.

dengi: (Russ.) Money. Colloquially, "soft money." Unstable national currencies or korp scrips. "Trash dengi" refers to currency subject to runaway inflation.

DL: "Download." Anything that moves data from the Net to a local data store, including financial transactions.

dyadooshka: (Russ.) Grandfather. Gramps. Old-fashioned. Colloquially, an old-timer, someone with a 20th-century attitude.

drig: (Obsc.) Copulation. A common expletive.

Echeverista: A member of the Cuban revolutionary movement, headed by Rafael Echeveria, devoted to releasing Cuba from U.S. control.

ecoterrs: Ecoguerrillas.

ecus: ECU: Economic Community Credit Units; hard currency.

eurotaler: ECU of United Europe.

faex: Excrement. A common expletive.

flatblack: A NERCC Enforcer

fold: Actual currency, in hardcopy scrip: bills, folding money.

Gauss: To shoot with a Gauss needle weapon. "Gauss out": to fall down after being shot with a Gauss needle weapon.

gig: Gigabyte: one billion bytes or 1,000 megabytes.

Glavkosmos: Russian Space Agency

go dodo: To become so obsolete as to be extinct.

'hayo gozaimas: (Jap.) Hello.

headset: A sensie performer.

heat: The authorities.

'hood: Neighborhood.

hot rig: A cyberdeck that was created on the street instead of a nanotech lab.

indesp: Industrial espionage.

keiretsu: A corporation, cartel, conglomerate.

khorosho: (Russ.) Good. OK. Fine.

K-mark: Keiretsu mark, or Korp mark. Currency issued by a multinational corporation.

korp: From Russian "korporahtseeya," meaning multinational corporation. A keiretsu.

korpo: A corporate employee.

krovvy: (Russ.) Bloody.

livewire: Informal term of address, complimentary or sarcastic according to context.

loco: Local company, an independent business with no korp connection.

Low C: Insulting slang term for someone with a lower Citizenship Scale than the person speaking.

Talkin' One-and-Twenty

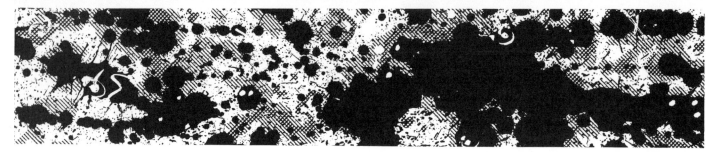

The Low Six: The six Reserved states created after the U.S. annexed Mexico.

mil-spec: Designating something built to military specifications.

mileetsya: The military.

minshy: From Russian "menshyeh," meaning "small." Generally means "small time," "second rate."

nak-nik: From Russian "nachal'nik," meaning supervisor, boss. A low- or mid-level manager.

neocoke: A more potent form of cocaine, made from the cocanova plant.

neodollar: ECU of the U.S. and its North American trading partners.

neofeudalism: A fancy name for local rule by the strongest faction.

nerk: Any agent, officer, or bureaucrat of the NERCC.

null zone: Any area where local law does not apply.

nullo: A U.S resident who doesn't have a Citizenship Scale rating – i.e., a Zero, whose identity does not exist in the National Data Banks (see p. C21).

nyek: From Russian *nyeh'kulturny,* meaning uncultured. Unhip, uncool.

oldvid: Archival footage.

one-and-twenty: The 21st century. Also, an up-to-date attitude or product.

oo'zhas: (Russ.) Awful. Terrible. Kakoy' oo'zhas: That's awful. "Too bad." Usually used sarcastically.

paryen: (Russ.) Pal. Friend. Chum. (pl. paryeni)

praz'navoon'yeh: (Russ.) Celebration. Party.

prog, proggie: Agents or officials of the Provisional Government.

ProGov: The Provisional Government of the United States.

proles: Proletariat; literally the working class; the underprivileged.

raw meat: Street slang for someone with no cyberwear, or even no obvious cyberwear.

ronin: A street op with a rep as a fighter. A loner, without affiliation to a gang or tribe. Like a samurai but without an honor code or reputation.

rubyen: ECU of the CIS and Japan.

rumbler: A professional gladiator.

samurai: A skilled street fighter, usually heavily modified. Muscle for hire with a reputation for trustworthiness and an honor code.

sarariman: (Japlish) Korp employee.

sensie: A popular type of entertainment involving reliving another's sensory experiences through an implant chip.

shaikujin: (Jap.) "Good citizen." A taxpayer, "suit," sarariman. A korp employee.

shash: Someone (dead or alive) used to supply parts to a body bank. From Russian *shashlik,* literally meaning "shish-kebab."

shield: Bodyguard.

shy: A broker. Short for "shyster," a lawyer, or "shylock," a loan shark.

slam: Collapse, major setback, disaster. Originally referred to economic collapse, but now in general use for anything from a corporate bankruptcy to a personal disaster.

smyertniki: Killers. Specifically refers to Net assassins for korps and government agencies, assigned to take out illicit netrunners.

sneetch: Snitch, informer.

Snoh'veem Goh'dum: (Russ.) Happy New Year.

street treat: A cheap firearm. A "Saturday Night Special."

stoh?: An interjection that means roughly "really?"

suit: A straight citizen, a white-collar worker, usually middle class or higher. By implication, a korper or government employee.

tapper: A broker specializing in selling information.

Tchort: (Russ.) Literally "devil." A common expletive.

TD: Tolliver's Disease.

tekniki: A technician or anyone who repairs technology.

Ten-Tan: Slang for Kosmozavot Tenno Tanjo, the Russo-Japanese orbital facility.

terabyte: 1,000 gigabytes: one trillion bytes.

thriddie: 3-D, three-dimensional.

Toller: Tolliver's Disease.

Touchdown: Tolliver's Disease.

'traff: From Spanish *"narcotraficante"* (trafficker in narcotics). A member of the powerful crime cartels of the South American region, most of which have branched into other areas of crime.

Triad: A criminal organization based on the structure of the Chinese secret societies (also called "tongs"). Influential throughout Southeast Asia and the Pacific Rim.

valuta: (Russ.) Literally "foreign currency." Colloquially, any hard currency, either electronic or scrip: ecus, K-marks, etc.

virgonomics: Contraction of "virtual ergonomics." Any control system that creates a virtual environment, without using neural interfacing, that allows the user to access a computer without using analog controls.

wizzie: Contraction of WYSIWYG, "what you see is what you get," a type of virtual display

Yak: The Yakuza, either as an organization (the Yak) or individual members (a Yak).

zavvy: From Russian "zavye'dooyooshee," meaning a manager. An upper-level sarariman.

zek: An executive.

zeroman: Assassin.

INDEX

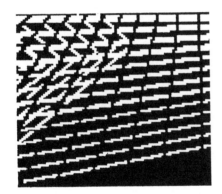

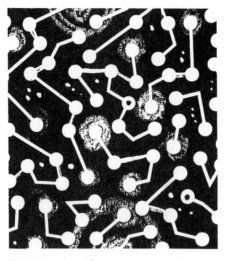

Index